IMAGES
of America

LAKE REGION

BRIDGTON, HARRISON, OTISFIELD, WATERFORD, AND BRIDGTON AND SACO RIVER RAILROAD

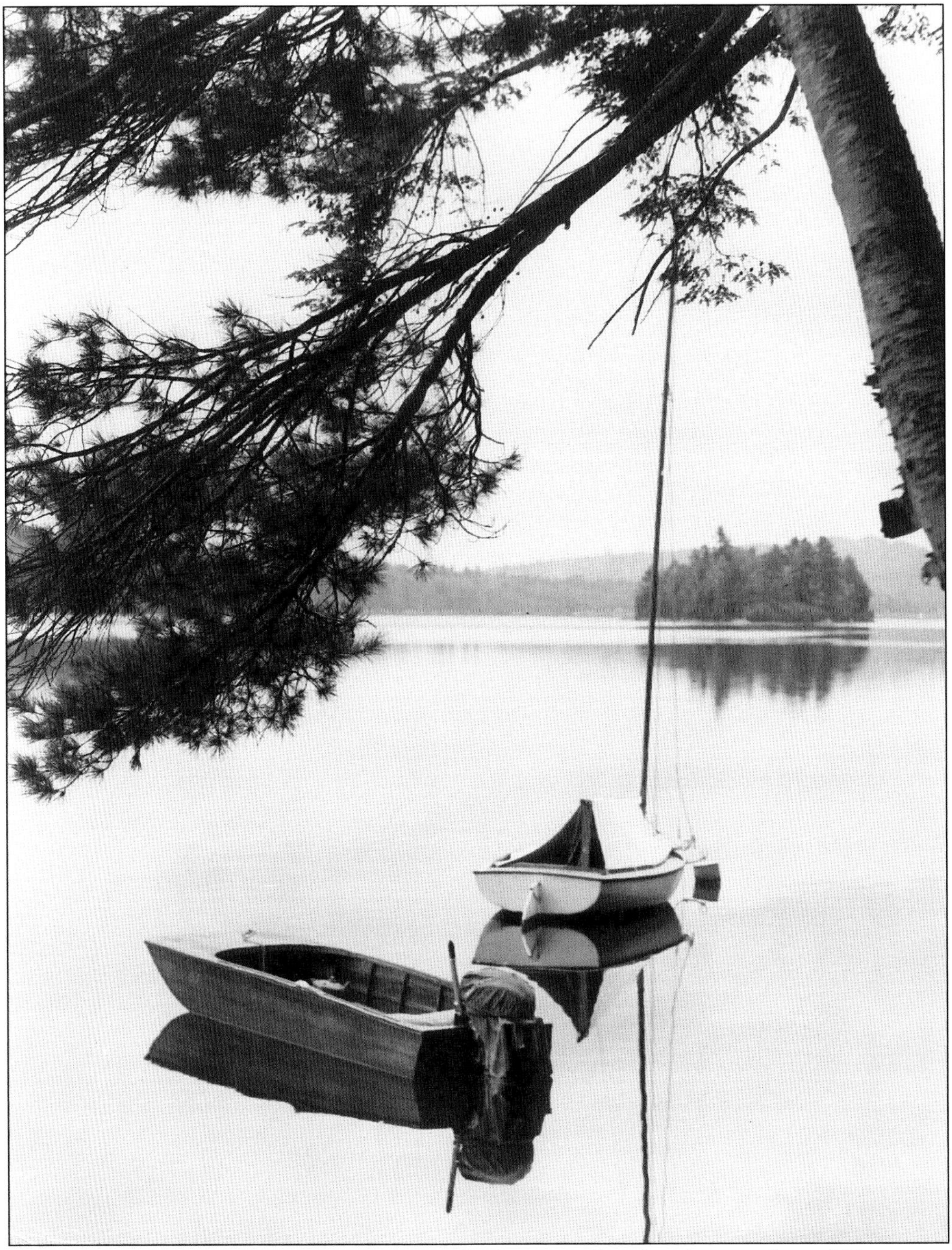

Serendipity, c. 1935. Not even a whisper of a breeze ruffles the glassy surface of Thompson Pond at The Cape in Otisfield.

Front Cover: A spectacular panorama from Pleasant Mountain in Bridgton, c. 1938.

IMAGES
of America

Lake Region

Bridgton, Harrison, Otisfield, Waterford, and Bridgton and Saco River Railroad

Diane and Jack Barnes

ARCADIA
PUBLISHING

ISBN 978-0-7385-1261-7

Published by Arcadia Publishing
Charleston, South Carolina

Printed in the United States of America

Library of Congress Catalog Card Number: Applied for

For all general information contact Arcadia Publishing at:
Telephone 843-853-2070
Fax 843-853-0044
E-mail sales@arcadiapublishing.com
For customer service and orders:
Toll-Free 1-888-313-2665

Visit us on the Internet at www.arcadiapublishing.com

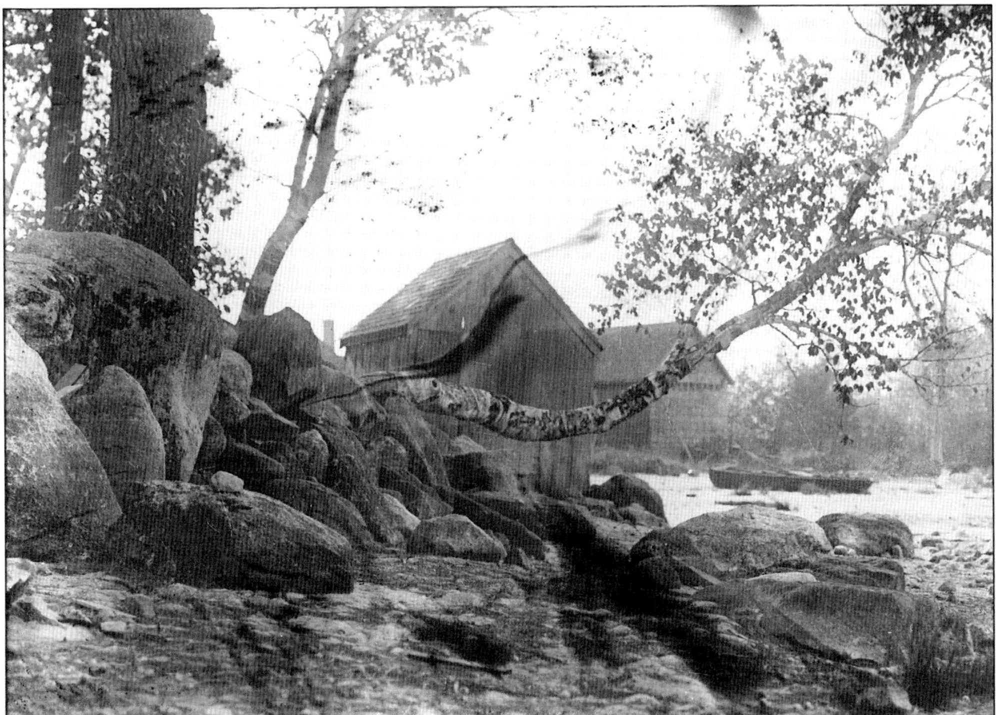

CHIAROSCURO, c. 1925. A white birch clings tenaciously to a crevice along a darkened rocky stretch of shoreline on Crystal Lake in Harrison.

Contents

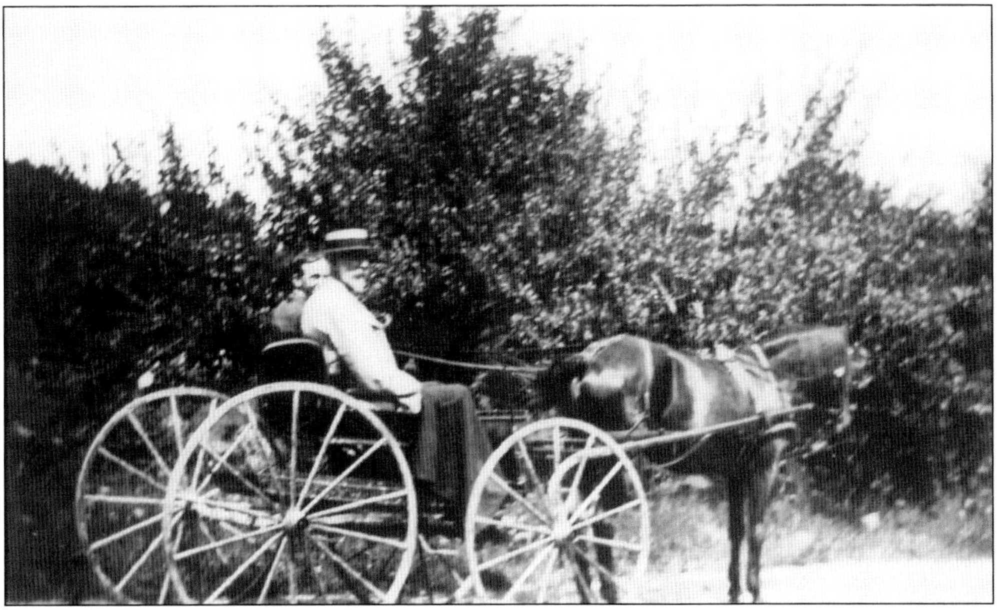

ON A HOUSE CALL, C. 1910. Dr. Joseph L. Bennett, a much beloved native of Bridgton, devoted 37 years of his 50-year medical career practicing in Bridgton.

Acknowledgments

We should like to express our profound appreciation to the Bridgton, North Bridgton, Harrison, Hiram, Otisfield, and Waterford Historical Societies, the *Bridgton News*, the Bridgton Public Library, Bridgton Academy, the North Bridgton Library, the management at Shawnee Peak at Pleasant Mt., and the Knight Library in Waterford Flat. We should also like to thank the many individuals who so willingly shared memorabilia, photographs, and research material. We are especially grateful to Eula Shorey, Ned Allen, Hazel Cook, Esther Kilborn, Arthur Kilborn, Esther Gyger, Judy Blake, Eleanor Parker, Randy Gleason, John and Elaine Fabello, and Col. and Mrs. Allan P. Richmond for the Bridgton chapter; Mary Carlson, Jean Higgins, Gary Searls, David Card, and Maida Card for the Harrison chapter; Jean and David Hankins, Ethel Turner, Dorothy Lombard, Martha Connell, Virginia Jillson, and Lita Henley for the Otisfield chapter; Nancy Marcotte and Bill Fillebrown for the Waterford chapter; and Bob MacDonald, Hubert Clemons, Raymond Cotton, Merle Douglas, June Allen, and Timmy Allen for the chapter on the narrow gauge railroad. Leona Greene of Sebago and Randy Bennett and Stan Howe of the Bethel Historical Society were invaluable sources of information throughout. Special thanks goes to Richard Fraser of Poland for his expertise on antique automobiles and to Joyce Bibber of Gorham for her expertise on architecture.

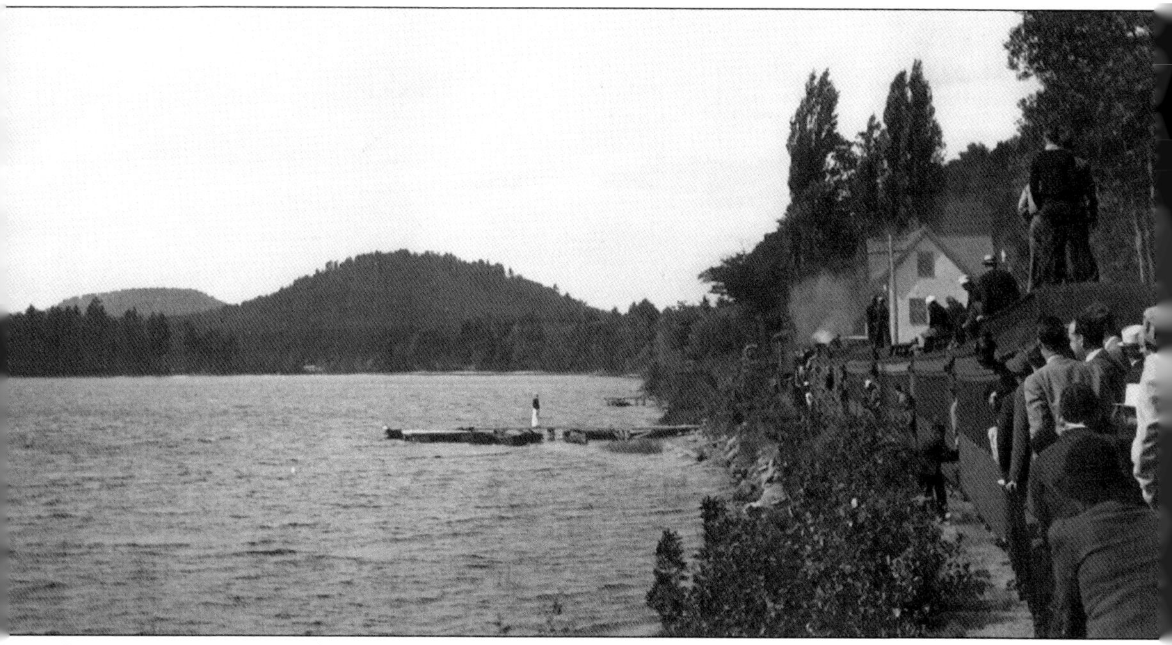

Railbuffs, c. 1940. A large group of railbuffs are enjoying a stop at Hancock Pond in West Sebago during a leisurely outing on the Bridgton and Harrison Railway.

Introduction

The four towns that are featured in this work—Bridgton and Harrison in Cumberland County and Otisfield (since 1978) and Waterford in Oxford County—indirectly owe their existence to some of the veterans of the ill-fated British colonial campaign to capture Quebec from the French in 1690 and terminate the French and Indian menace. But because the French and Indian Wars continued until the British General Wolfe captured Quebec in 1763, little effort on the part of their heirs was made to survey areas north of Windham and Fort Pearsontown (Standish Corner) until after the Peace of Paris was signed. In fact, only a few intrepid individuals and families settled in the Lake Region until the eve of the Revolutionary War and its aftermath when Maine became a part of the Commonwealth of Massachusetts.

Penetrating the hinterland, which included the four Lake Region towns, was an arduous task. Some of the earliest settlers trekked all the way from Massachusetts on foot, packing only what they could carry on their backs along meandering deer and Native American trails.

These early settlers had their hands full building their rude cabins and clearing enough land to sustain themselves and their animals, and little thought was given to road building. It was not until around 1790 that the road from Standish via Flintstown (Baldwin-Sebago) to Bridgton was made wide enough for horse- and ox-drawn wagons. By the early nineteenth century Bridgton had become the crossroads of the east-west and north-south stagecoach routes, although travel by stage was extremely uncomfortable.

The four towns comprising the Lake Region and the towns surrounding Sebago Lake, however, were blessed by a highway of connecting lakes, rivers, and ponds—beginning with Sebago Lake and, after 1830, Portland Harbor (when the Cumberland and Oxford Canal was opened). Both Bridgton and Harrison are located partly on Long (Pond) Lake. Bear River linked Waterford City (South Waterford) with Long Lake. Crooked River, which forms a confluence with Songo River just before the locks, provided an artery as far as Edes Falls (until Naples was incorporated in 1834 it was a part of Otisfield) and to some degree all the way to North Waterford and beyond. Little wonder that mill owners and farmers very early on were motivated to produce more than could be consumed locally. Both people and goods could reach Portland by the all-water route from almost anywhere in the Lake Region in three days or less.

All four towns, Waterford and Otisfield to a greater degree, benefitted when the Atlantic and St. Lawrence (Grand Trunk) Railroad reached Oxford, Paris, and Bethel in 1851 and Vermont by 1853. The Lake Region, however, continued to rely heavily on the all-water route until after 1870, when the Portland & Ogdensburg Railroad reached Sebago Lake Village (the railroad reached Fryeburg by June of 1871). But it was not until the little two-footer, the Bridgton & Saco River Railroad, was built from the junction in Hiram on the Saco River through a portion of Sebago and Denmark to Bridgton and then to Harrison that the Lake Region really felt the impact of the railroad era.

Coinciding with the construction of the Portland & Ogdensburg Railroad and the Bridgton and Saco River Railroad was the development of steamboat transportation from Sebago Lake Station to Bridgton and Harrison, largely due to the foresight of Charles E. Gibbs of Bridgton. Thousands of vacationers and excursionists traveled by water to the Lake Region, especially when the Sebago Lake, Songo River, and Bay of Naples Steamboat Company was managed by Charles Goodrich.

The ever-growing popularity of the automobile and the rapid improvement of roads and highways ushered in a new phenomena—tourism, and consequently the popularity of both overnight cabins and summer cottages—and sounded the death knell for the steamships, the narrow gauge railroad, and many hotels. Agriculture, once the mainstay of these four towns, is today negligible, and few vestiges remain of the old mills that were humming within the memories of many, although several modern industries operate today in Bridgton. Fortunately, the modern era has altered but little much of the beauty of the Lake Region, an all-season resort area; and, if anything, places such as Harrison Village, North Bridgton, and Waterford Flat are more attractive than ever.

We welcome you to the scenic Lake Region, geographically and historically linked to Sebago Lake and the Oxford Hills.

One

Bridgton

First Settled: 1768
Incorporated: 1794
Population: 4,307
Principal Settlements: Bridgton, South Bridgton, Sandy Creek, North Bridgton, The Ridge

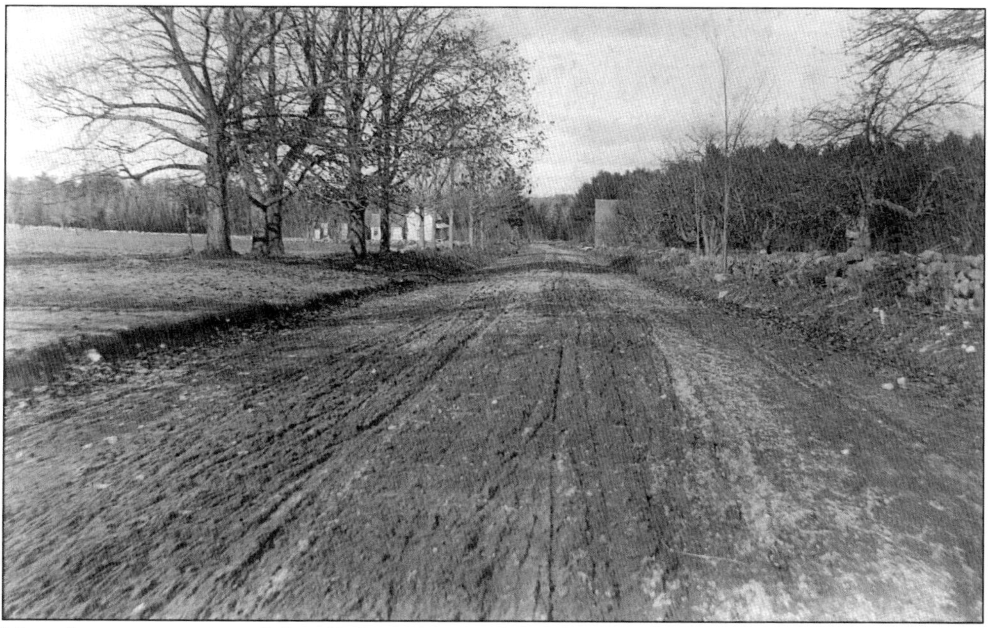

MUD SEASON, C. 1920. Like all the other roads in the area, the Roosevelt Trail (now 302) was a river of mud as soon as the snow melted each spring. Automobiles were useless until the roads dried out, and it was a challenge even to transport supplies and produce by ox cart at this stage. Little wonder the completion of the narrow gauge railroad from Hiram to Bridgton by 1883 and on to Harrison in 1898 was so important to the Lake Region. And even after the road had dried out, considerable freight and thousands of excursionists were transported via the waterways extending from Standish to Harrison. This section of the road runs through Side City in Bridgton near the Burnham-Packard farm, built over two centuries ago. The road was paved in the mid-1920s.

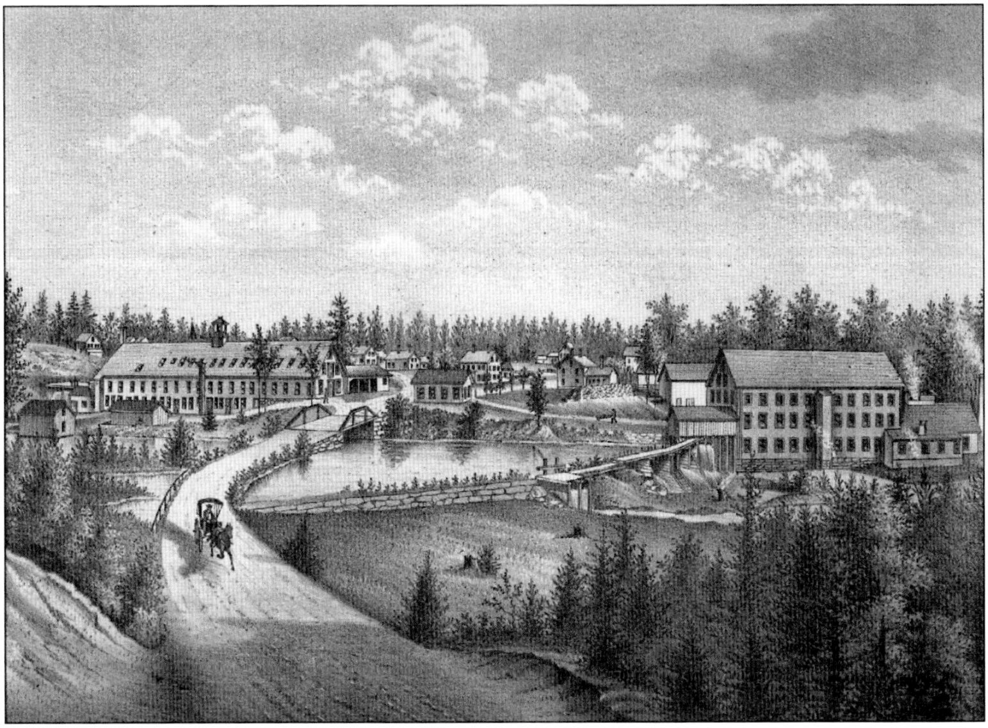

THE FOREST MILLS COMPANY, C. 1880. The Forest Mills complex, located at power sites eight and nine on Stevens Brook, played a vital role in the economy of Bridgton as well as adjacent towns for at least a half century. The company was established in 1861 by English-born George Taylor and William Fenderson Perry, both of whom served in the state legislature. Taylor died in 1878, and the following year the Forest Mills Company, which manufactured assorted fine woolen products, was incorporated and continued to prosper under Perry's leadership until his death in 1906. The mills then rapidly fell into dire straits and shut down completely in 1911. At some point the mills were reopened by the American Woolen Company, and for a short time in the mid-1930s shoes were manufactured here before the complex was abandoned.

It was the sinuous Saco River, despite its numerous rapids, that provided the initial artery leading to the eventual settlement of Bridgton—an artery that had been explored to some extent as early as 1642. Originally Bridgton was called Pondicherry, perhaps because of the effusive wild cherry trees in the area. The name was soon changed to Bridge's Town and then refined to Bridgton in honor of Moody Bridges, the proprietor most responsible for securing the land grant from the Province of Massachusetts in 1761. Bridges personally participated in the surveying of the township (along with Thomas Perley and Benjamin Milliken) shortly after Col. Joseph Frye (Bridges was married to his niece) surveyed what became Fryeburg. The pioneer settler, however, was Capt. Benjamin Kimball, a veteran sailor from Ipswich, Massachusetts, who on June 10, 1768, settled on 435 acres granted to him by the proprietors in North Bridgton. He built a house—which also served as a tavern—on the edge of Long Pond (Lake), ran a store, bartered with the local native tribes and forthcoming settlers, and conveyed goods and settlers on his small sailing vessel from Pearsontown (Standish) on Sebago Lake to the head of Long Lake until his death in 1802. Other early settlers were David Kneeland, Enoch and Noah Stiles, Enoch Perley, and Dr. Samuel Farnsworth, Bridgton's pioneer physician.

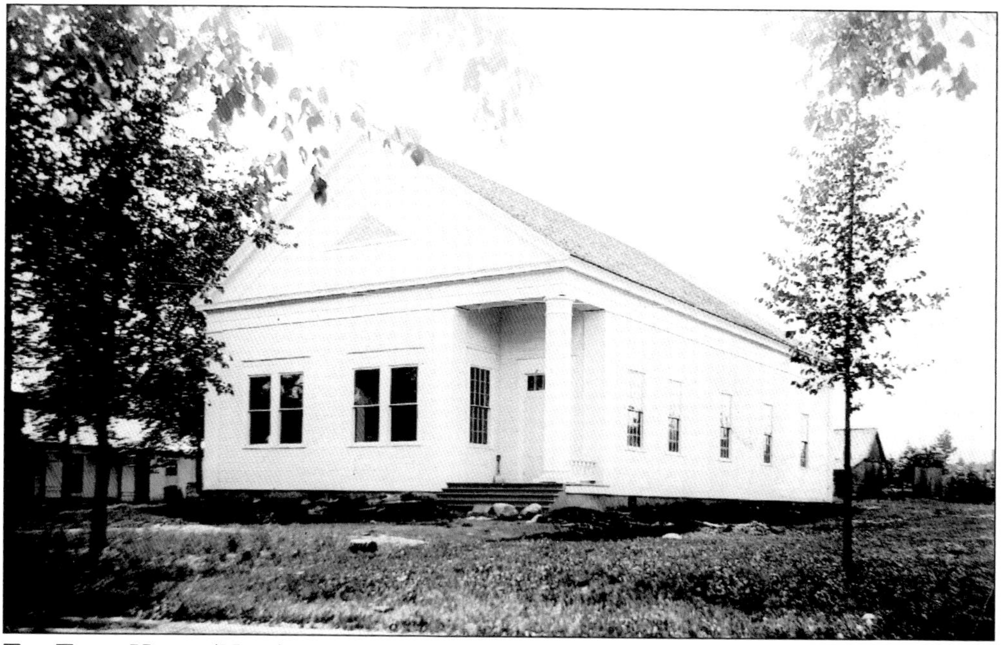

THE TOWN HOUSE (HALL), C. 1910. It was originally constructed in 1851 from lumber sawed at the Walker sawmill, located at the First Power Site on Stevens Brook. This photograph was taken after the building on North High Street was remodeled in 1903. Besides serving as a house for pure democracy, school and public dances were held here, and the B.H.S. Black Hawks played home basketball games here until the high school closed in 1969. It continues as a hall of democracy and a community recreational center.

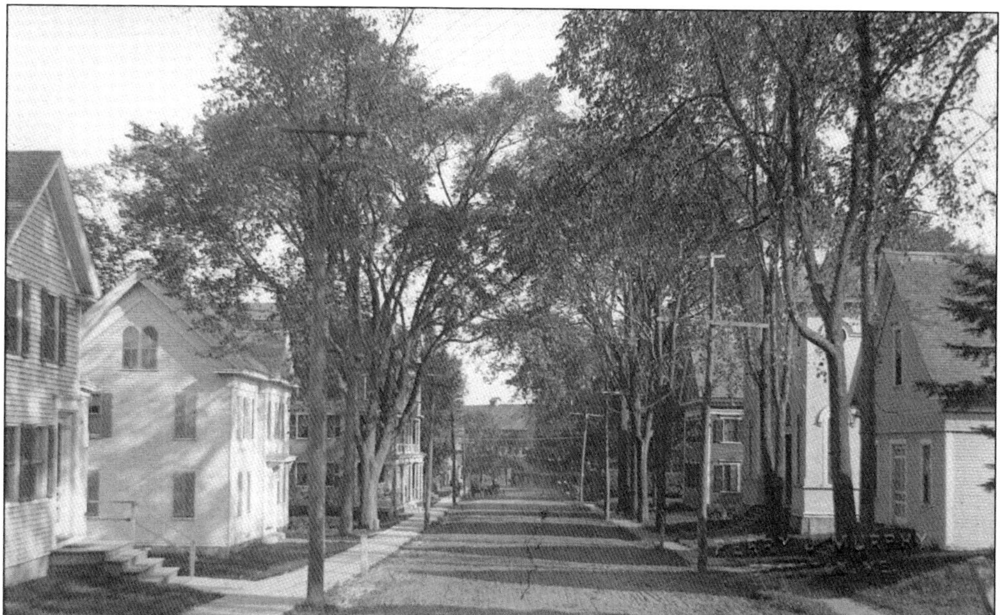

DOWN MAIN STREET TO TANNERY BRIDGE, C. 1890. This view of elm-shaded upper Main Street was taken from Main Hill. Tanning was a vital industry to Bridgton for several decades. A large mill was first built at the bridge in 1836. The Billings Tannery operated here until 1884.

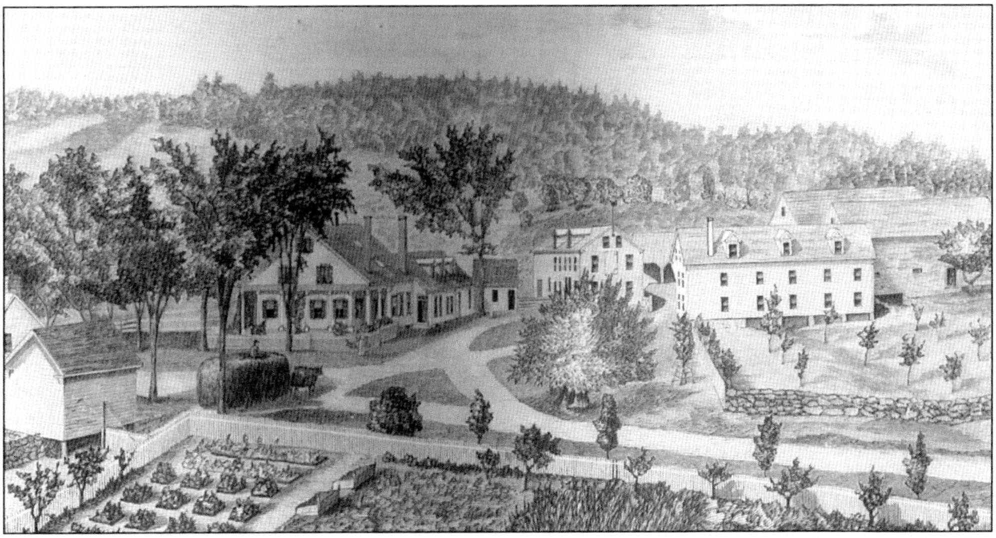

GEN. JOHN PERLEY'S FARM, C. 1880. John Perley (1779–1841), who was brigadier general of the Massachusetts militia and of the Maine militia when it became a state in 1820, commissioned Lyman Nutting of Otisfield in 1832 to design this imposing Greek Revival mansion opposite his father's farm (Enoch) in South Bridgton on what is now Route 107. Sadly, these lovely buildings, part of the John Gyger farm, were razed in 1964.

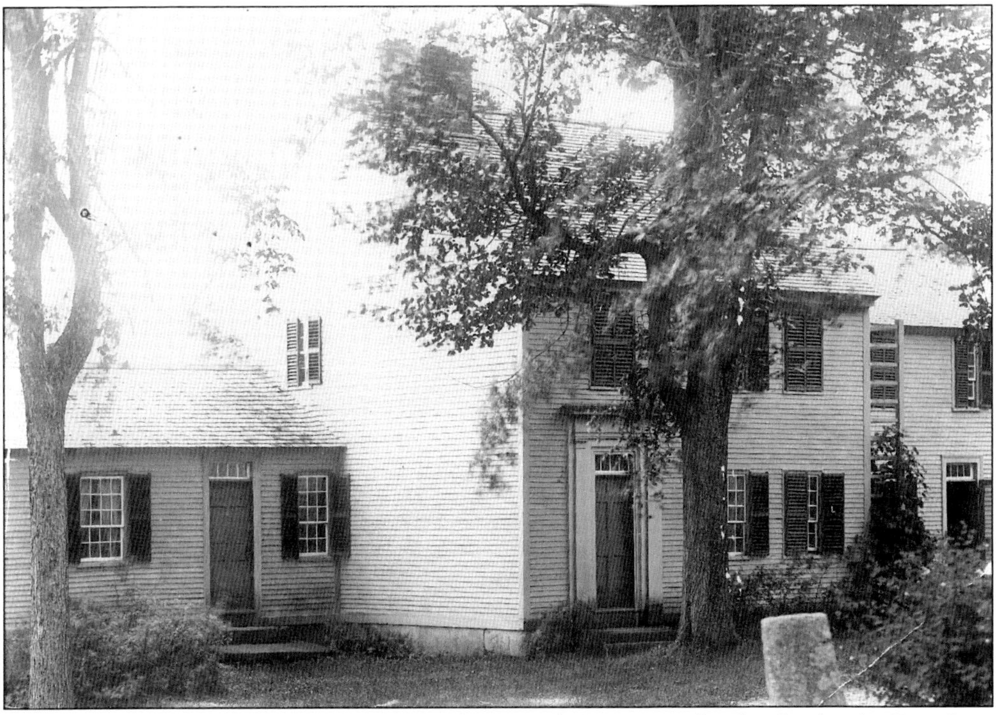

THE ENOCH PERLEY HOUSE, C. 1900. At the age of 27, a year after he fought the British at Lexington on April 19, 1775, Enoch Perley built a cabin on a large tract of land in South Bridgton. He succeeded Moody Bridges as proprietor's clerk in 1777. When his home burned in 1780 with all the records, he built this impressive house (now the Gyger house) across the road. Enoch played a key role in town affairs until his death at the age of 80 in 1829.

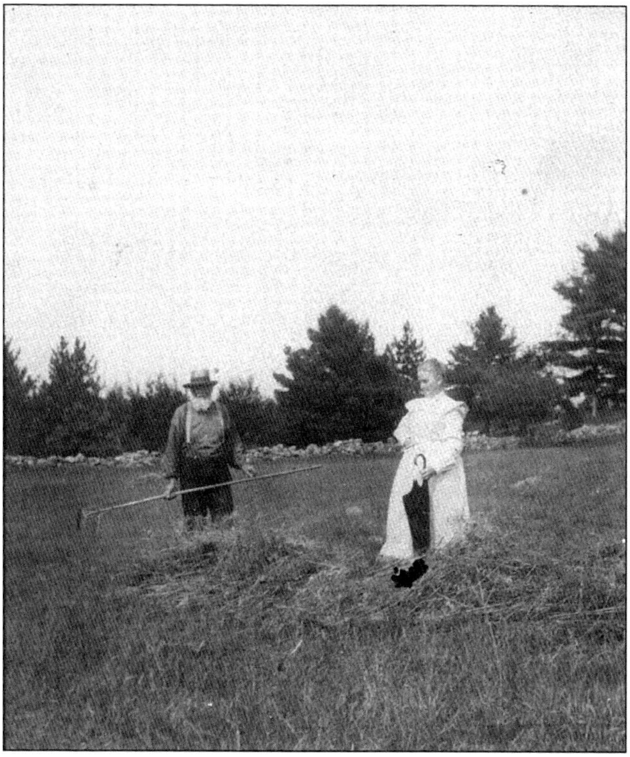

RAKING HAY ON CHOATE HILL, c. 1885. Spofford Ingalls pauses for a moment for some unknown photographer from raking a windrow of scatterings with a wooden rake he very likely made himself while his wife, holding an umbrella, stares rather pensively down at the crest of hay. Perhaps she has brought him an ice-cold mixture of ginger, molasses, and water called haymaker's switchel—a real old-fashioned thirst quencher on hot summer days. The Spofford farm still remains on Choate Hill in South Bridgton.

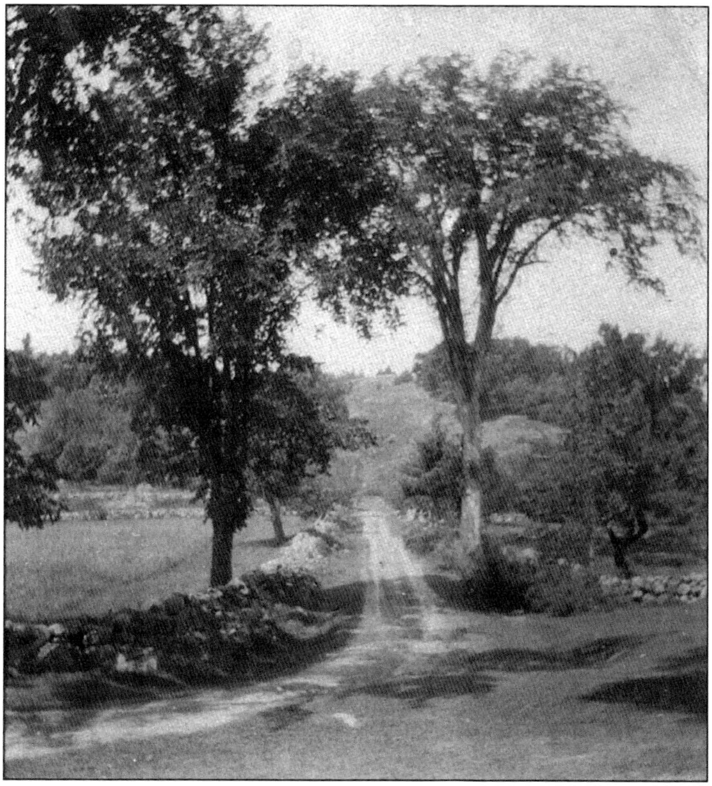

A BEND IN THE ROAD, c. 1885. Here at a bend in this narrow carriage road paralleled by stone walls, one is afforded a halcyon view of Choate Hill in South Bridgton and the Spofford Ingalls farm at the summit.

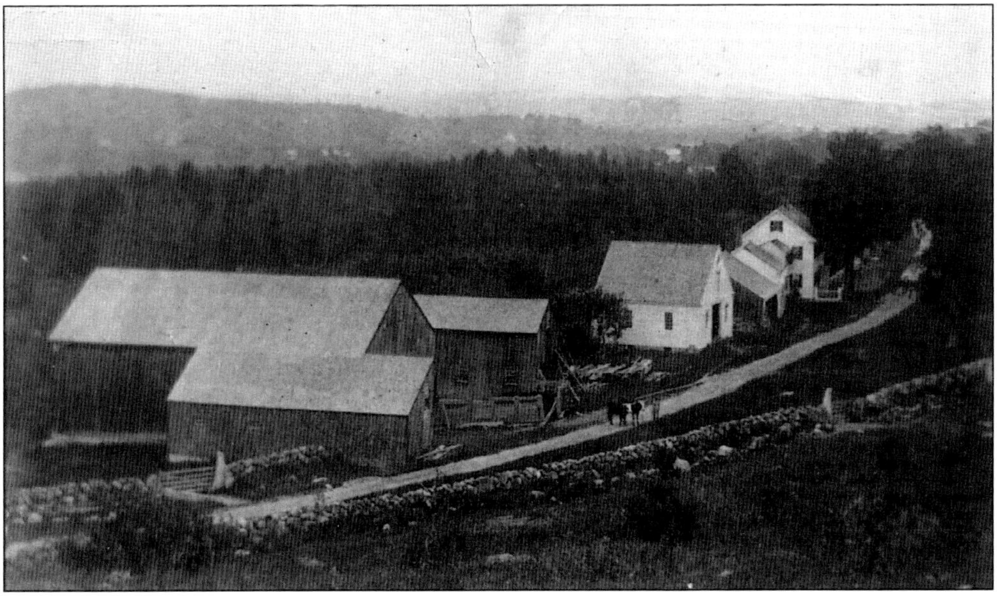

The Phineas Ingalls Farm, c. 1900. Located in South Bridgton, this was a paradigm of the typical postage stamp hill farms that were carved by early settlers in a surprisingly short period of time out of a vast wilderness with the aid of the simplest of tools and stout oxen such as the "brockel"-faced pair in the middle of the road. The glacial soil provided adequate pasturage for sheep and cattle and was especially well suited for apple growing. It was, however, poorly suited for mechanized farming.

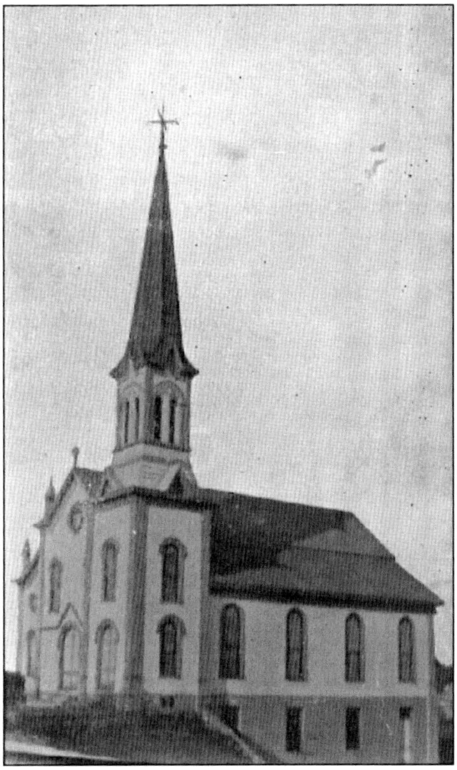

The South Bridgton Congregational Church, c. 1915. This structure, with its imposing spire and Gothic design, was erected opposite the site of the original meetinghouse built in 1826. It was dedicated July 14, 1871, and is still in use.

On August 26, 1784, Enoch Perley, Jacob Stevens, Jesse Knapp, James Stevens, Reuben Burnham, and John Peabody met in the latter's house in South Bridgton and formed Bridgton's first church. For many years thereafter church services were held in private homes; and until a minister could be found, deacons conducted the services.

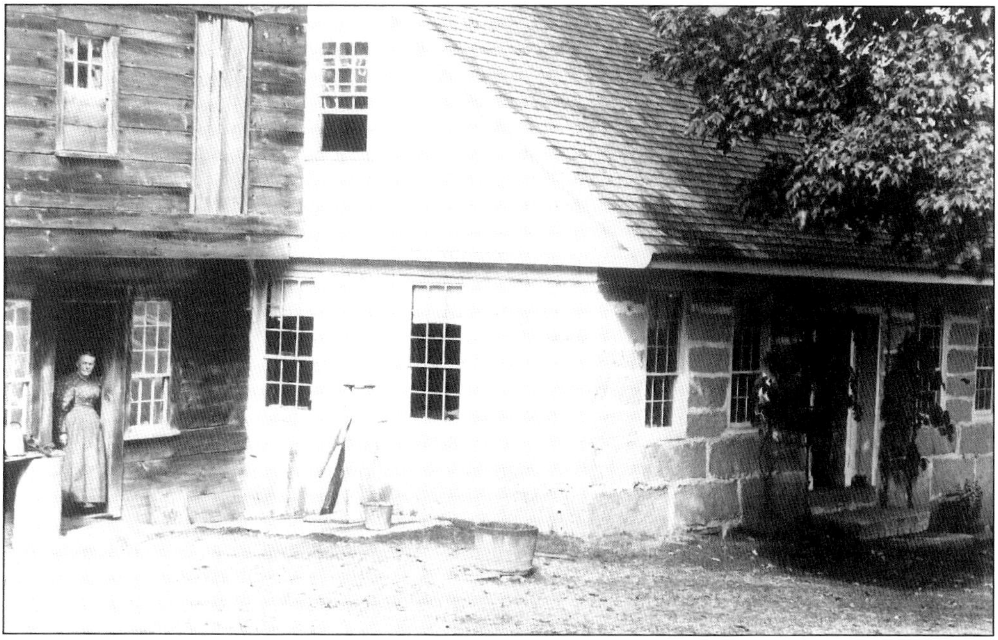

The Stone House, c. 1910. "I will build a house to withstand all winds and weather," George Mead Sr. declared after his first house on Mead Hill blew down. So, around 1830, he split granite stone and erected this unique, English style house (presently owned by the Richmonds) on the north side of Burnham Road. Perhaps even more unique to the area, George and Lucinder Mead imported mulberry trees to feed the silk worms they raised in the cellar to produce their own silk! The woman in the doorway is thought to be Mrs. Maynard Irish, a later resident.

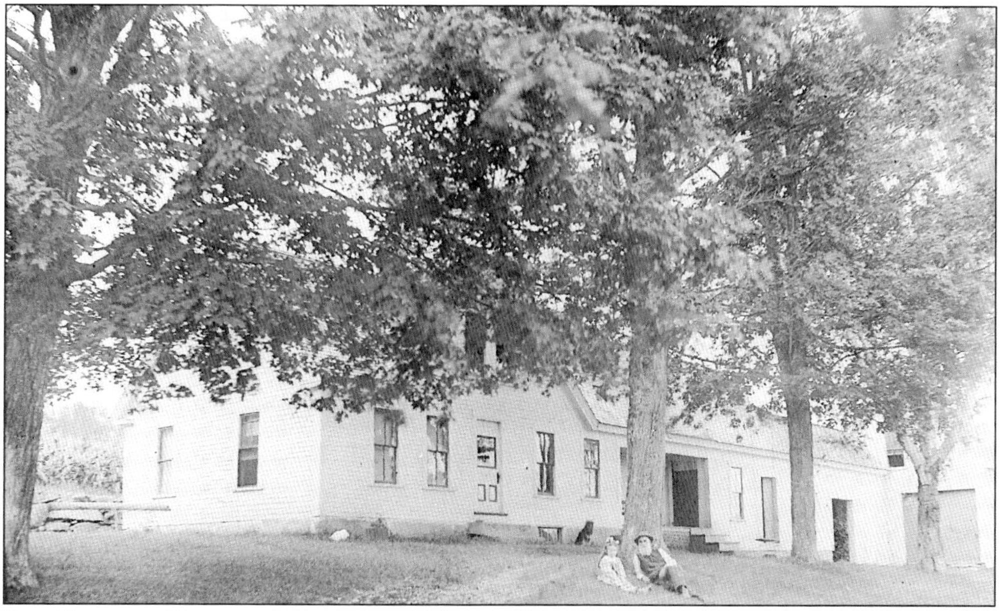

The Kilborne Homestead, c. 1890. Albert Kilborn, a noted apple grower, is pictured here with his granddaughter Evelyn. The house was built by Albert's father, Jesse Kilborn, on the Burnham Road.

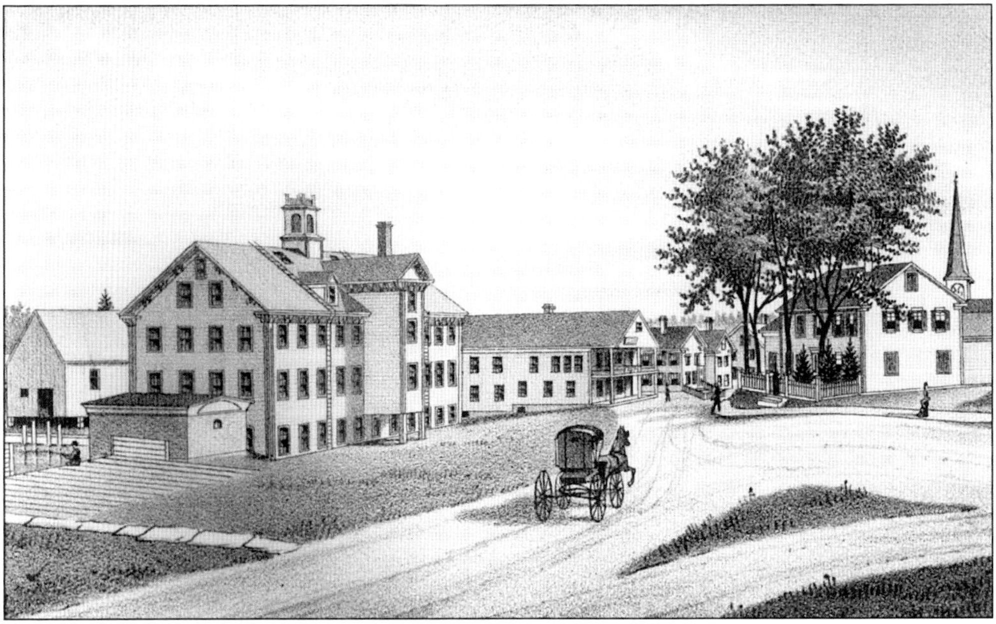

THE RESIDENCE AND MILLS OF RUFUS GIBBS, C. 1880. Rufus Gibbs (1800–1892) was born in a section of Bridgton that later became a part of Harrison. He was truly a pioneer, entrepreneur, and noted philanthropist. He began as a tanner at the Enoch Perley farm in South Bridgton and for a while operated the tannery at Tannery Bridge. He soon got into the lumber business and real estate. He was one of six local business men to organize Bridgton's first bank in 1869, and he was the backbone of Bridgton's woolen industry.

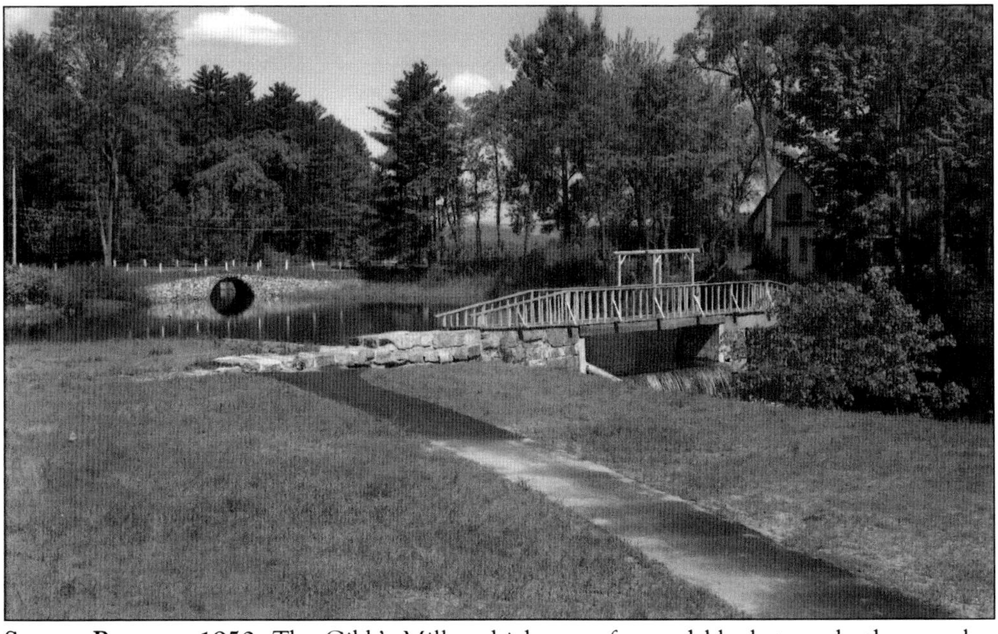

SHOREY PARK, C. 1950. The Gibb's Mills, which manufactured blankets and other woolen products, were razed in 1941, and the area once known as the First Power Site at the foot of Highland Lake later became Shorey Park in memory of Henry A. Shorey.

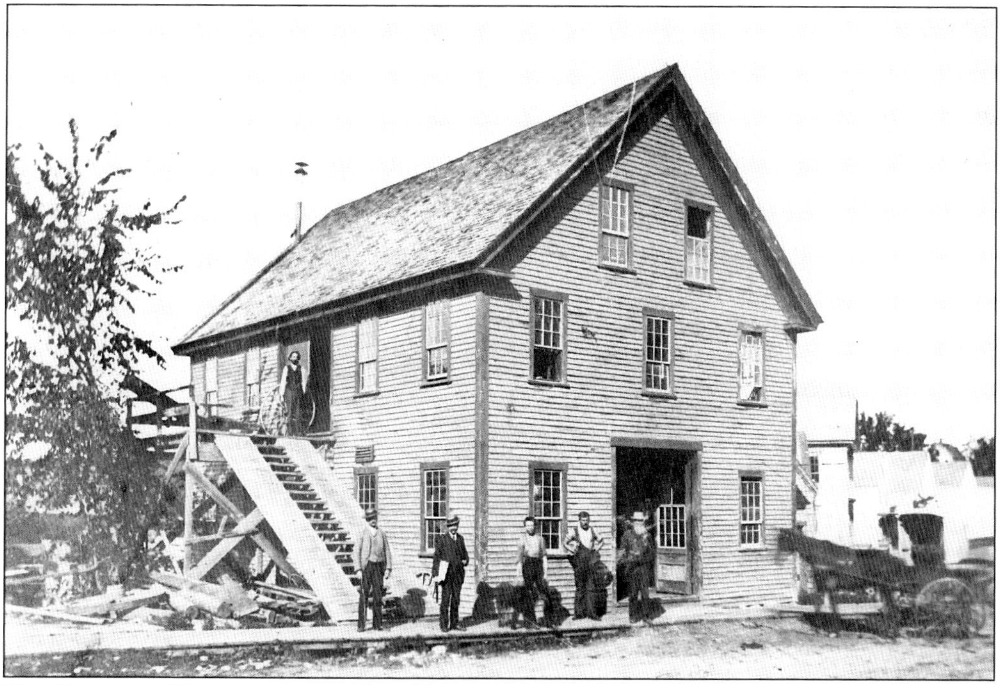

THE *BRIDGTON* NEWS, C. 1895. The oldest uninterrupted business in Bridgton and the oldest independent newspaper perpetually owned by a single family was established by Major Henry A. Shorey on September 9, 1870, soon after his printing press, type, and other printing equipment arrived by canal boat at Plummers Landing down on Long Pond. In 1895 Major Shorey obtained this building on Main Street, where Shorey Park is now located, and set up the newspaper office on the first floor. The building was torn down in 1988.

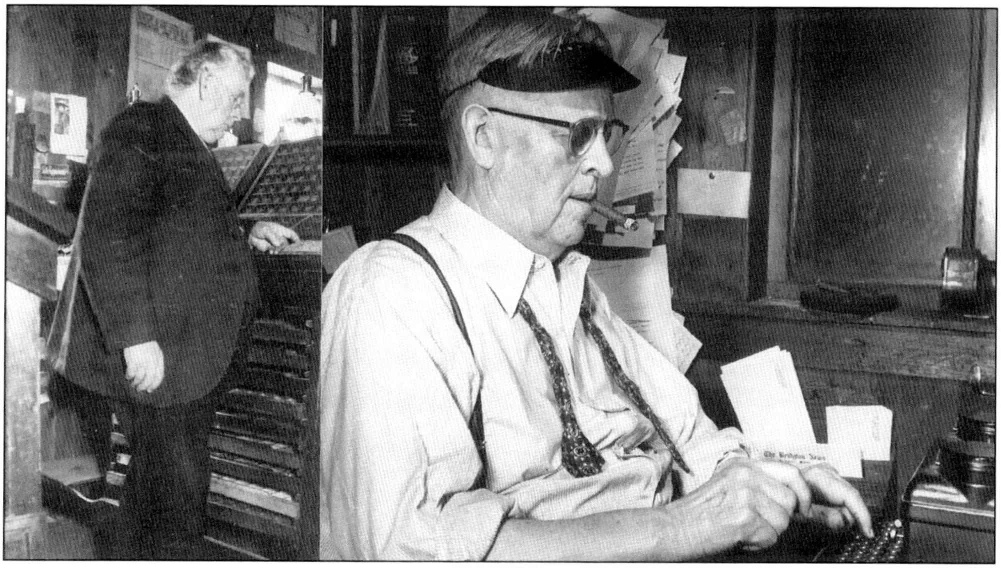

MAJOR SHOREY (LEFT). The Major ran the paper for 53 years before turning it over to his son, Harry A. (right), in 1923. The Major was 83. Harry died in 1953, and the newspaper was taken over by his son, Henry the III, aided by his wife, Eula. Their son Stephen is presently at the helm.

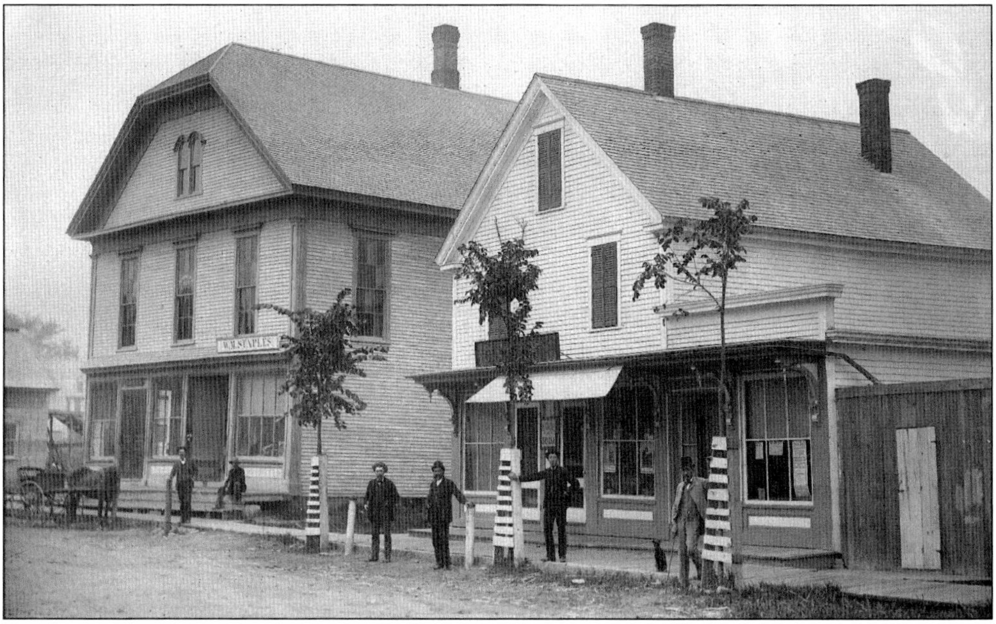

THE STAPLES-HARRIMAN BLOCK, C. 1887. In 1885 Winburn M. Staples (hand on a hitching post in front of his store) and Abel H. Harriman purchased this property on the corner of Main and Nulty (destroyed by fire in 1875) from William Larrabee and built this block. The west side of the first building on the ground floor was the new post office. On the east side the partners ran a fruit and grocery store. Upstairs was the Knights of Pythias Lodge No. 10. Note the wooden sidewalk. The block burned February 11, 1898.

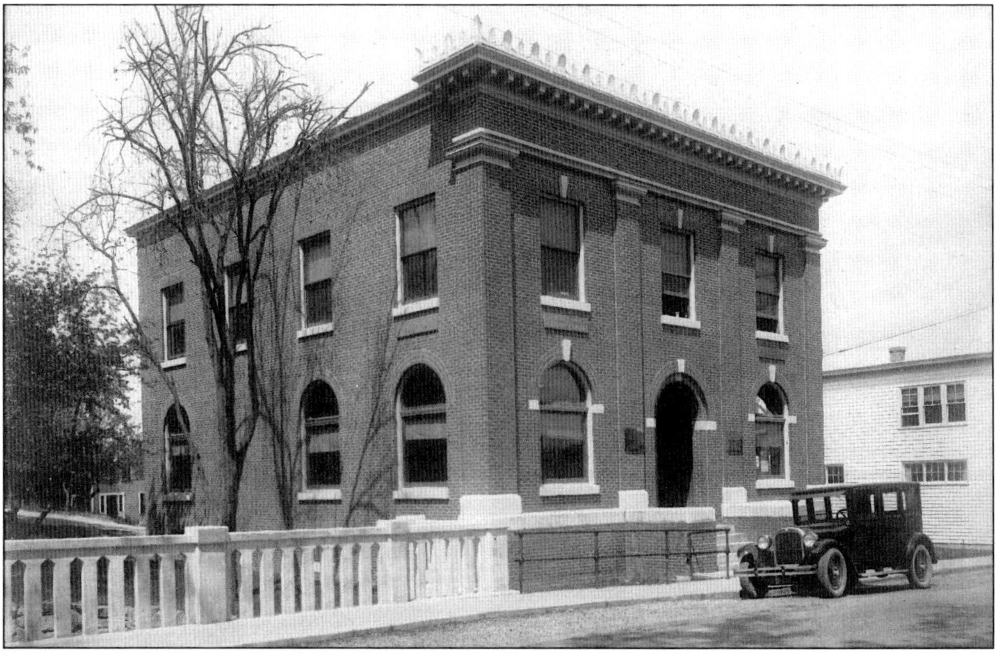

THE CASCO MERCANTILE TRUST COMPANY, C. 1932. This bank building was erected in 1907 next to Tannery Bridge on Main Street. In 1965 it became the municipal office, court, and jail. It is currently the Brookside Whole Health. The automobile is a 1932 Chevrolet.

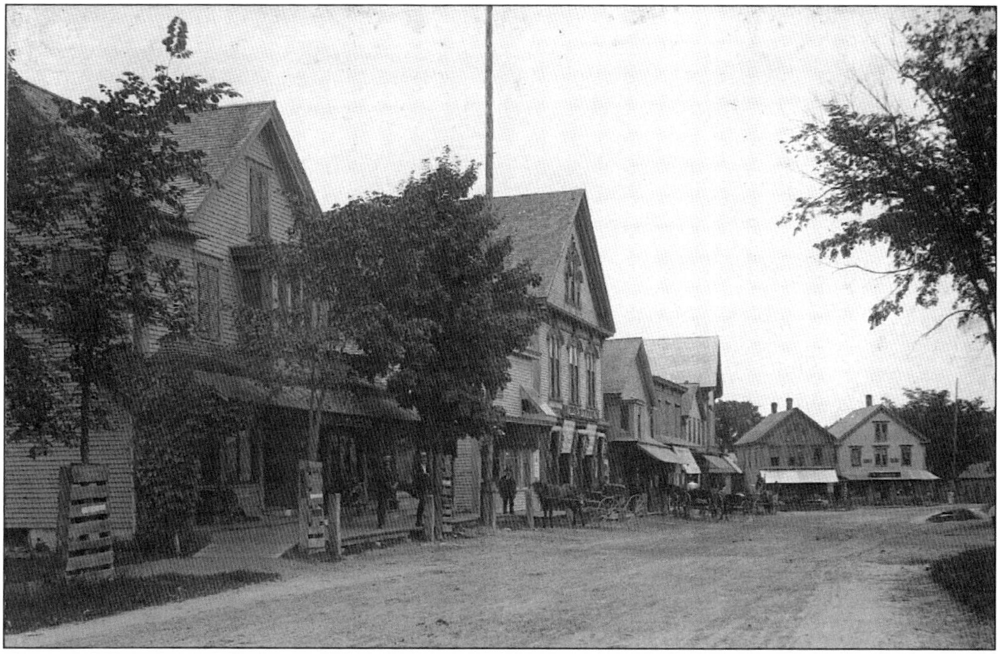

PONDICHERRY, C. 1900. Except for down at Pondicherry Square, the lower half of Main Street, traditionally referred to as Pondicherry, remains much the way it was before the advent of the automobile. In 1985 the Wales & Hamblen building, which at this time housed the IOOF on the second floor, was listed on the National Register of Historic Places.

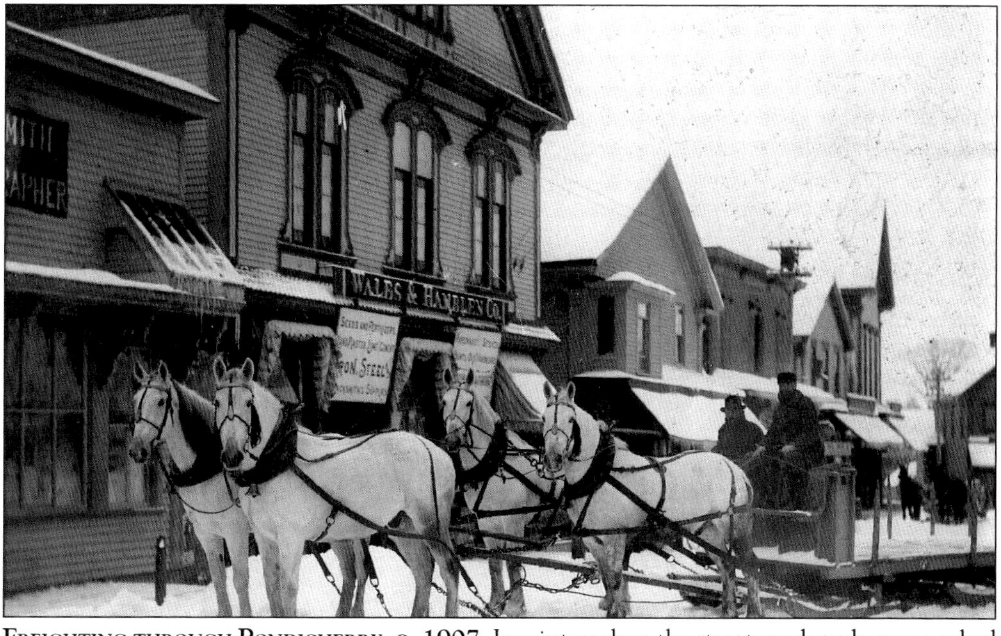

FREIGHTING THROUGH PONDICHERRY, C. 1907. In winter when the streets and roads were packed down by snowrollers, goods and freight could be easily transported. This impressive four-horse team and bobsled, owned by Henry Fessenden and driven by Walter Hill (of South Bridgton) and Louville Johnson, hauled corn boxes from Knapp's Mill at Fosterville in South Bridgton to the corn shop in Bridgton Center.

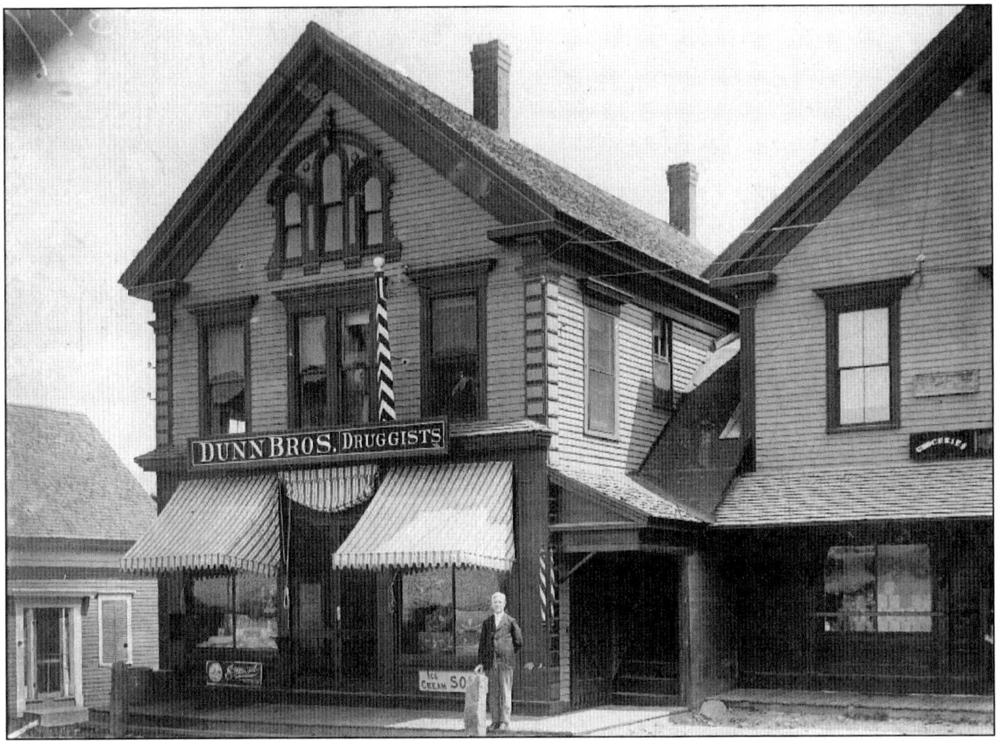

Pondicherry Square, c. 1895. Will Dunn of Harrison rests his hand on a split-stone granite hitching post in front of the drugstore he and his brother Charles had purchased from Frank P. Bennett in 1892. Charles soon thereafter left the business. The building burned in 1916, but Will immediately rebuilt and continued as a pharmacist until his death in 1937.

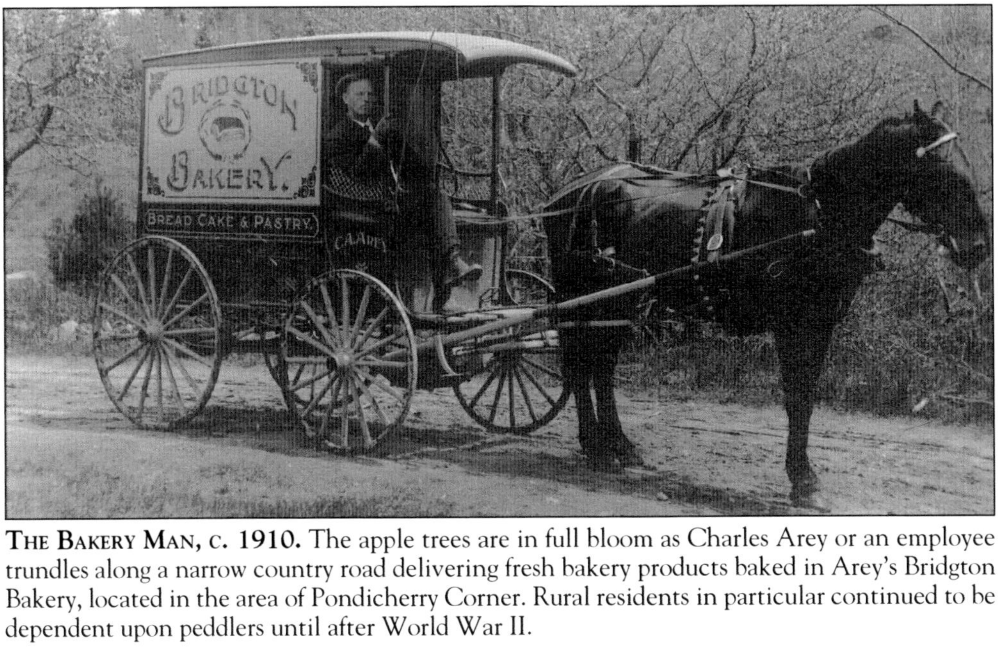

The Bakery Man, c. 1910. The apple trees are in full bloom as Charles Arey or an employee trundles along a narrow country road delivering fresh bakery products baked in Arey's Bridgton Bakery, located in the area of Pondicherry Corner. Rural residents in particular continued to be dependent upon peddlers until after World War II.

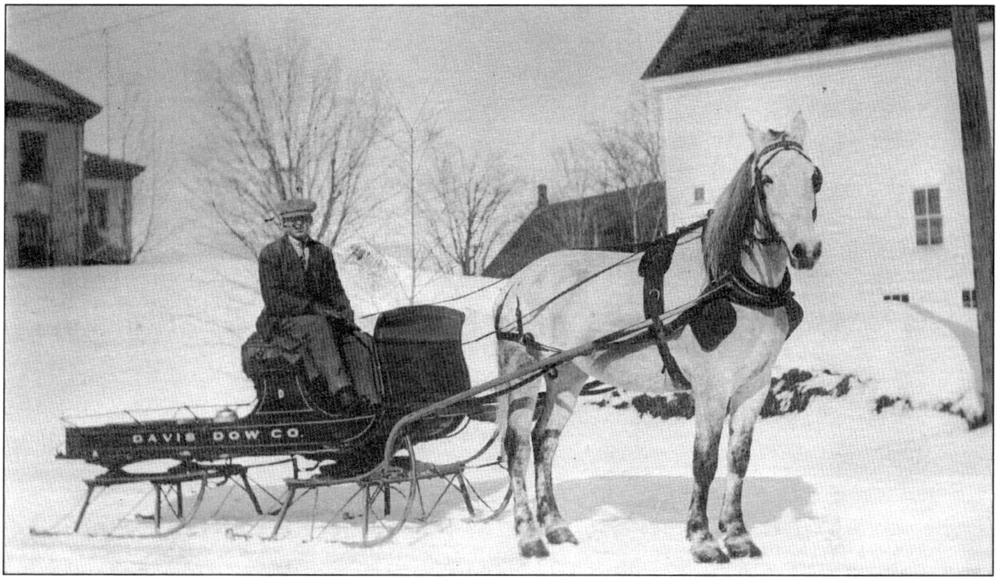

WINTER DELIVERY, C. 1910. As soon as the first appreciable snowfall blanketed town and country roads, sleds and sleighs replaced wagons, carriages, and even the automobile until the 1920s. Walter Davis of Lovell and Walter Dow of Portland ran a grocery store on the first floor of Gibbs Hall on Main Street. In 1913 they also began showing the first movies to come to Bridgton at the Opera House.

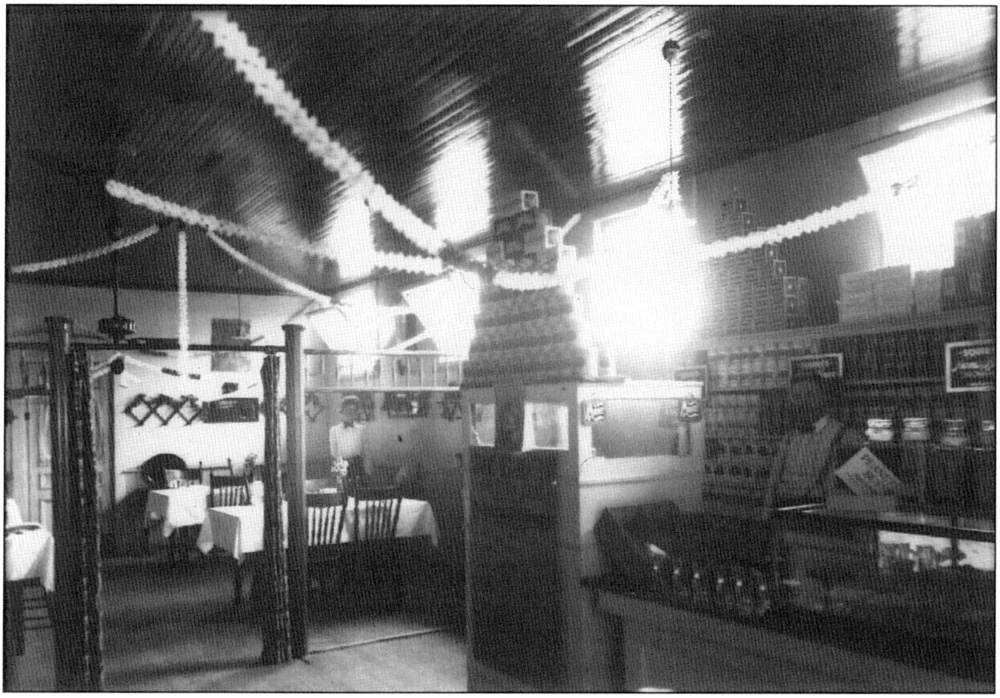

WARREN'S MARKET, C. 1927. Rue Warren of Brownfield purchased this building from Ned Holden of Sweden, and for the next 58 years Rue and his descendants ran an old-fashioned grocery and meat market. In the early years they also ran a restaurant. The market did not close until 1984, and the building is now a part of Chalmers Insurance and Realty.

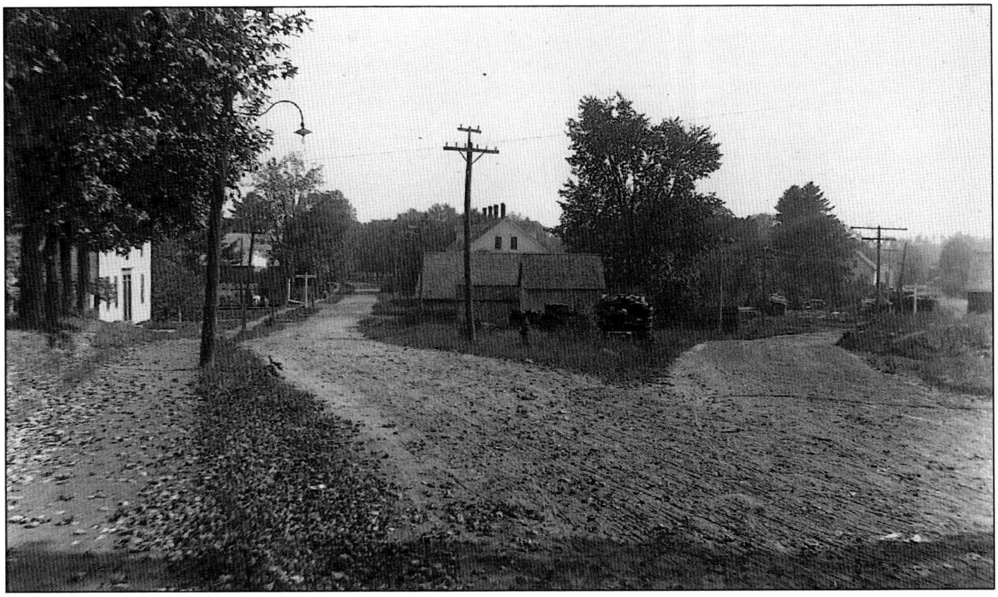

The Beehive Block, c. 1910. This was a suitable name for the area at lower Main Street and Mill Street during the many years that looms clattered at the Forest Mills and later the American Woolen Company. Both the mill buildings and the company houses are visible.

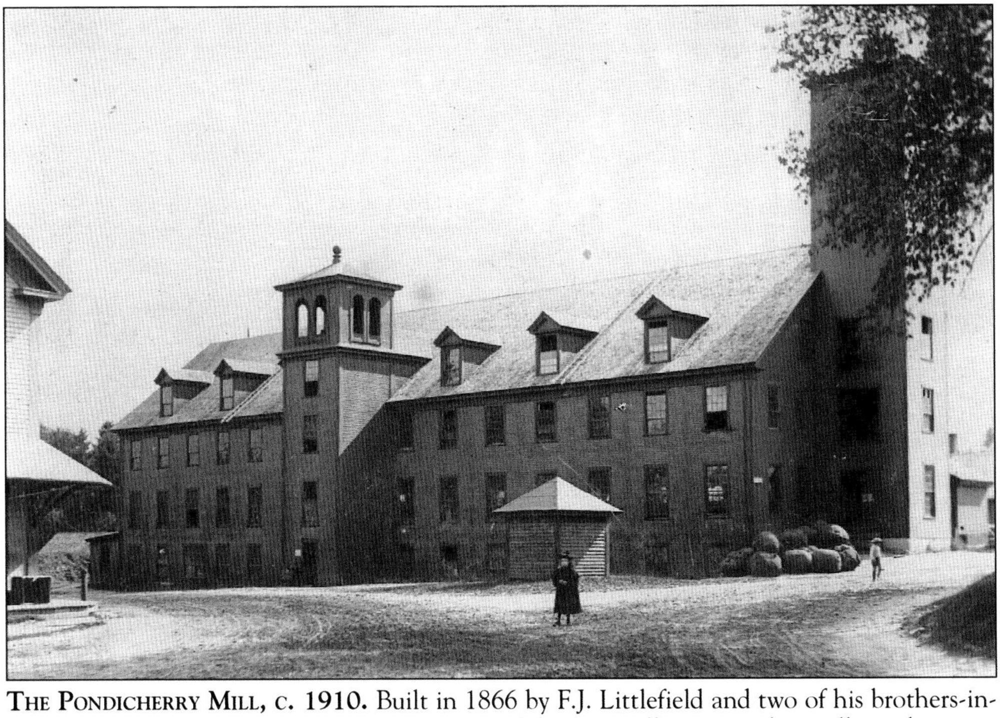

The Pondicherry Mill, c. 1910. Built in 1866 by F.J. Littlefield and two of his brothers-in-law, this was considered at the time to be one of the most efficient woolen mills in the state. In 1873 Rufus Gibbs formed the Pondicherry Company, merging this mill and the Cumberland Mill. Over the years the mill passed through several ownerships. Like the Forest Mills, it was a major employer, and when the mills converted to steam power, it was the Bridgton & Saco River Railroad that kept them supplied with coal. This building was razed in 1965.

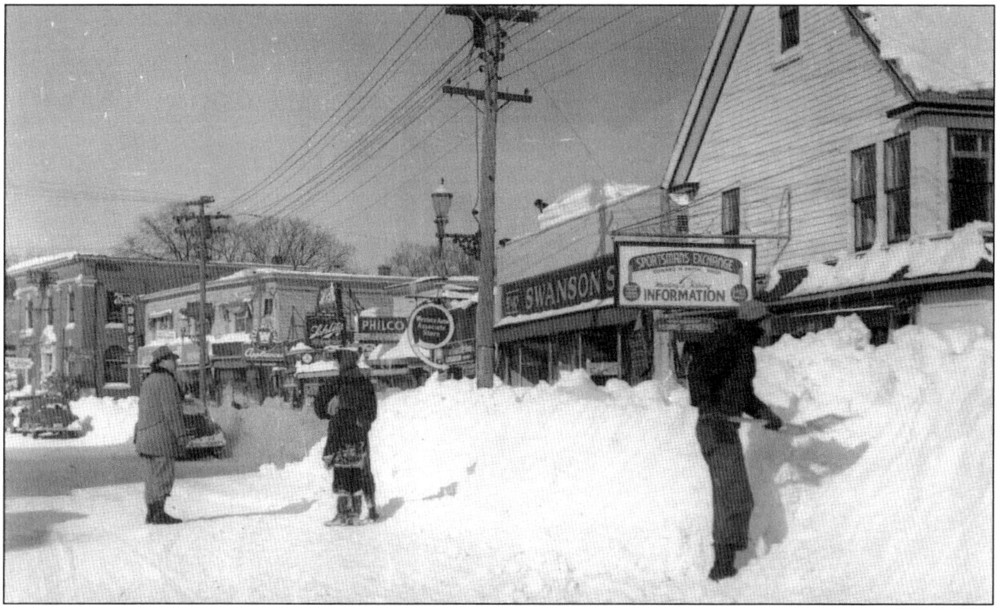

DIGGING OUT, FEBRUARY 18, 1952. The merchants of upper Main Street were faced with the unenviable task of cleaning up from a blizzard that had raged for 30 hours, paralyzing much of Maine. Many were saddened when the weight of another severe winter destroyed the popular State Theater in 1969.

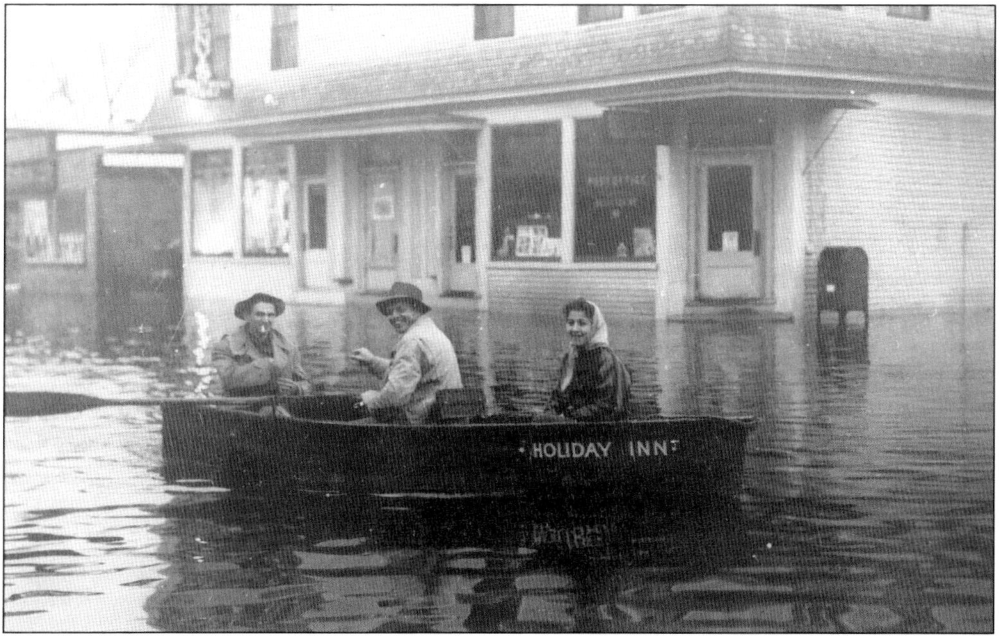

BOATING DOWN MAIN STREET, MARCH 27, 1953. The following winter the snowfall also was heavy. Excessive early spring rains resulted in the rapid melting of the snow, causing the water level of Highland Lake to rise. The upper part of Stevens Brook could not contain the deluge of water pouring in, and Post Office Square on Main Street and Depot Street were transformed into a miniature Venice. Although the merchants here in the Square suffered severe losses, these three people are obviously enjoying a rare boating experience.

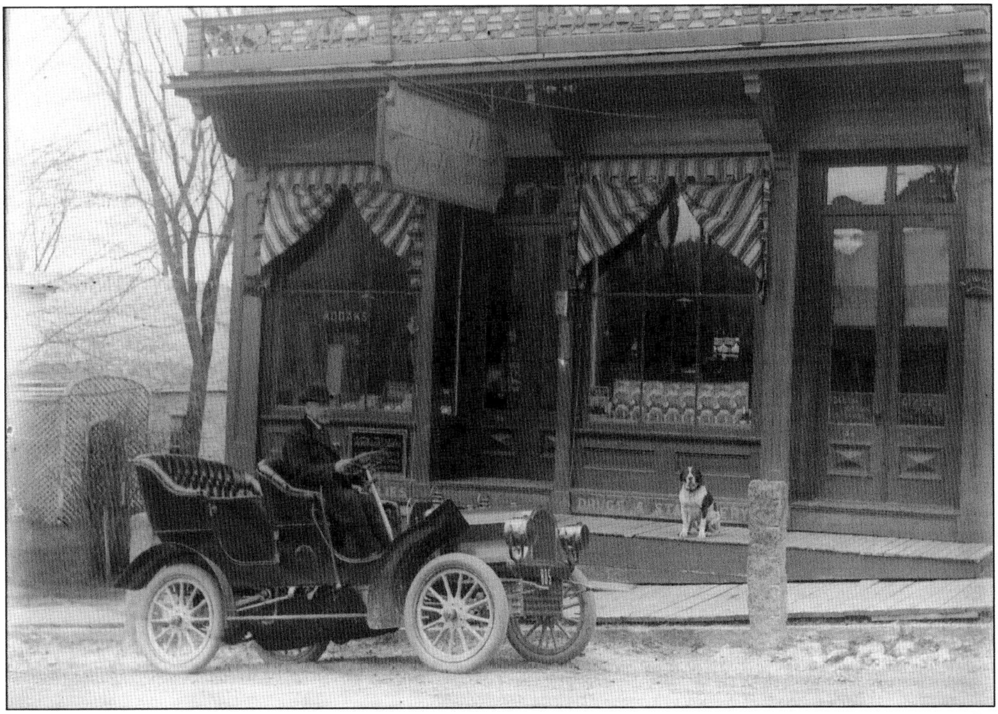

UP MAIN HILL, C. 1905. Dr. Frank E. Stevens, one of the first car owners in Bridgton, sits proudly behind the wheel of his 1905 Buick. In 1892 Dr. Stevens purchased this building (damaged in the fire that destroyed the adjacent Moses Block) from F.H. Hazelton and continued running a drugstore on the first floor. Dr. Asaph Walker practiced dentistry on the second floor. Today the building is an antique shop.

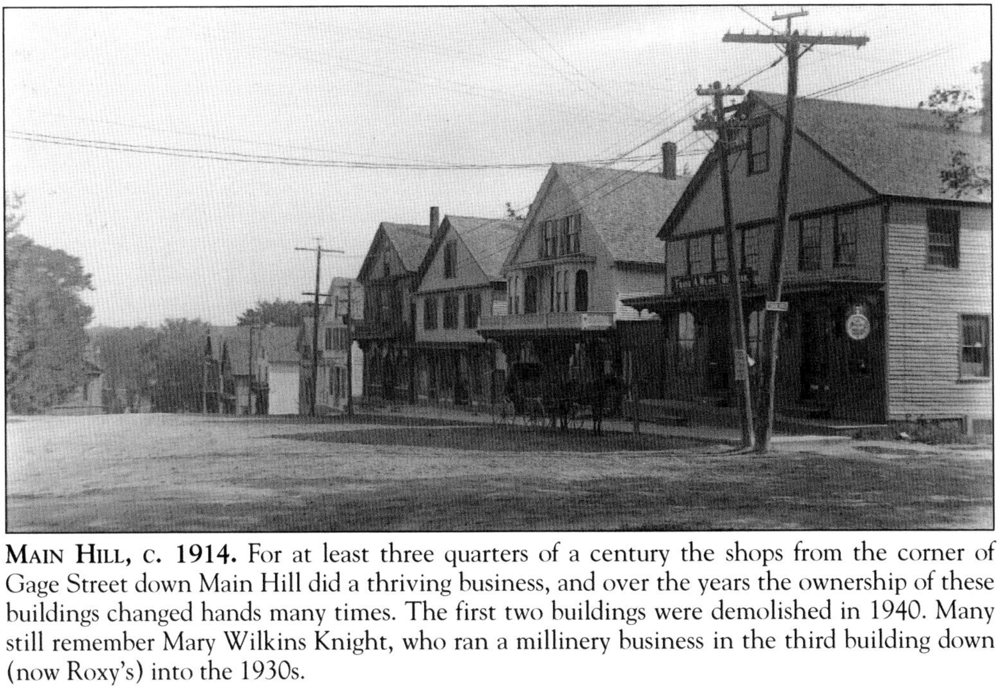

MAIN HILL, C. 1914. For at least three quarters of a century the shops from the corner of Gage Street down Main Hill did a thriving business, and over the years the ownership of these buildings changed hands many times. The first two buildings were demolished in 1940. Many still remember Mary Wilkins Knight, who ran a millinery business in the third building down (now Roxy's) into the 1930s.

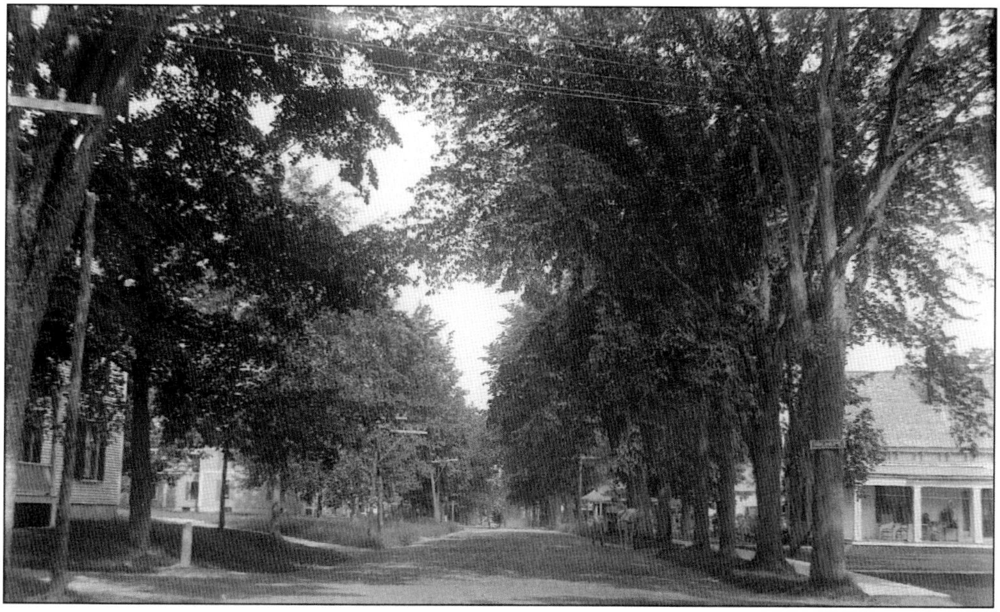

North High Street, c. 1890. This photograph was taken shortly after Jacob Stevens set the industrial wheels in motion along Stevens Brook that generated significant wealth in Bridgton. In 1774–75 Reuben and Simeon Burnham arrived in the area, which was the main artery to Fryeburg and Conway, and in an amazingly short time High Street developed into a residential locale for some of the wealthiest and most distinguished Bridgton families. (Because of the Dutch Elm disease, the majestic elms were cut down in 1968.)

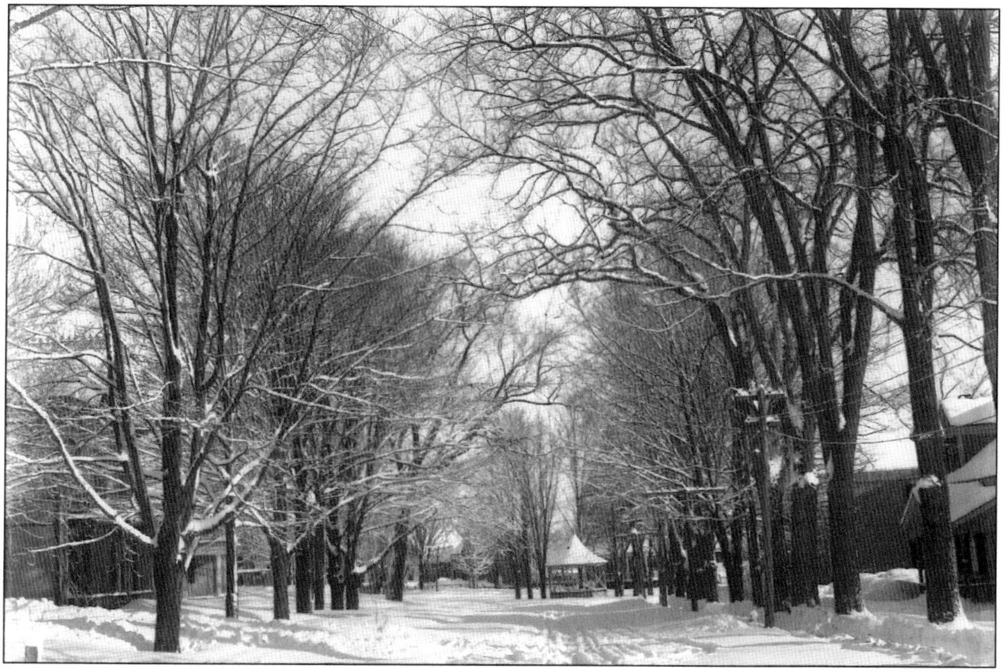

South High Street, c. 1890. The street is shown here beneath a fresh layer of unsullied snow. "Carpenter's Bandstand" (built in 1877) is visible where the Civil War monument now stands. High Street presents a marvellous study in local architectural history.

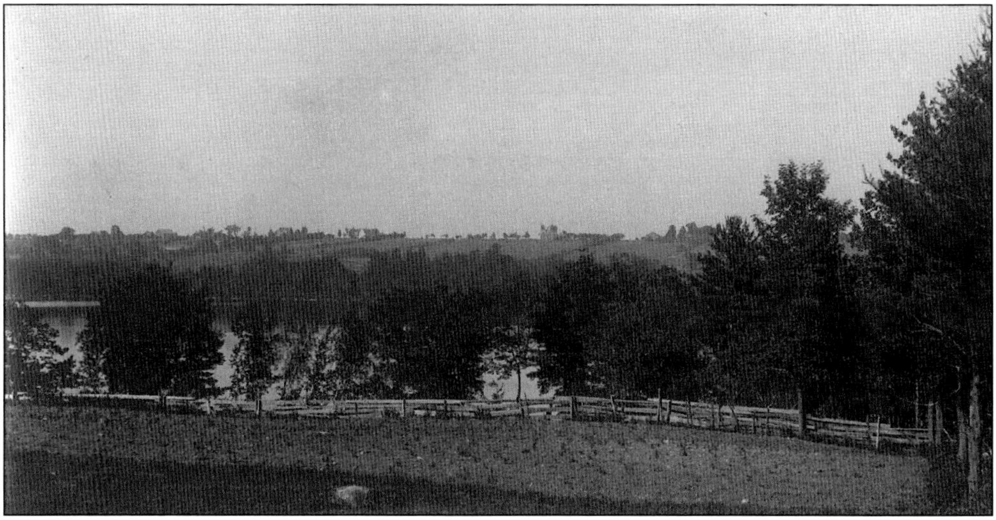

Upper Ridge, c. 1895. Agriculture still prevailed in the area of the Ridge overlooking Crotched Pond (Highland Lake) when this photograph was taken, and hay was still the primary crop. Abraham Kneeland, the son of David Kneeland, is credited with being the first settler on the Ridge.

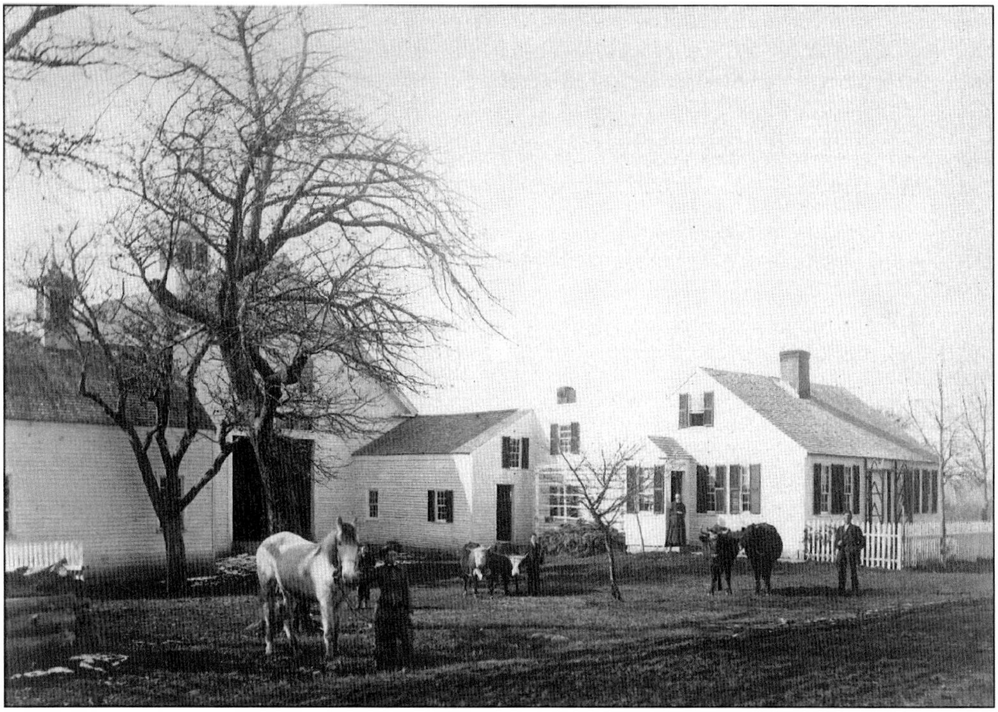

The Ingalls Farm, c. 1877. The farm is located on Lower Ridge, near the spot where David Kendrick was mortally wounded in a struggle with a Native American who coveted his wife's kettle (they were the first married couple on the Ridge, and David was the only known victim of a Native American conflict in the Lake Region). Edwin Ingalls is standing near the yoke of Red Durhams with his son Willis beside the white-faced steers. Roxy, his second wife, is holding the beautiful white horse.

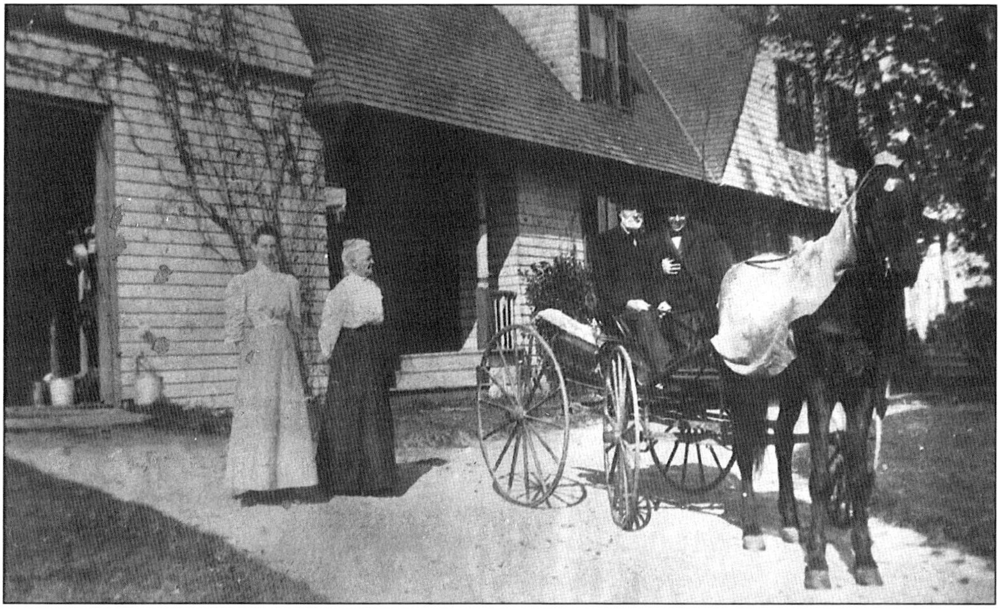

The Trufont Estate, c. 1890. Ineluctably, distinguished families from "away" discovered the ineffable scenic beauty of The Ridge. In 1889 Lilla Trufont, the wife of Charles M. Trufont, purchased from Julia (Smith) Davis the farm that in 1796 had been the property of Isaac Johnson, a farmer and blacksmith. The house and barn built later by Nathanial Bradstreet were then moved and the Trufonts replaced them with this impressive summer home. Presumably at least some of these people are Trufonts.

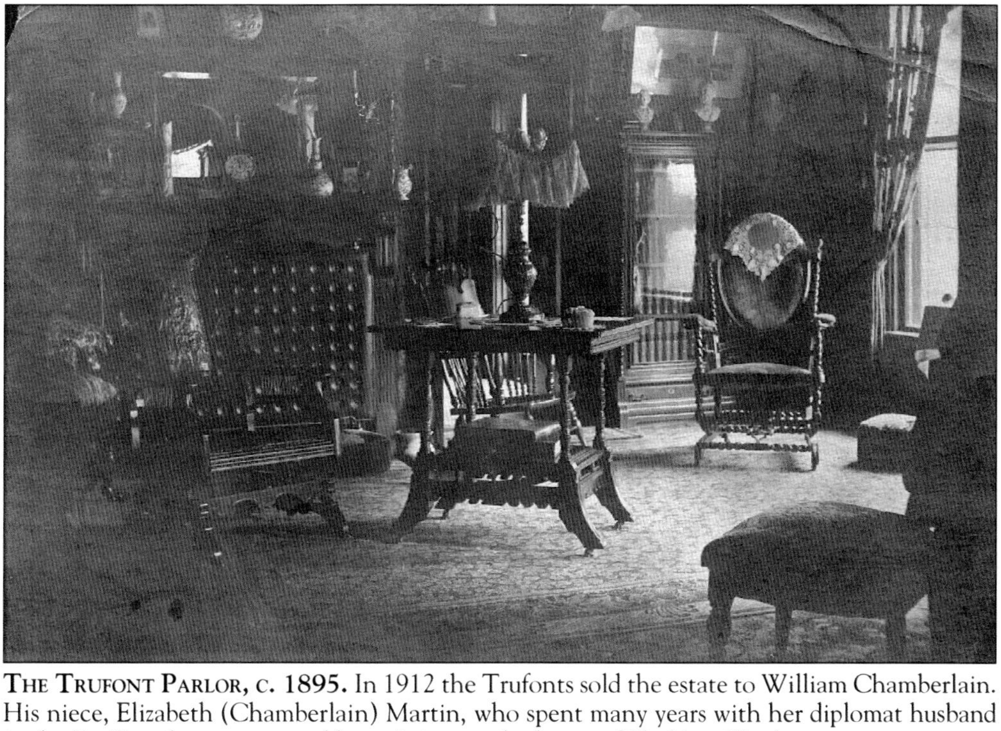

The Trufont Parlor, c. 1895. In 1912 the Trufonts sold the estate to William Chamberlain. His niece, Elizabeth (Chamberlain) Martin, who spent many years with her diplomat husband in the Far East, later summered here. It is now the home of Sheldon Chaikin.

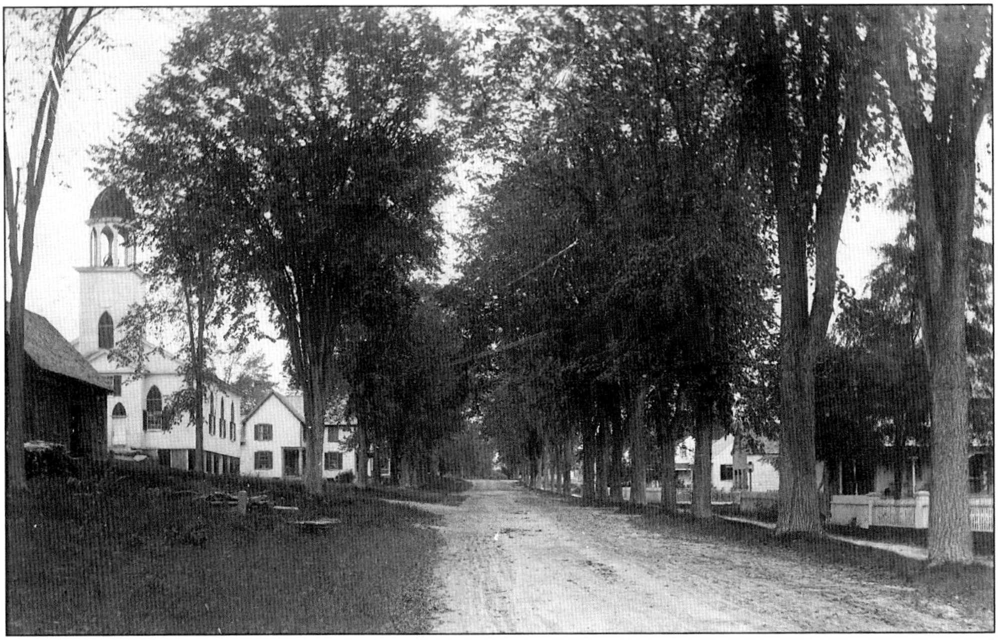

North Bridgton, c. 1890. This was an attractive little village; and, except for the removal of the stately elms because of disease in 1968 and the paving of Route 37, the lovely hamlet has been little altered. The dirt road was a great improvement over the first trail that was cut through here in 1766, linking Bridgton to Waterford. The Gothic-trimmed Congregational church was built in 1834.

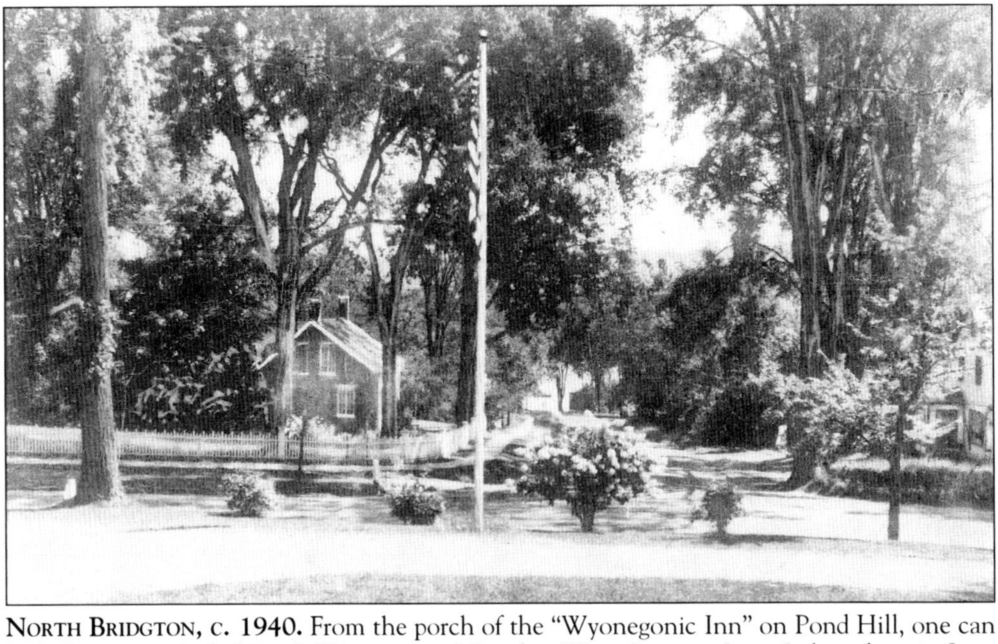

North Bridgton, c. 1940. From the porch of the "Wyonegonic Inn" on Pond Hill, one can look down tree-shaded Pond (Wyonegonic) Road to West Cove on Long Lake, where in June of 1768 Benjamin Kimball (34) built his boat landing and log house. He ran an inn and trading post here until he died at the age of 68. The lovely brick house, now owned by the Parkers, was built by Col. George W. Cushman in 1820 with bricks from his brickyard.

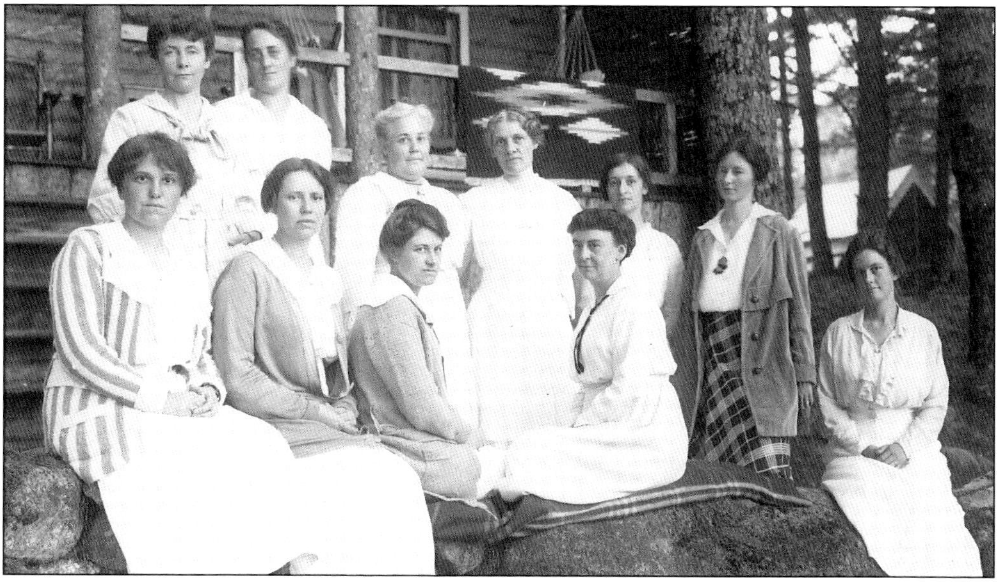

A NORTH BRIDGTON CONGREGATIONAL CHURCH PICNIC, C. 1920. From left to right, these women are as follows: (front row) only Mrs. Blake, seated to the far left, has been identified; (back row) Mrs. McComick, Mrs. Whitman, Mrs. Spooner, Mrs. Taylor, and Helen Hamlin (who lived to be 103 years old).

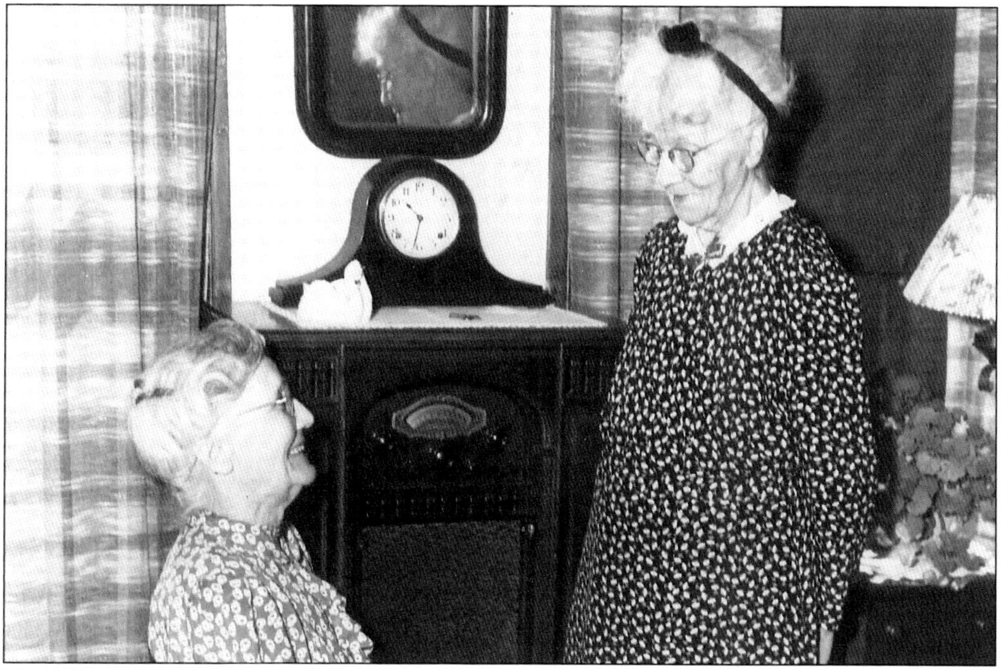

THE WHITEHOUSE SISTERS, 1949. Julia (Whitehouse) Chadbourne (age 95) looks down at her younger sister, Lilla (Whitehouse) Marr (age 82), "because she is so young and has so much to learn." Julia graduated valedictorian from Bridgton High School and was a member of the first graduating class of the Gorham Normal School (USM). She taught for many years in the area. She was an accomplished poet and journalist, and at the age of 100 (shortly before her death) she was still writing weekly for the *Bridgton News*.

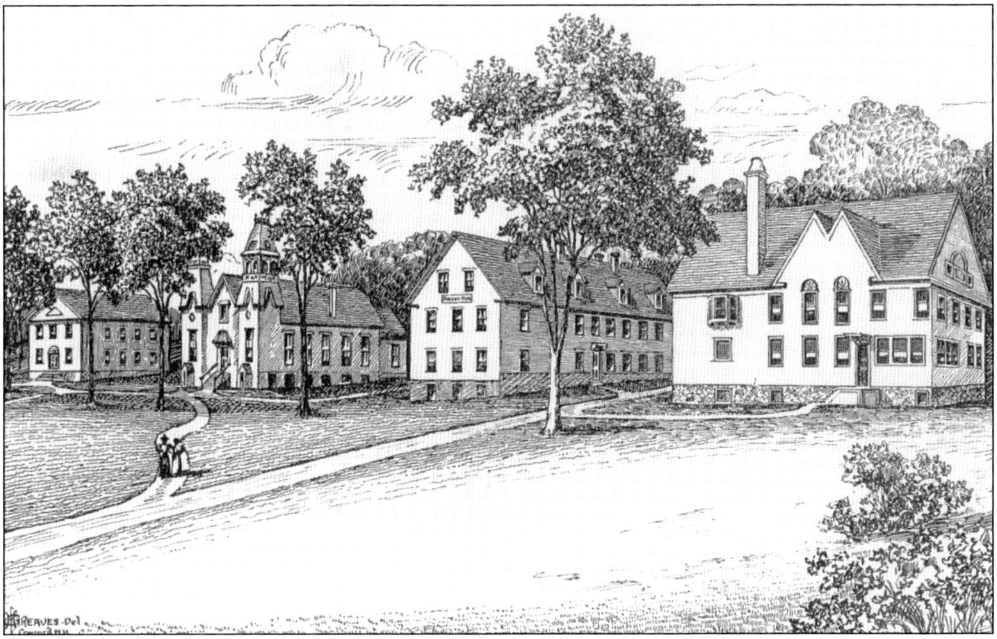

Bridgton Academy, 1892. The academy has played a prominent role in the North Bridgton community almost from the time the first classes were held in 1827 in the first building to the left (now the administrative building). Incorporated in 1808, the academy held classes from 1811 to 1827 on the third floor of the old Masonic Building next to Samuel Andrew's stone store down at West Cove. Newly constructed Ingalls Hall to the right (burned in 1969) was one of the best equipped gymnasiums at the time in the state.

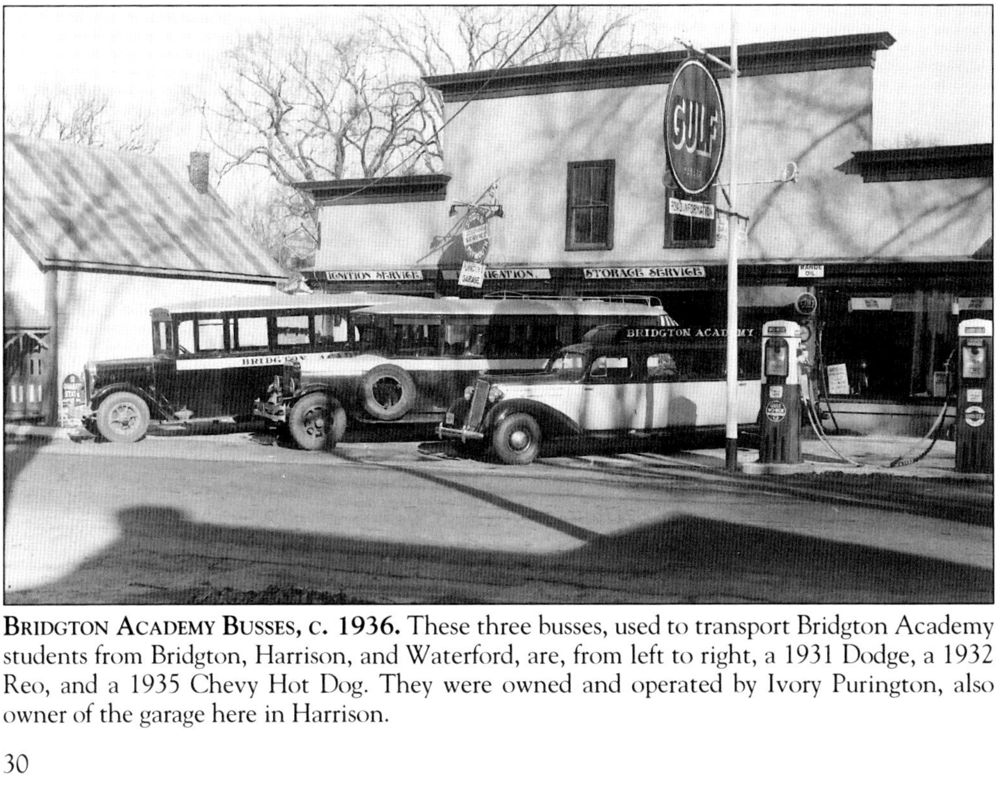

Bridgton Academy Busses, c. 1936. These three busses, used to transport Bridgton Academy students from Bridgton, Harrison, and Waterford, are, from left to right, a 1931 Dodge, a 1932 Reo, and a 1935 Chevy Hot Dog. They were owned and operated by Ivory Purington, also owner of the garage here in Harrison.

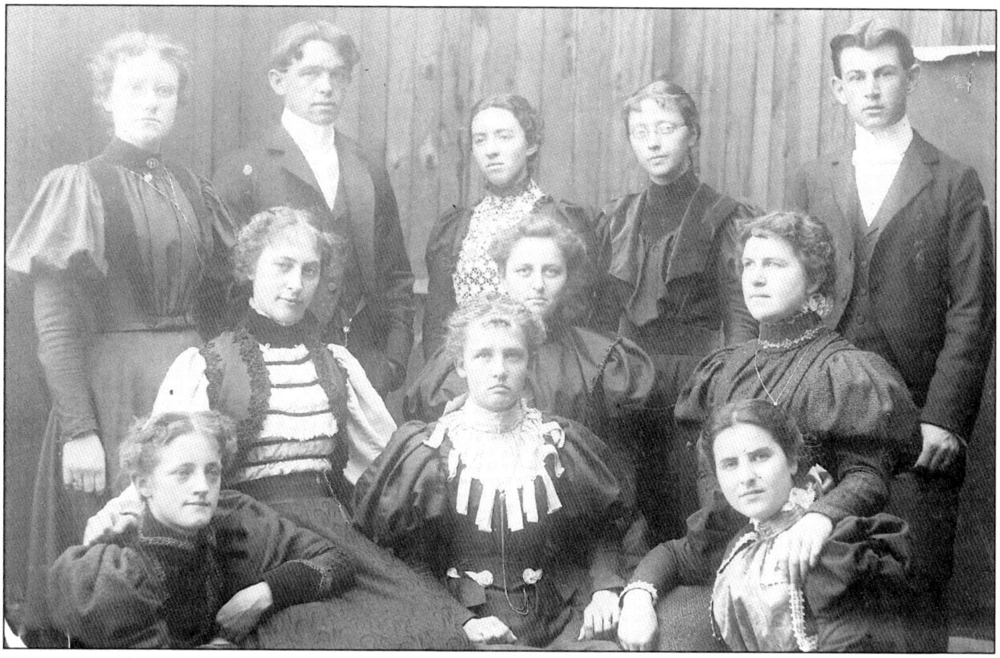

Bridgton Academy Scholars, 1897. These students are, from left to right, as follows: (front row) Bertha Pitts, Grace Skillings, and Carrie Hubbard; (middle row) Anne Weston, Blanche Cole, and Ethel Stanford; (back row) Jose Ricker, Harry Watson, Alice Paine, Bertha Greene, and Arthur Stanley. The number of girls is a reminder that the first dormitory (Farnsworth Hall) burned in 1896. The first dormitory for boys was not built until 1933.

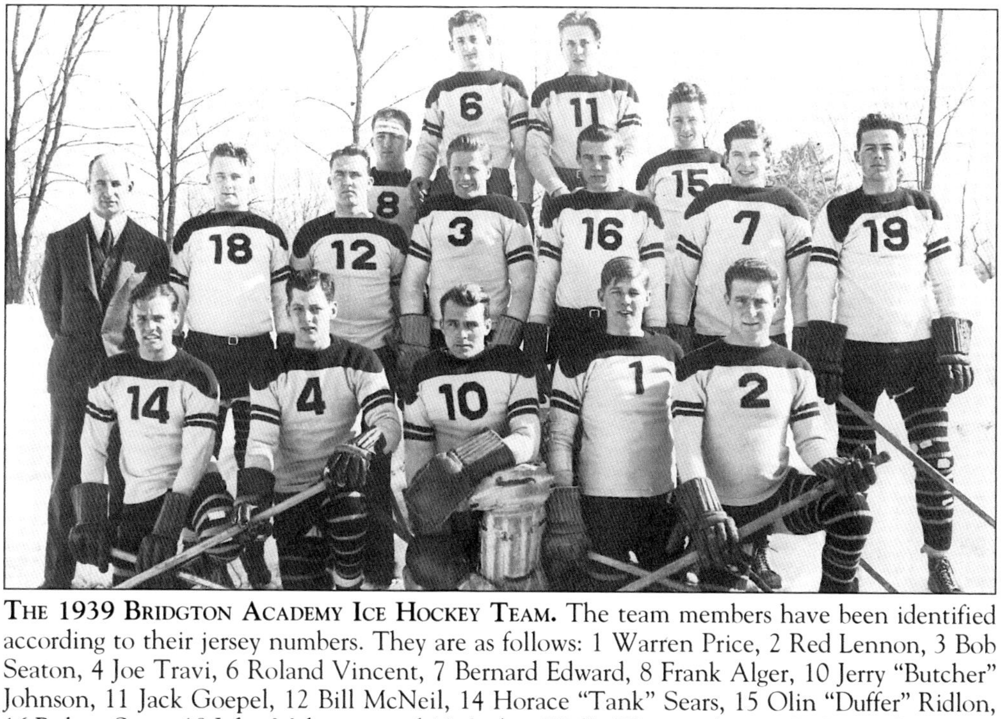

The 1939 Bridgton Academy Ice Hockey Team. The team members have been identified according to their jersey numbers. They are as follows: 1 Warren Price, 2 Red Lennon, 3 Bob Seaton, 4 Joe Travi, 6 Roland Vincent, 7 Bernard Edward, 8 Frank Alger, 10 Jerry "Butcher" Johnson, 11 Jack Goepel, 12 Bill McNeil, 14 Horace "Tank" Sears, 15 Olin "Duffer" Ridlon, 16 Robert Sears, 18 John Mahoney, and 19 Arthur Wells. The coach is Leslie B. Griffin.

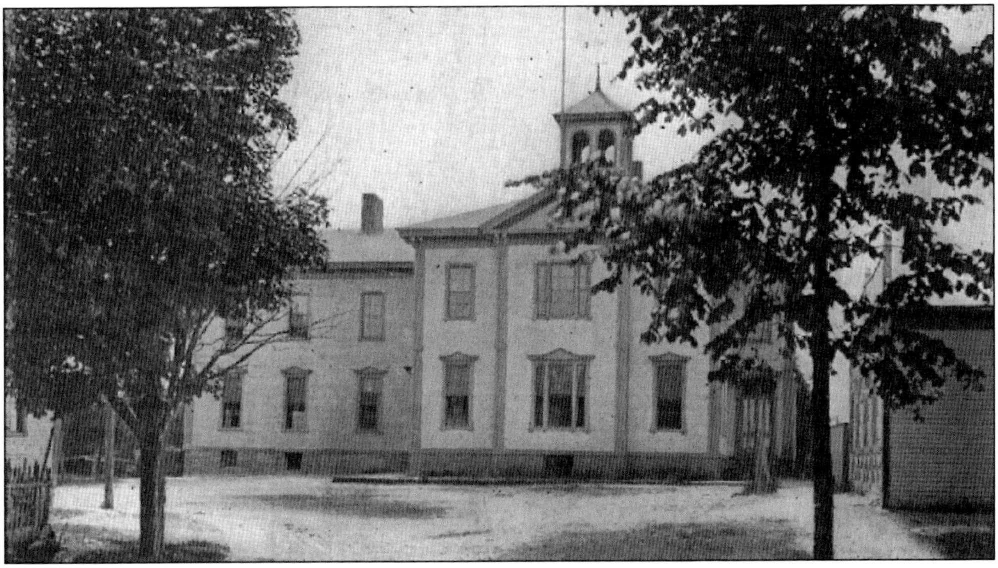

Bridgton High School, c. 1916. Despite opposition, the original high school building (shown here without the wing) was built in 1872. Before that, most students in the town who wanted a secondary education attended Bridgton Academy. In the beginning water was drawn from a local well and drunk from a tin dipper. There was no artificial lighting. A new high school was built in 1949 on the site of the old railroad yard, but this building continued to be used until the Lake Region High School opened in September of 1969. It was torn down in 1990.

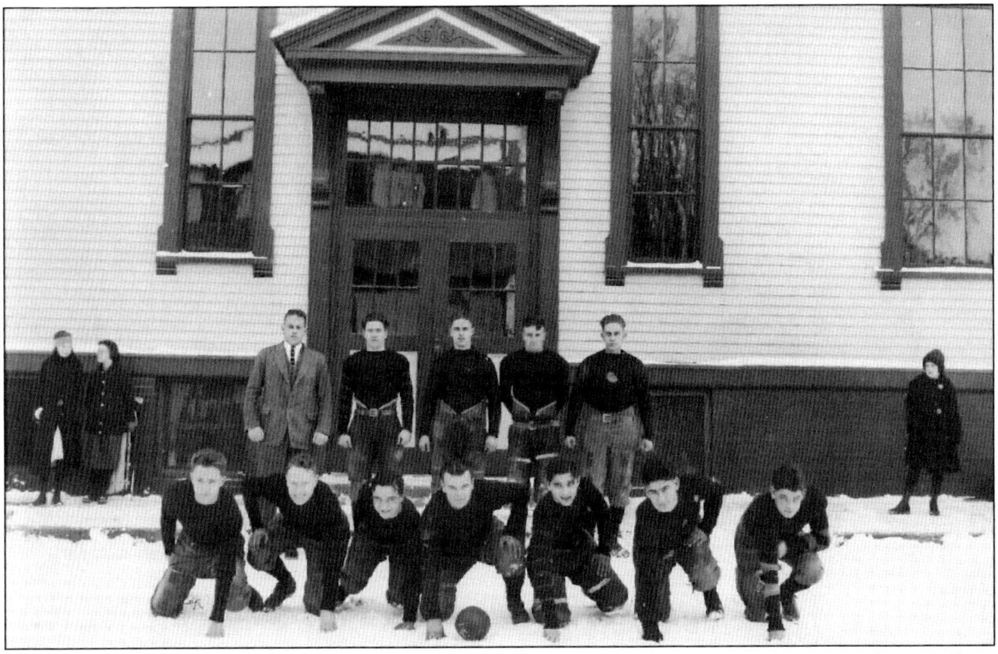

The 1924 Bridgton High School Football Squad. The team members are, from left to right, as follows: (front row) L. Moynihan, J. Ames, S. Gallinari, R. Browne, L. Gallinari, W. Knight, and W. Cockburn; (back row) Coach Milan Herrick, H. Berry, H. Richardson, H. Warren, and J. McDonald.

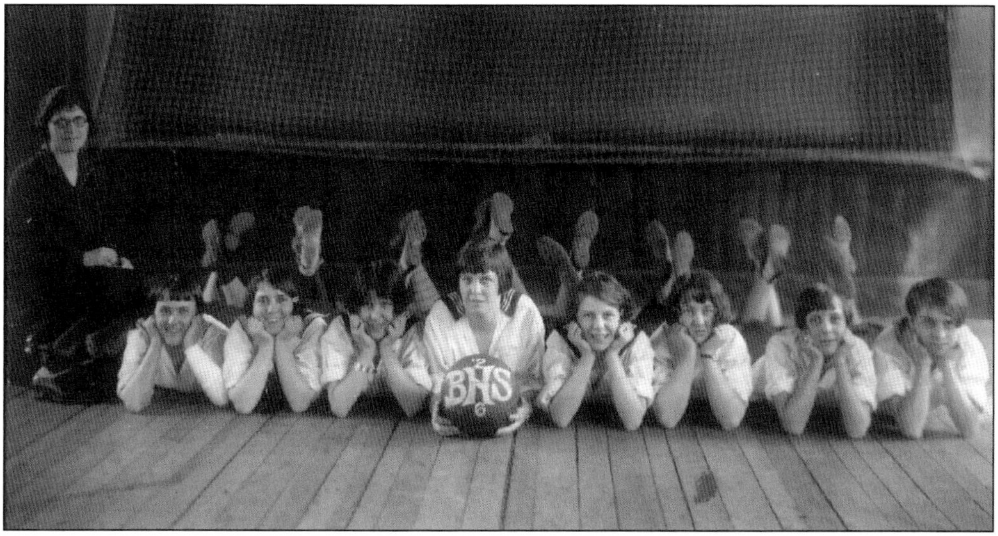

THE 1926 LADY BLACK HAWK BASKETBALL TEAM. Shown are, from left to right, Coach Helen Hill, Hazel McDaniels, Arline Hill, Dorothy Embick, Genella Dodge, Marie Embick, Eva Sylvester, Theo McDaniels, and Beatrice Humphries.

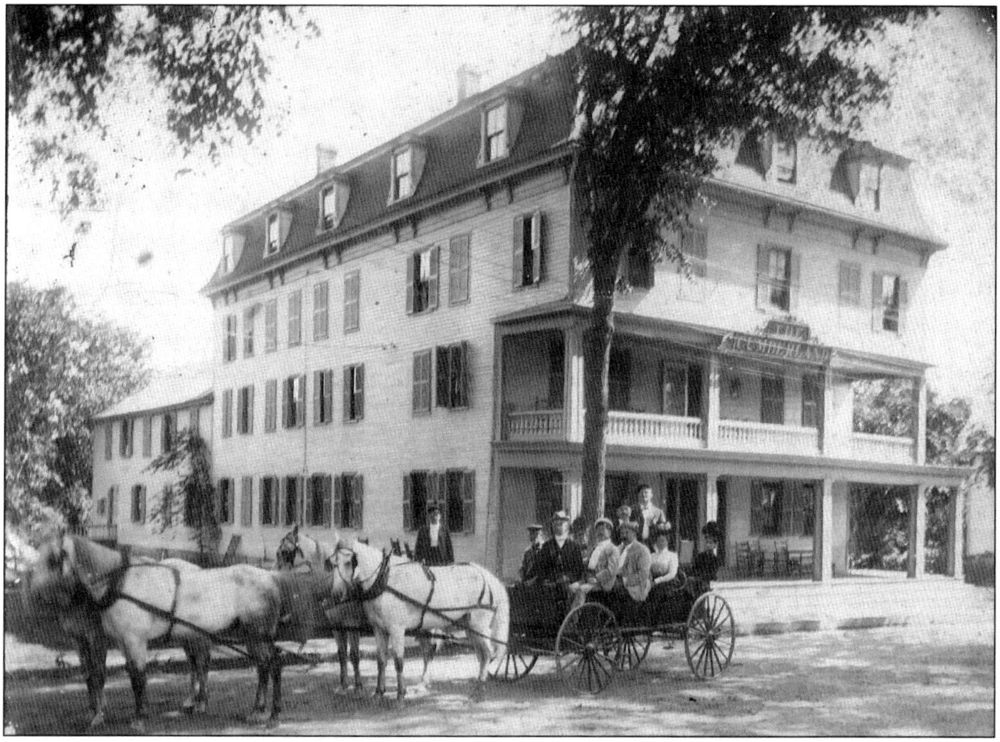

THE CUMBERLAND HOTEL, C. 1890. Located on the corner of Main and Bacon, this hotel was a popular place for guests to repose and dine, especially during the many years it was operated by Marshal and Joshia Bacon (and later by Marshal's three children). Marshal purchased the hotel in 1858 from Rufus Chase and greatly expanded it over the years. Very likely those in the open wagon are guests either headed out on an excursion or to the railroad station. The building was demolished in 1970.

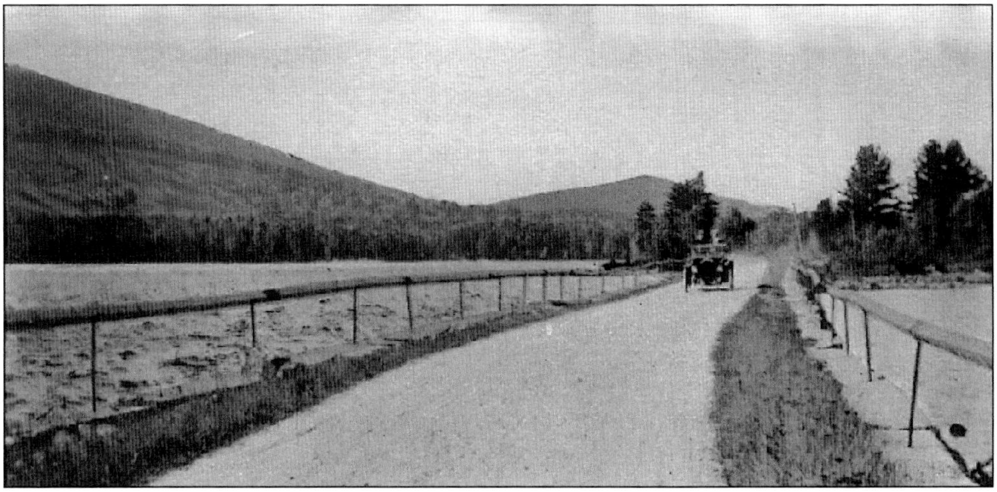

Moose Pond, c. 1914. The growing popularity of the automobile and the improvement of roads gave impetus to tourism in the Lake Region. Bridgton, with nine different ponds either totally or partly within its confines, became a mecca for summer visitors. An early vintage car is put-putting toward Bridgton across Moose Pond on the causeway (Route 302), first built in 1835.

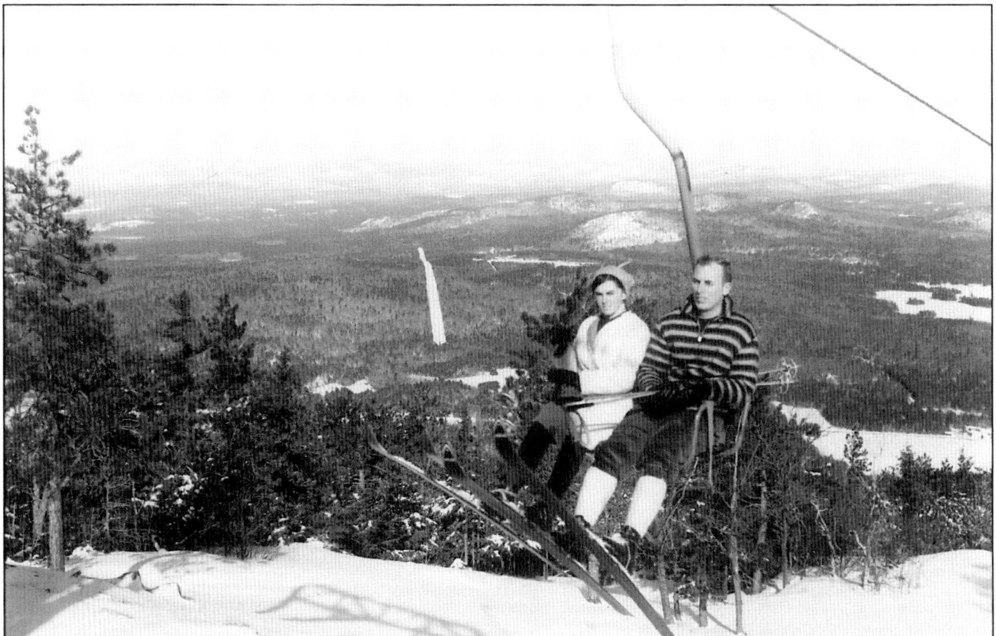

Pleasant Mountain Ski Slopes, c. 1953. The second oldest ski area in Maine, Pleasant Mountain officially opened in January of 1938. Harry Sampson, headmaster of Bridgton Academy, along with his students and the help of the CCC and WPA, began clearing the forested slope in 1937. Russ Haggett and other civic leaders helped make Pleasant Mountain and Bridgton a popular ski resort. In 1988 the area was renamed Shawnee Peak at Pleasant Mt.

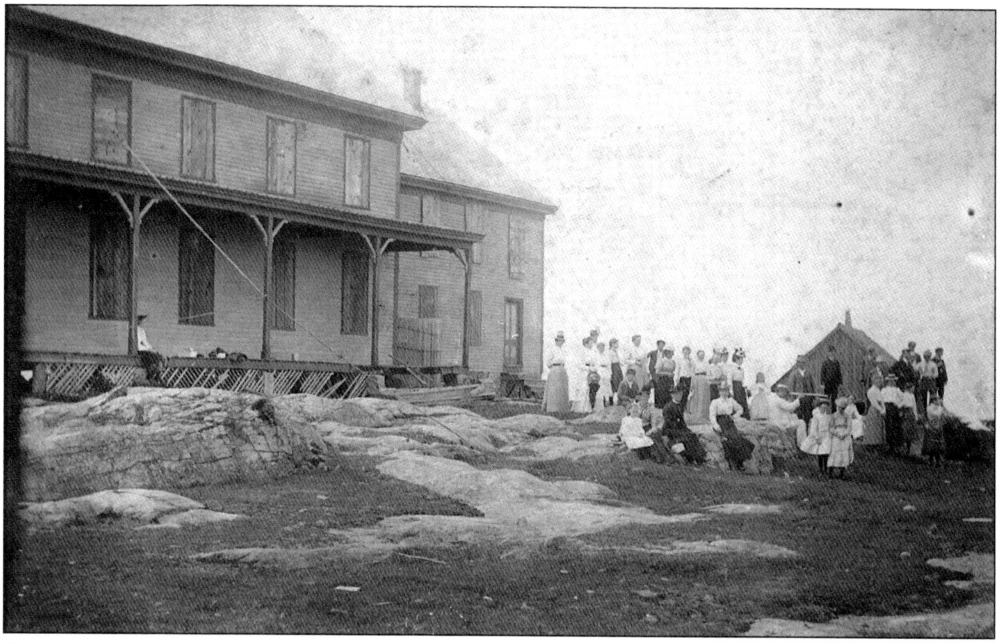

THE PLEASANT MOUNTAIN HOTEL, 1897. Long before Pleasant Mountain began attracting ski enthusiasts, the splendid view from the summit of the mountain unfolding in every direction began attracting the more adventuresome. In 1845 Caleb Warren erected a crude shelter on "Green Pinnacle." In 1850 he sold the property to Joseph Sargent, who converted the shelter to a bowling alley and constructed a two-story hotel that burned in 1860. In 1872 Charles E. Gibbs bought the property and erected this 26-room hotel. It was demolished in 1908. A church group is shown here having a picnic.

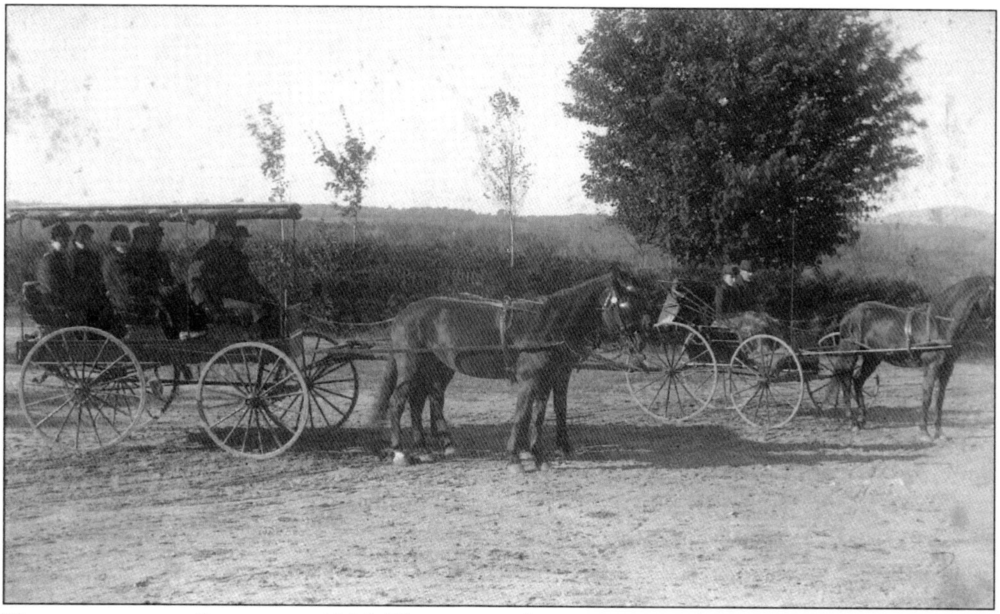

HEADING FOR THE SUMMIT, C. 1895. This group of excursionists is being conveyed to the foot of Pleasant Mountain either to endure a rough ride up the precipitous trail to the hotel or ascend it "shanks mare."

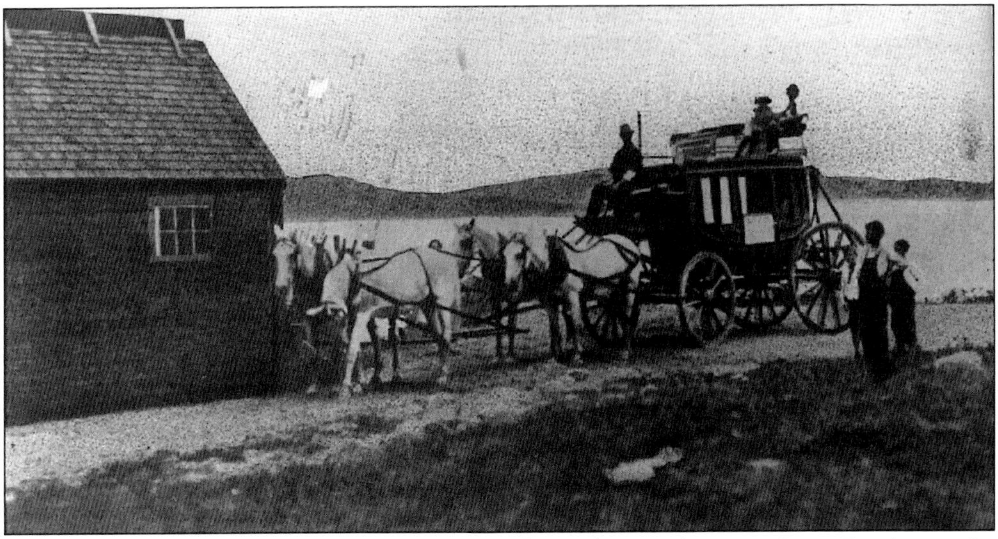

PLUMMERS LANDING, C. 1890. The landing was located in Bridgton on Long Pond near the homestead of Eli Plummer, a colorful canal boat captain. Both freight and passengers were loaded and unloaded here. Vacationers came to Bridgton via the steamboats from Sebago Lake Station (Standish) and were transported by stagecoaches to either farms that took in summer boarders, or to the Pleasant Mountain Hotel, the Cumberland House, or—after Charles Cobb closed the Pleasant Mountain Hotel—the Bridgton House on Main Hill.

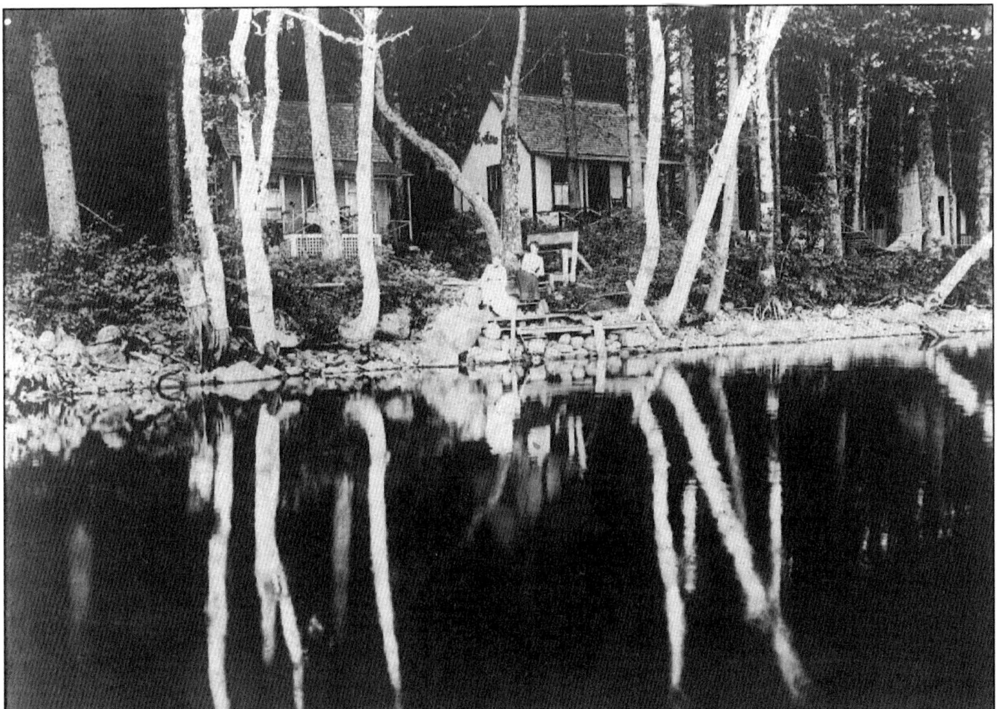

HIGHLAND LAKE (CROTCHED POND), C. 1930. Shortly after the turn of the century, cottages began to sprout up along the shores of the lakes and larger ponds in the Lake Region. These rental cabins were located near Richardson's Motel.

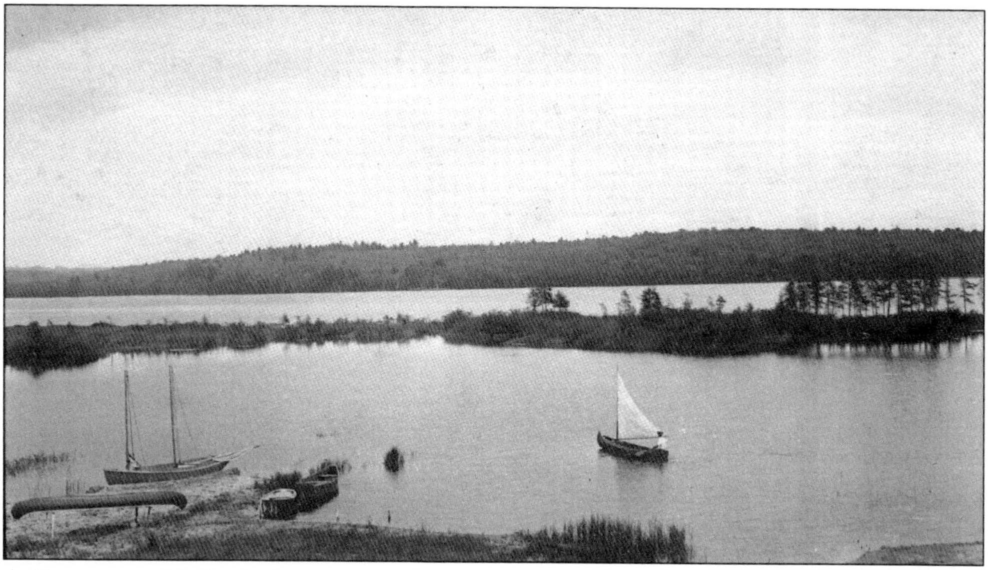

A View from McKay's Landing on Long Lake, c. 1910. Long Lake, earlier called Long Pond, is approximately 12 miles long and is linked to Sebago Lake by Chute's River at the Naples Causeway, Brandy Pond, and the serpentine Songo River. Before the advent of the inboard and outboard motors, the silence of wooded ponds and lakes was only occasionally broken by the cry of a loon. The towns of Naples, Bridgton, and Harrison have shorelines on the lake.

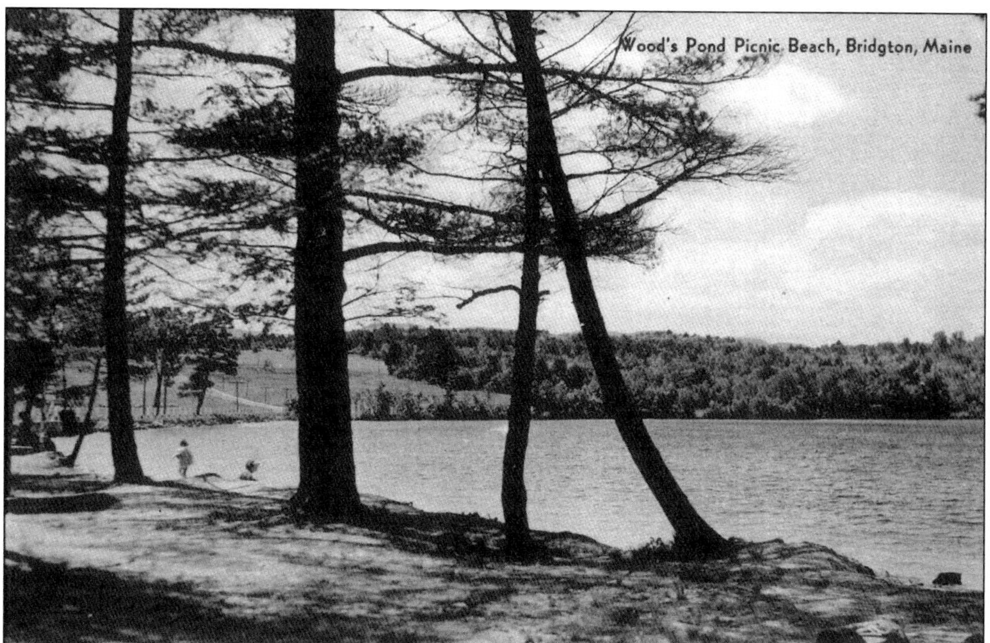

Woods Pond Picnic Beach, c. 1950. Located on Route 117, this popular recreational site includes a protected swimming area. It is reputed to be named after Solomon Wood of Boxford, Massachusetts, who, along with five assistants, surveyed Bridgton in 1763.

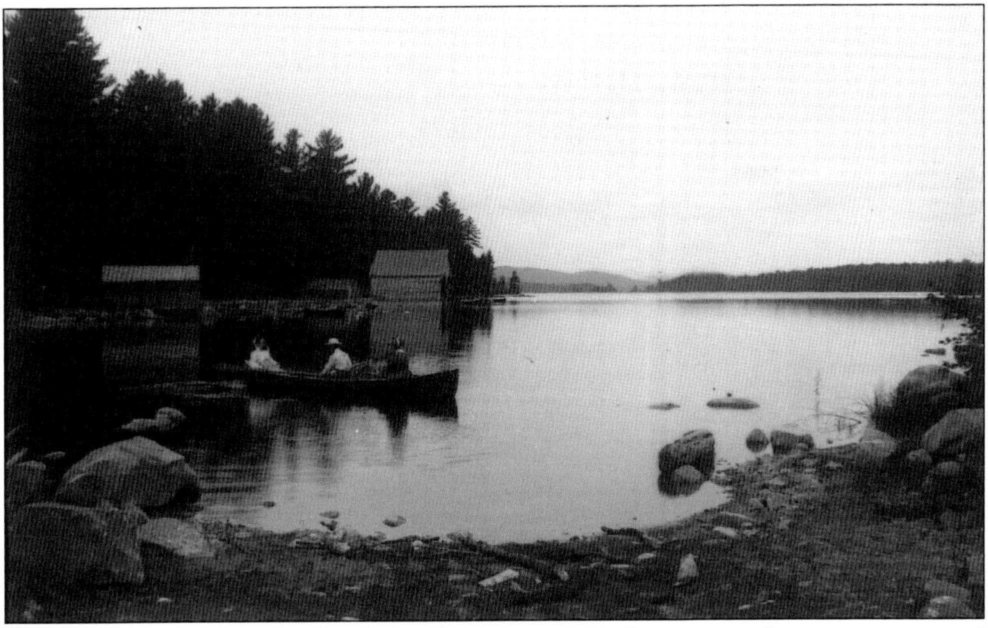

HIGHLAND LAKE, C. 1900. Ever since the late nineteenth century, when vacationers and sportsmen came by water to Plummers Landing and then by stage to Ingalls Grove and Indian Spring to rough it in tents, this lovely body of water has enhanced Bridgton as a vacation center. Especially in the 1940s a goodly portion of Bridgton's annual Winter Carnival was held here, including speed skating events. The lake fed Stevens Brook, turned the mill wheels, floated logs to the sawmills, provided ice for domestic and commercial use, provided power to generate the first electricity (1898) on Main Street, and was the source of water for the first water system in 1902.

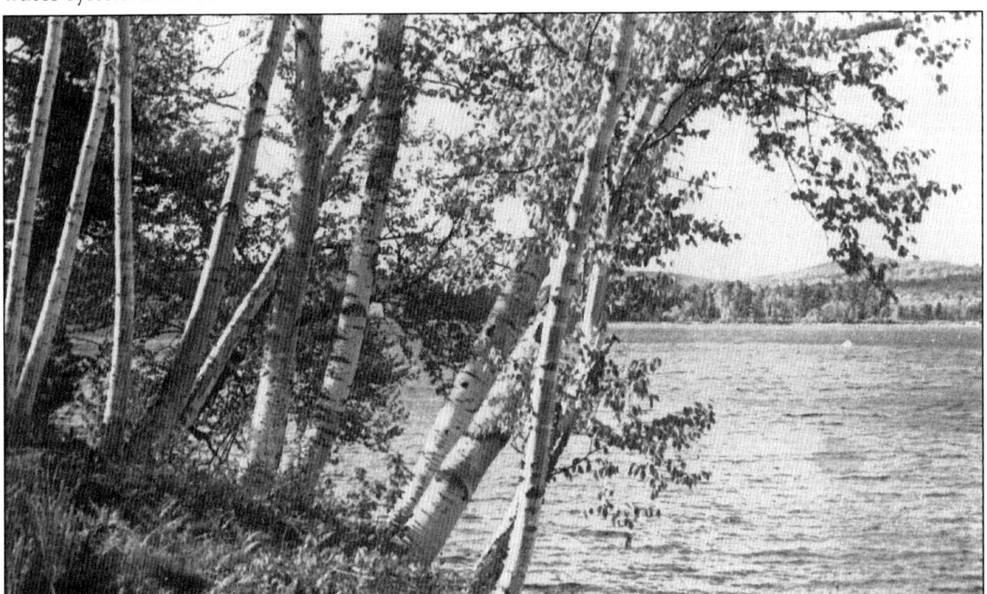

INFINITUDE. White birches arch gracefully over the rippled waters of Moose Pond in the shadows of Pleasant Mountain.

Two

Harrison

First Settled: 1792
Incorporated: 1805
Population: 2,200
Principal Settlements: Harrison Village and Bolster's Mills

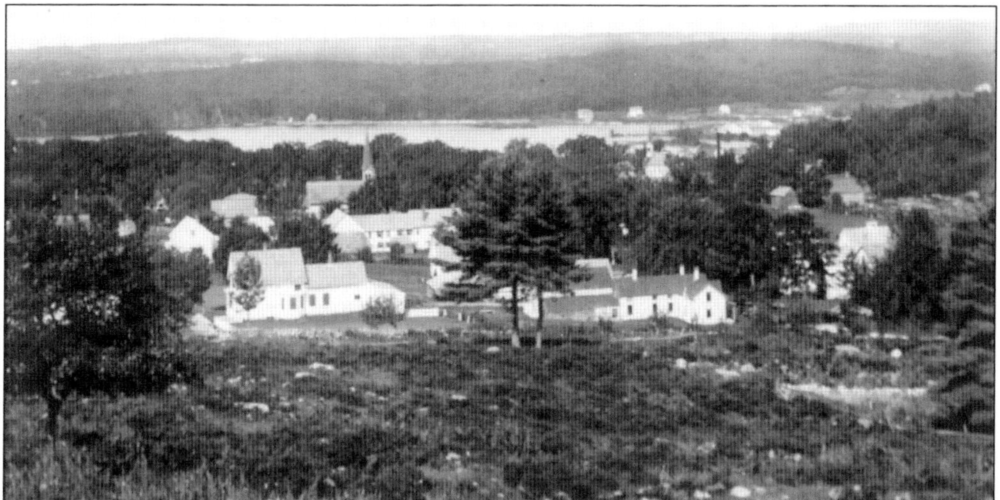

HARRISON VILLAGE FROM DAWES HILL, C. 1920. This panoramic view of Harrison Village, located on the upper end of Long Pond or Long Lake, clearly indicates why a few years after this photograph was taken, artists and other summer visitors would begin flocking to the area in increasing numbers. And long before the roads were paved, excursionists and vacationers could easily reach Harrison by taking the train from Portland to Sebago Lake Station and then boarding a steamer for the nearly 50-mile voyage up lakes and rivers to the head of Long Lake.

Dawes Hill was named after one of Harrison's first settlers, Cushing Dawes, from Duxbury, Massachusetts, who along with his wife, Mary, and his father, settled on a farm here on the hill. His son John was one of the original founders of the Free Will Baptist Church (now the Calvary Church), visible from the hill, as well as the Harrison Agricultural Mechanics Club.

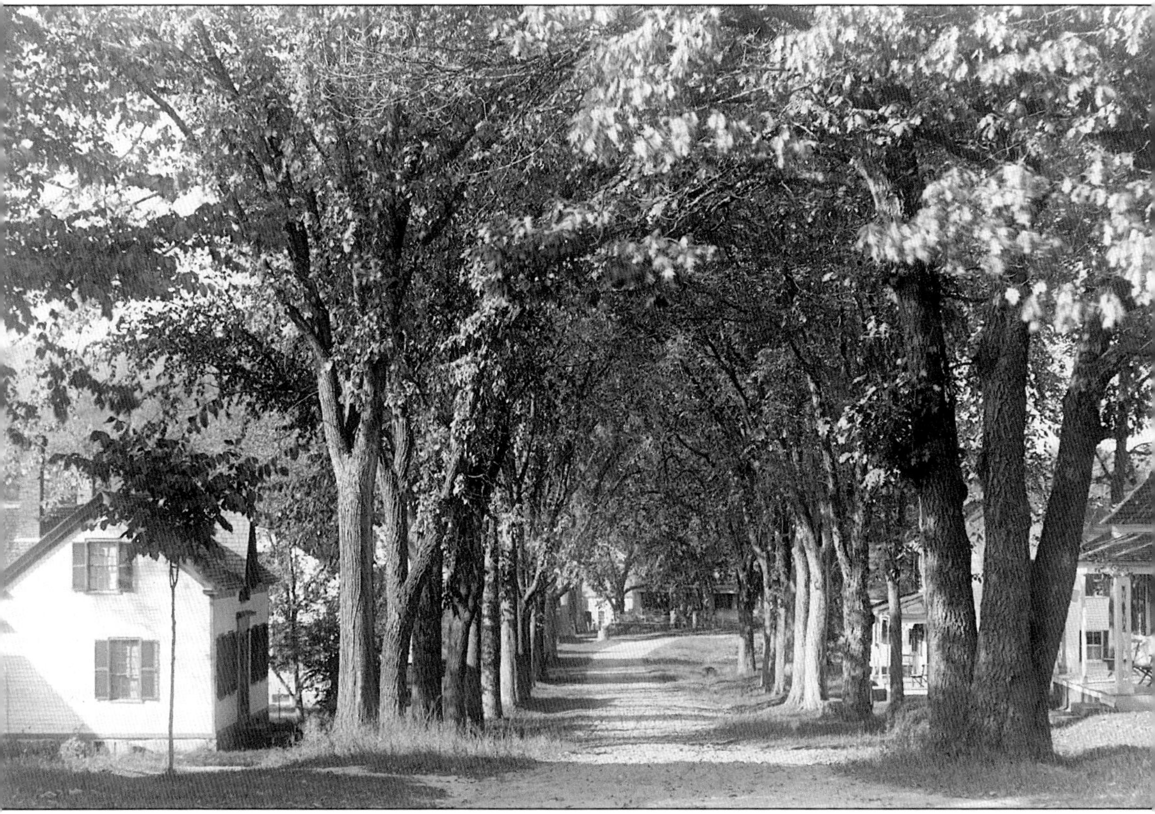

SMITH STREET. Smith Street virtually tunneled beneath an archway of stately elm trees that provided privacy and much-needed shade in summer to the residents of these well-maintained houses. There is something timeless about this peaceful scene, and it seems incredible that a century earlier there were but a few crude dwellings scattered about.

John Carsley Jr. and his brother Nathan are thought to have been the first settlers of Harrison. It is said that they came up to what is now Harrison in the fall of 1792 from their family home in Gorham. The following March, while the waterways were still frozen, they again made the long, arduous trek; but this time they came with their wives, began tapping maple trees and boiling the sap down into syrup and sugar, and very likely remained here in the crude cabins they erected from the trees cut and hewed into logs with little more than axes.

James Sampson, who built a cabin near the lake in 1800 and later erected the house that is thought to be the Crystal House, is considered to have been the pioneer settler of Harrison Village. His grandson, Christopher Sampson, captained the ill-fated *Fawn*, the first passenger steamer in the Lakes Region (1847–55).

Harrison, incorporated March 8, 1805, was carved out of portions of Otisfield and Bridgton and was named after Harrison Gray Otis of Boston, the nephew of the enigmatic James Otis.

Agriculture and forest-related industries early on became the mainstay of the town. And what really gave impetus to both was the completion of the Cumberland & Oxford Canal in 1830. For the first time Harrison residents and those in the adjacent Oxford Hills communities were provided with a relatively quick and easy way to convey themselves and their produce and products to Portland and return with much-needed supplies. Particularly the apple and wood product industries rapidly expanded, and Harrison quickly became a port town. A temporary setback for Harrison and the Lake Region occurred shortly after 1870 when the Portland & Ogdensburg Railroad put the canal out of business, but by 1898 Harrison was linked to what had become the Maine Central Railroad by the Bridgton & Saco River Railroad.

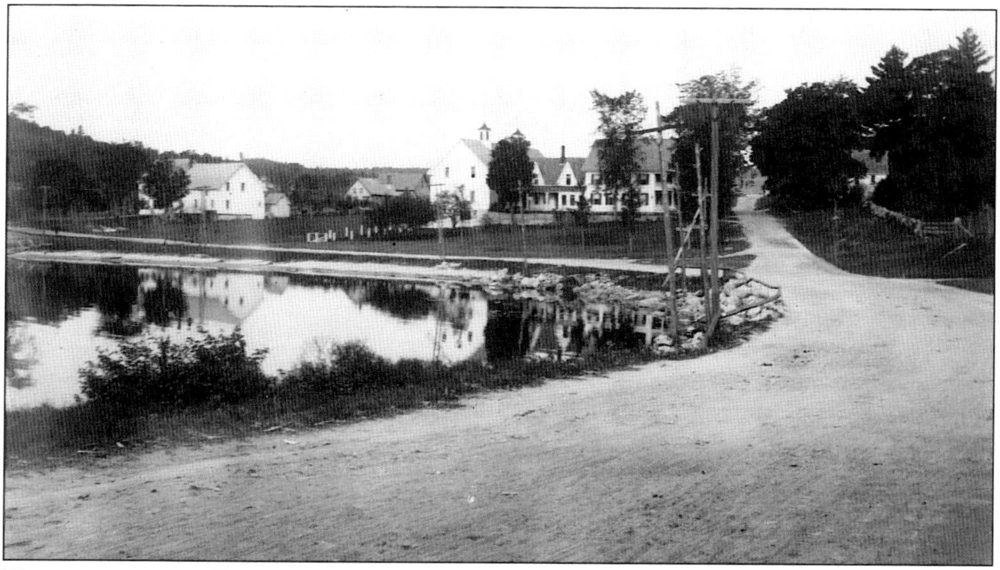

Harrison at the Head of Long Lake, c. 1920. The head waters of Long Lake mark the terminus of nearly 50 miles of waterways beginning with the Lower Basin in Windham and Sebago Lake Station. The expansive house and barn reflecting into the mirror-like waters were built by John Woodson Caswell, the father of J. Wallace Caswell. The house to the left was owned by John Witham at the time this photograph was taken.

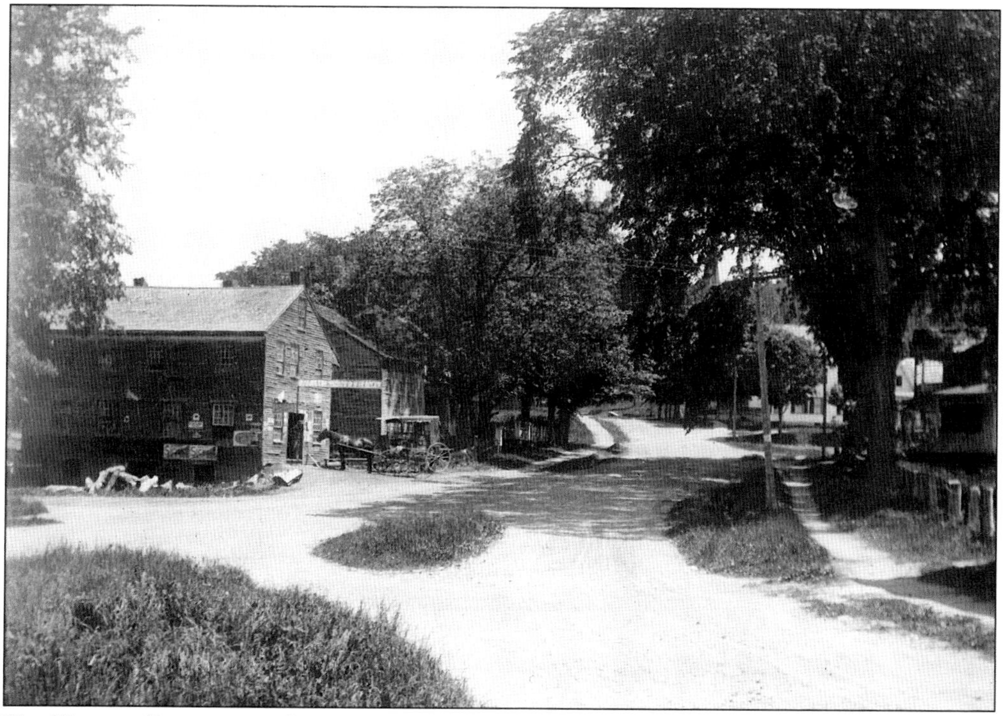

The Village Blacksmith Shop, c. 1895. No service industry was more vital to Harrison or any other rural Maine community until the advent of the automobile than the village blacksmith. This smithy, which earlier had been Robie's Store, was centrally located here in Harrison where the roads to Norway, Naples, and the Harrison Block converged.

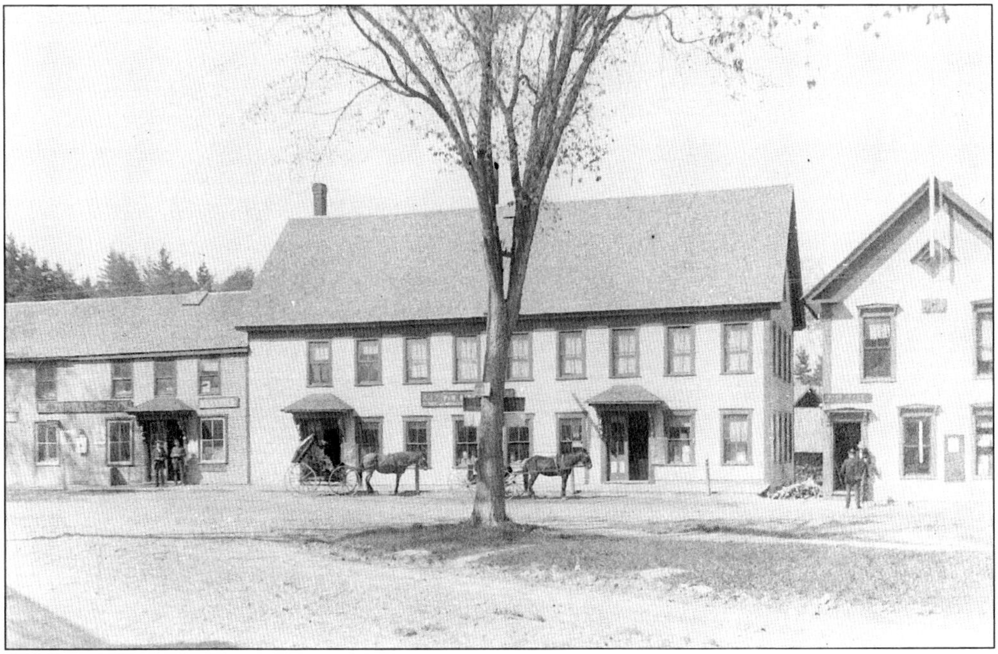

The Harrison Block before the 1907 Fire. The disastrous conflagration on May 14, 1907, left the original Harrison Block in smoldering ruins. On the right was the Reform Club Hall, built *c.* 1876 by the Temperance Union. The post office was located on the first floor, and the library was upstairs. The center section was Freeland Holmes Ricker's store. The building on the left was the store of Marshall Jordan & Son.

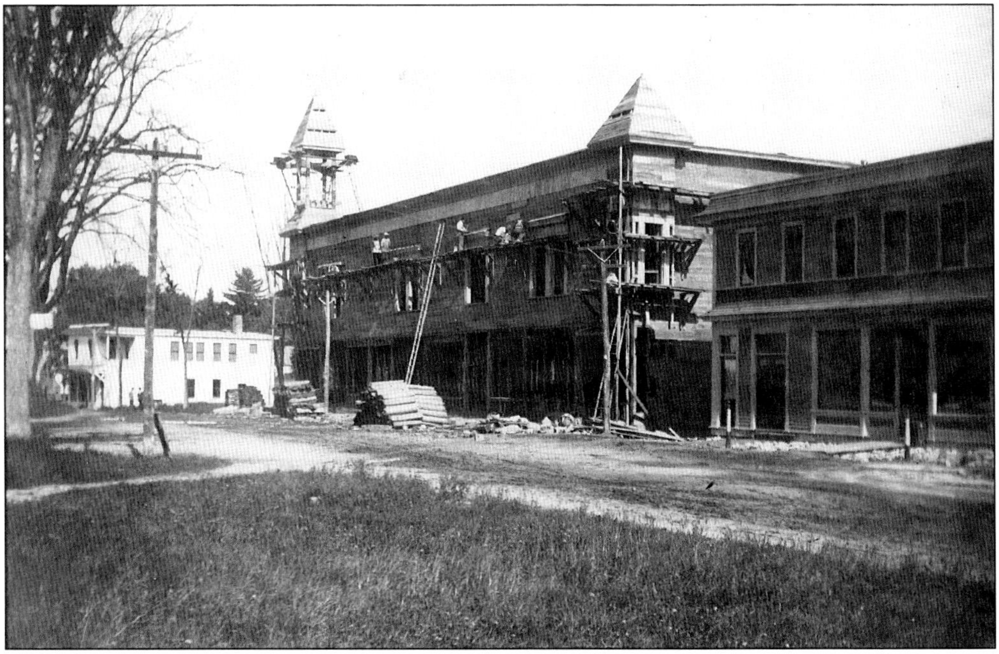

Rebuilding the Block, 1907. The ashes had hardly cooled before the Harrison Block began rising again like a phoenix. But on December 17, 1921, the IOOF Block and the F.H. Ricker store to the right became a blazing inferno.

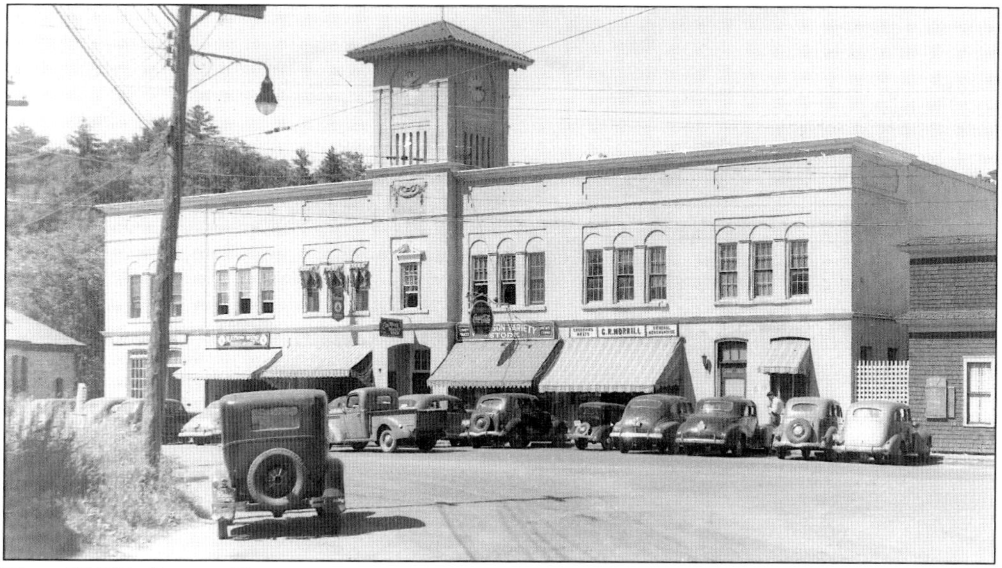

The IOOF Block Resurrected, c. 1938. Two disastrous fires in 14 years inflicted tremendous damage on the whole community. Nevertheless, a committee was formed to plan the rebuilding of the block. This time the Odd Fellows, with considerable financial help from J. Howard Randall, constructed Harrison's most distinguished landmark of concrete.

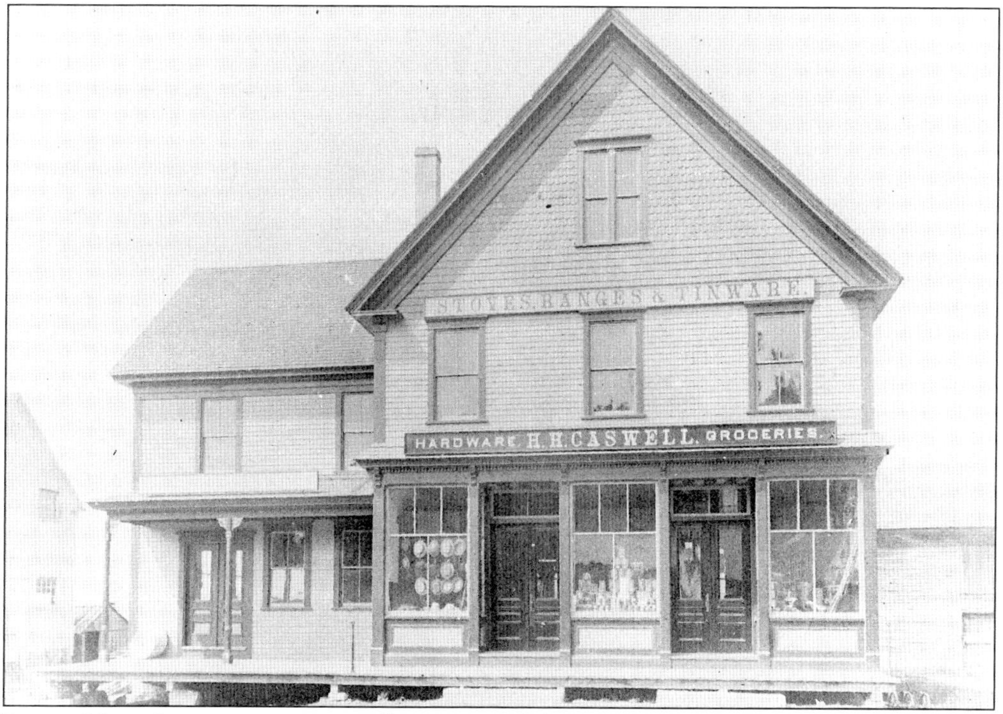

Lower Main Street, c. 1895. Hollis H. Caswell built this store around 1892 on the present site of Gary Searles's the Anchorage, using doors, frames, and windows made at his water-powered woodworking shop. He also operated a gristmill. In 1939 Ernest E. Ward converted the store into a dine and dance hall, but in 1942 he remodeled it into a 16-room house. The structure was torn down in 1983.

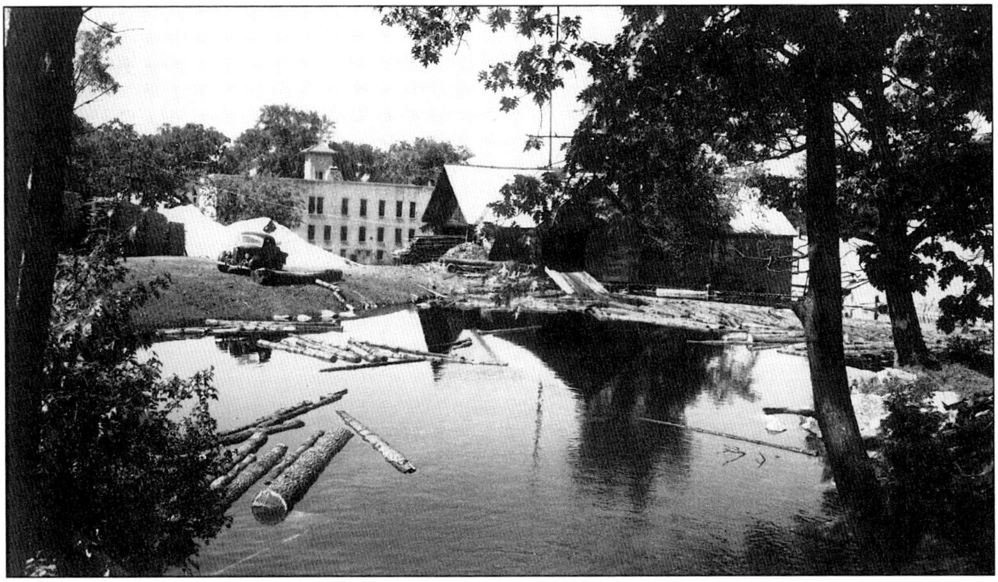

The Sumner Whitney Mill, c. 1938. It was sawmills like this one located at the foot of Anonymous Pond (Crystal Lake) that set early Maine settlements and communities in motion. The original sawmill on this site was purchased by Sumner Whitney from the firm of Philander Tolman & Co. on September 1, 1888. It was totally destroyed in the 1907 fire. Undaunted, Whitney rebuilt the mill, which by the time this photograph was taken was operated by George Skillings, sawing logs for the Dupont Company.

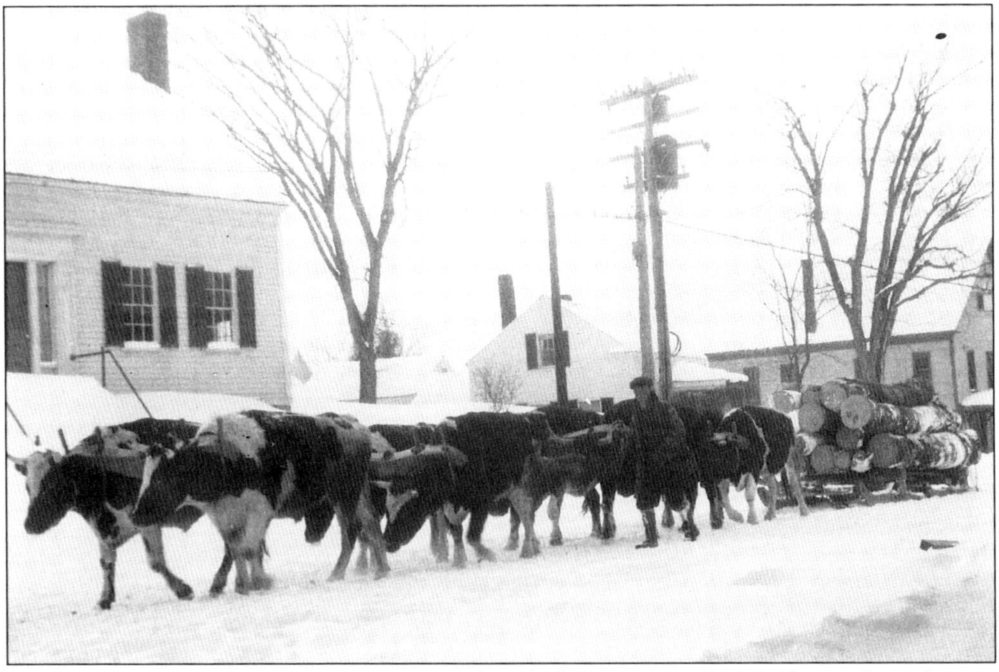

Heading for the Mill, c. 1920. An unidentified teamster is driving four yokes of oxen, effortlessly pulling a bobsled loaded with logs, through Harrison Village destined for the sawmill seen at the top of this page. The buildings, from left to right, are the Howard Sampson and Frank Whitney residences and the Grange Hall.

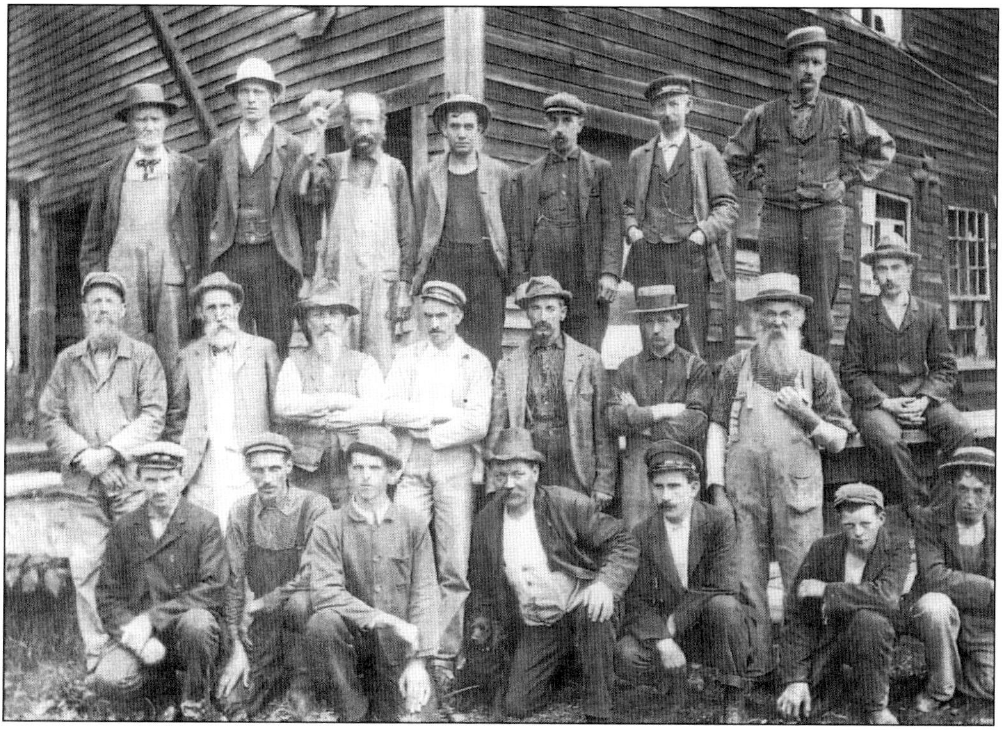

THE HARRISON CHAIR FACTORY CREW, c. 1895. From left to right are as follows: (front row) Mr. Rowe, Fred Allen, Daniel Wood, Walter Tibbets, William Wheeler, William Glines, and Willis Libby; (middle row) Charles Lee Brown, George Henry Brown, David Merrill, Mr. Seavey, Andrew Wheeler, George Martin, David Cobb, and John Blair; (back row) William Bennett, Bradford Kimball, Melvin Jordan, Charles Sumner Whitney, Harvey Whitney, Harry Whitney, and Wilmont Walker.

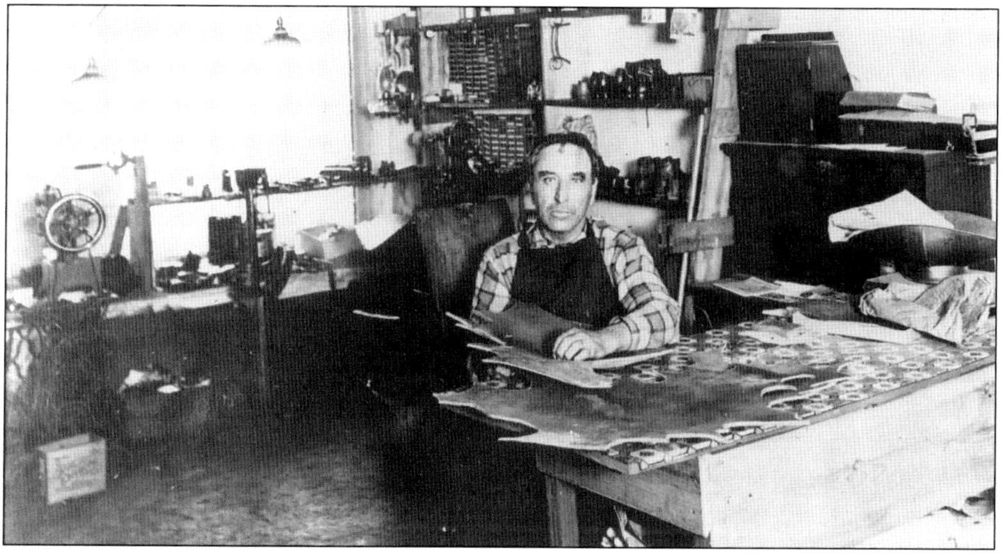

THE VILLAGE COBBLER, c. 1928. George Marshall Rand (1876–1938) is seated at his bench working on a piece of leather in his shop beneath the Harrison Block, where he made and repaired shoes and boots from 1927 to 1930.

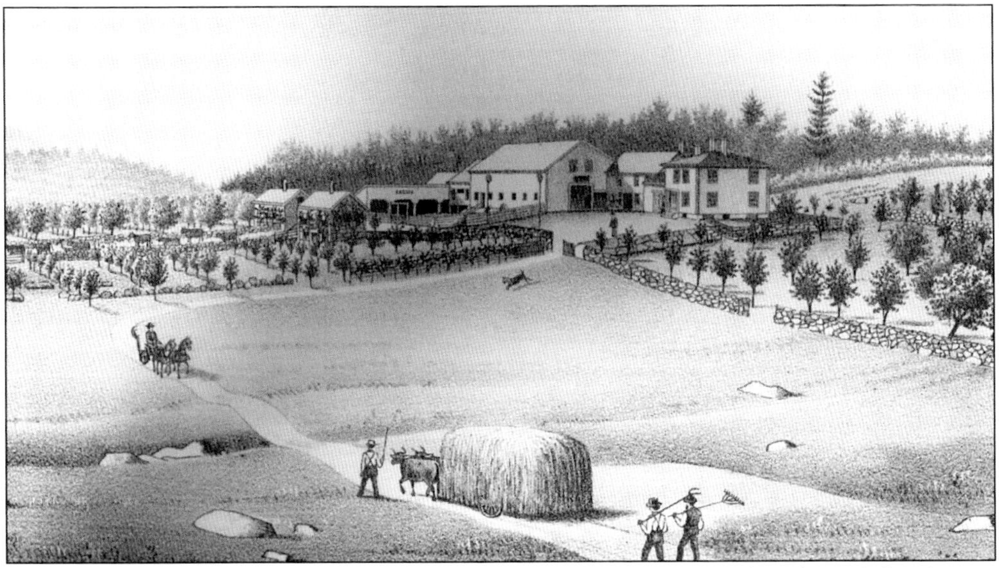

THE EDWARD K. WHITNEY FARM, C. 1870. This lithograph of the Edward Kendall Whitney farm at haying time clearly indicates why his agricultural practices were emulated by other farmers in the Lake Region and the Oxford Hills. He was a highly regarded breeder of Jersey cows and Chester hogs and a noted fruit grower, specializing in apples and pears produced from his own nursery stock.

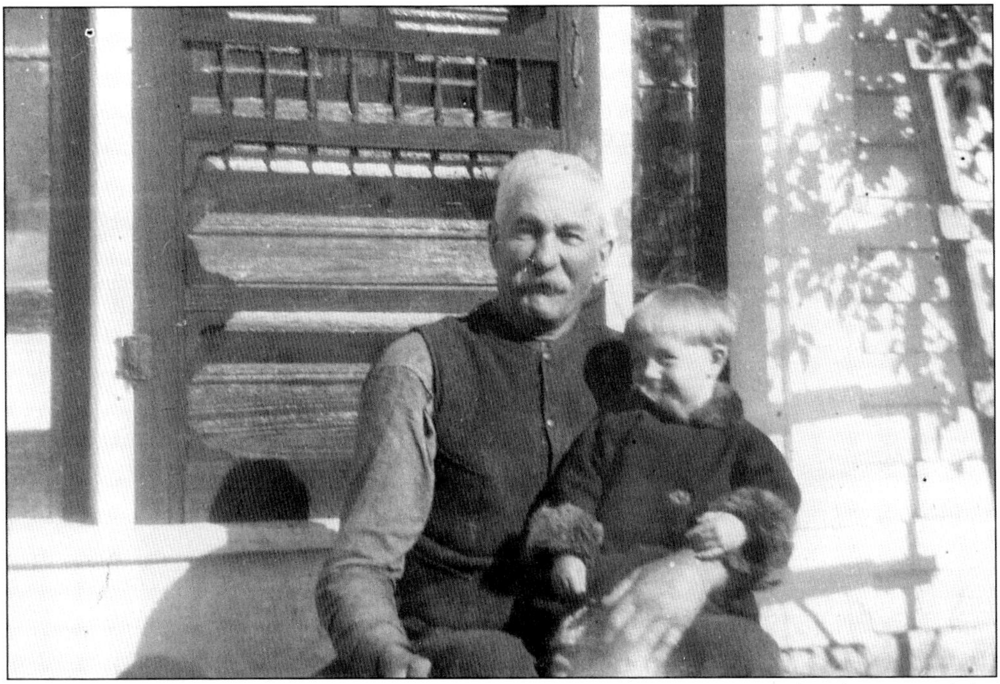

JAMES THOMES AND GRANDDAUGHTER, C. 1928. James Thomes sits on the doorstep of the family homestead owned by his grandfather (for whom he was named), proudly holding his granddaughter, Mary Etta Thomes, on his knee. Both the grandfather and granddaughter were born here. James was a successful farmer and lumberman, a prominent community leader, and a strong supporter of the Harrison-based Northern Cumberland Agricultural Society.

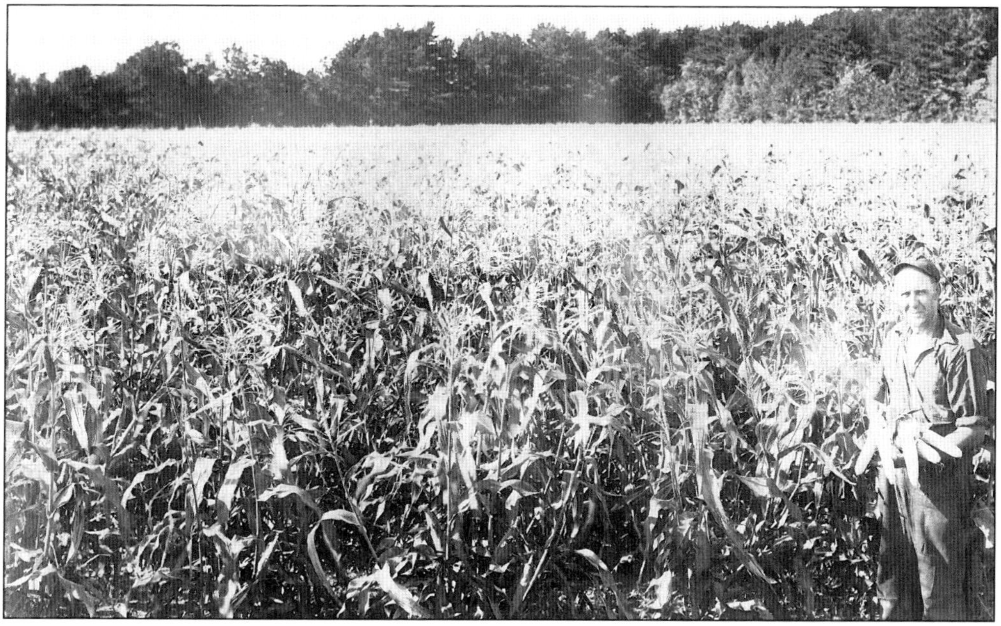

A Bountiful Corn Crop, c. 1940. Agriculture continued to be an important part of Harrison's economy until after World War II. Here Charles Seilonen, who was born in Finland in 1883 and settled in South Harrison in 1912, displays some of the corn he is in the process of harvesting from his lush field for the Harrison Corn Shop. The Seilonens were one of a number of Finnish families who settled in Harrison.

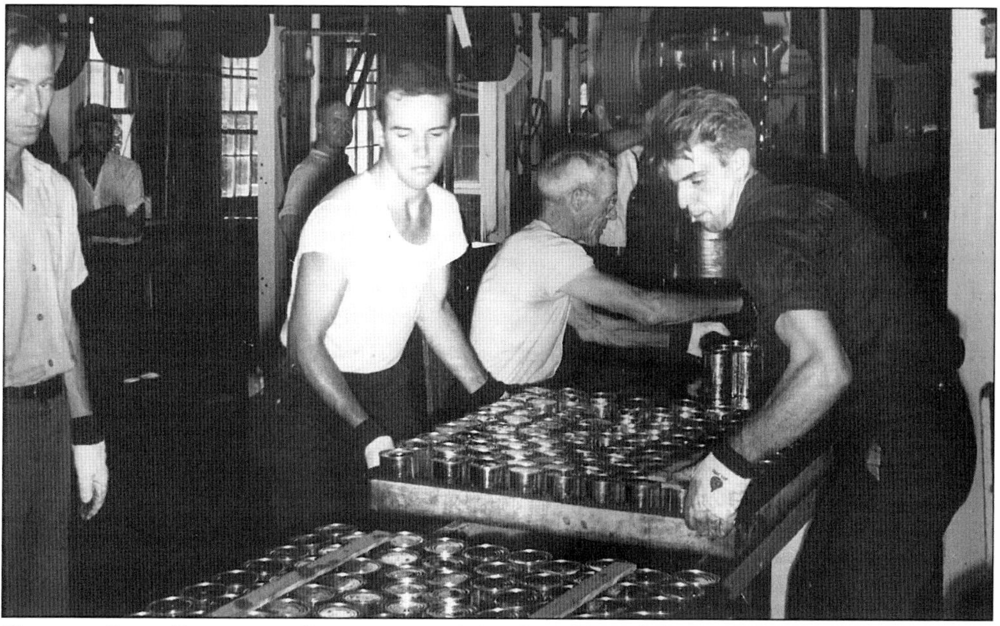

Cans of Corn Ready for Cooking, c. 1940. Oswald Luck (second from right), George St. John (far right), and two unidentified workers are lifting trays, each containing about 90 cans of corn ready to be moved on small trucks to the cooking retorts. The corn shops provided gainful summer employment for a number of local residents as well as a dependable income to farmers such as Charles Seilonen.

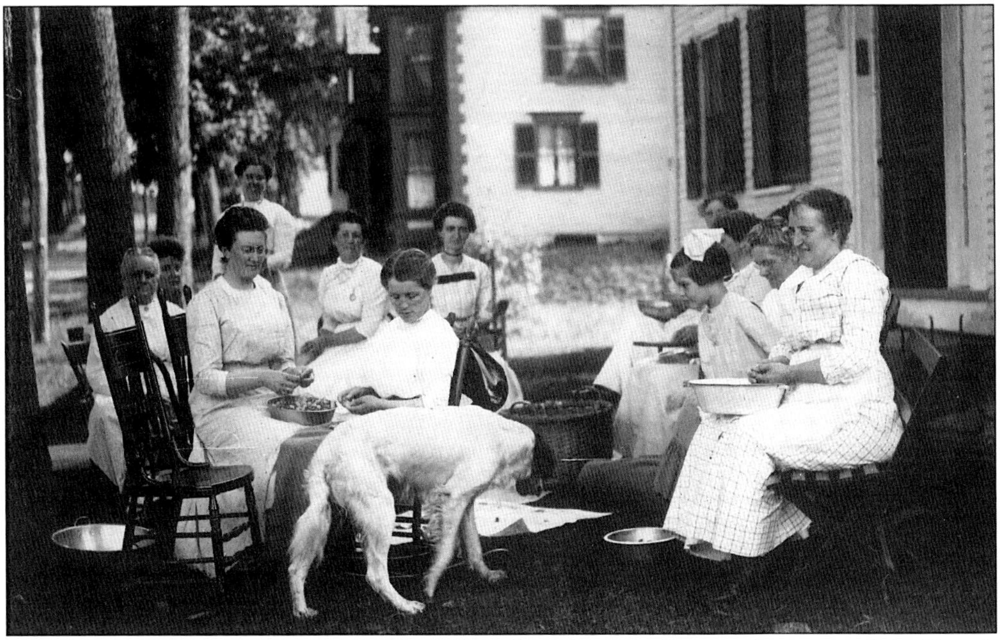

Shelling Peas, c. 1909. It is very likely that this photograph was taken around the Fourth of July. These women have gathered in front of the Wheeler House and are shelling peas for a family get-together or a community supper. Seated on the extreme left is Granny Greene; to the right near the door is Nell Davis.

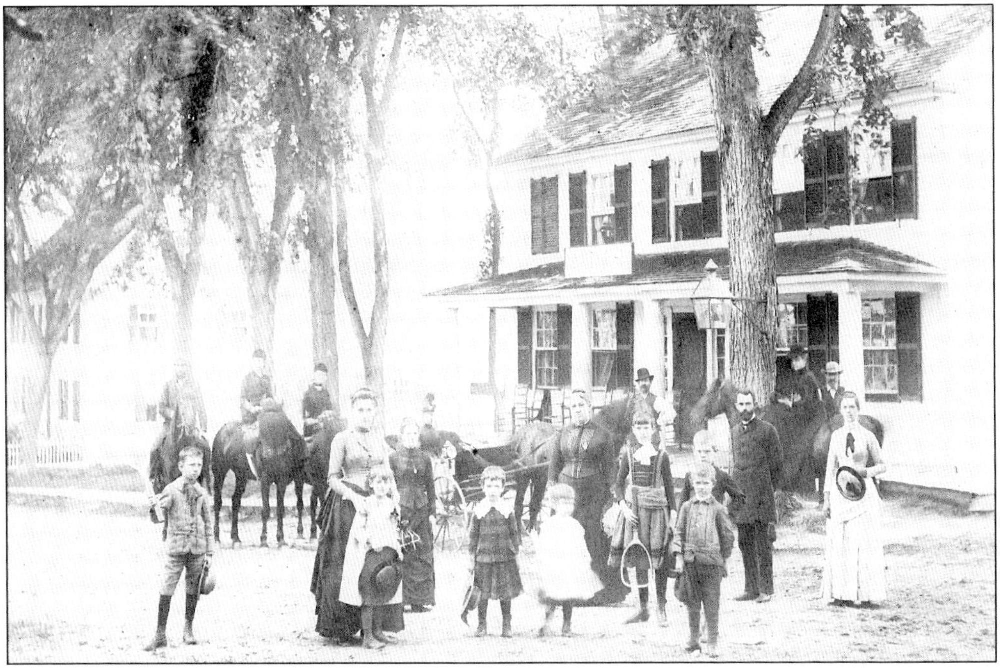

The Elm House, c. 1890. Almon Kneeland, who married Dorcas Sands of Standish in 1841, farmed there until he purchased this house in 1860 and converted it into an inn. Their son David and his wife, Caroline, operated it as the Elm House for 30 years. Their daughter Grace is mounted on the horse nearest the inn.

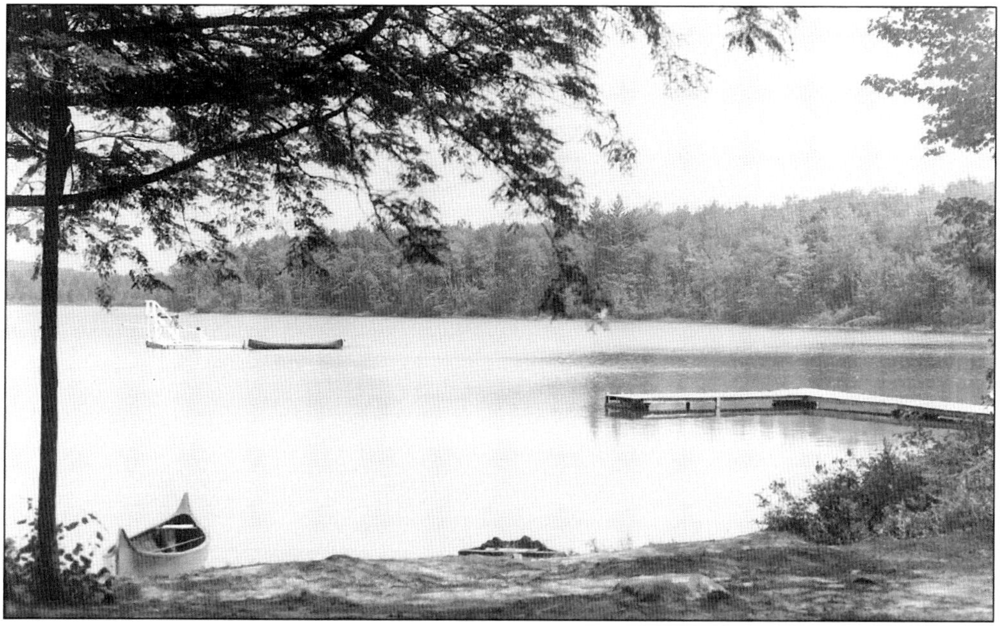

Camp Bendito Waterfront at Island Pond, c. 1940. The sylvan lakes and ponds throughout the Lake Region early in the twentieth century began attracting an increasing number of boys and girls camps such as Camp Bendito, founded in 1925. These camps afforded young people predominantly from middle- and upper-class families an opportunity to spend their summer vacations participating in a great variety of supervised activities in a healthful and wholesome environment.

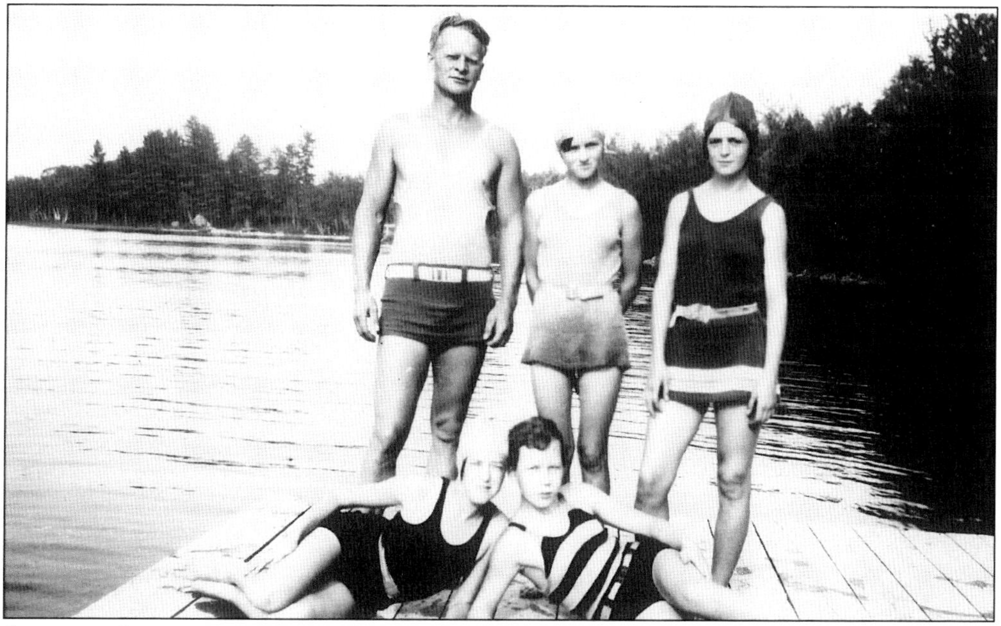

Swimming Lessons, c. 1927. Duke Overland is posing with one of his swimming classes on a dock on Crystal Lake. Standing next to him are Ruth Chapman and Ruby Chapman. In front of them are Maida Chapman and Florence Spaulding. Besides giving swimming lessons, Duke was a bookkeeper for local businesses.

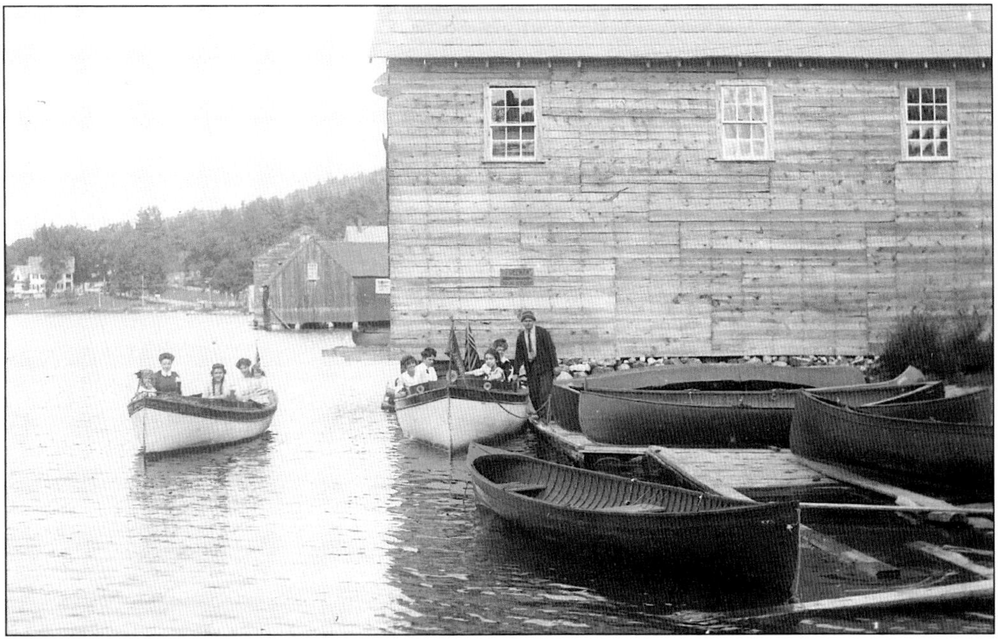

BOATING ON LONG LAKE, c. 1920s. Harrison, as well as the other towns in the Lake Region, attracted droves of fishermen, canoeists, and excursionists. Boat rentals, such as this one owned by Percy L. Smith & Co. on Long Lake, did a thriving business as soon as the ice was out until after Labor Day. Excursionists in the launches *Alice* and *Osceola* are about to head down Long Lake, perhaps to Naples.

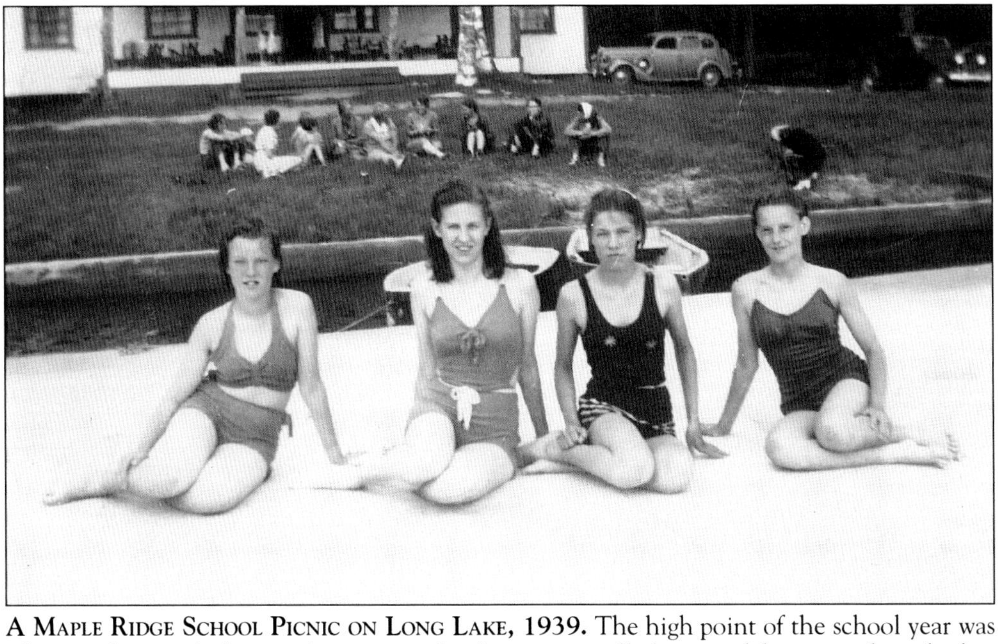

A MAPLE RIDGE SCHOOL PICNIC ON LONG LAKE, 1939. The high point of the school year was when teachers took their students on a school picnic, usually by some lake or pond on the last day of school. Besides teaching at the Maple Ridge School, Lida Carsley Trott—along with her husband, Arthur—ran Wildmere, a family camp on Long Lake. Posing from left to right are Phyllis Scribner, Constance Thomes, Idyllene Smith, and Catherine Scribner.

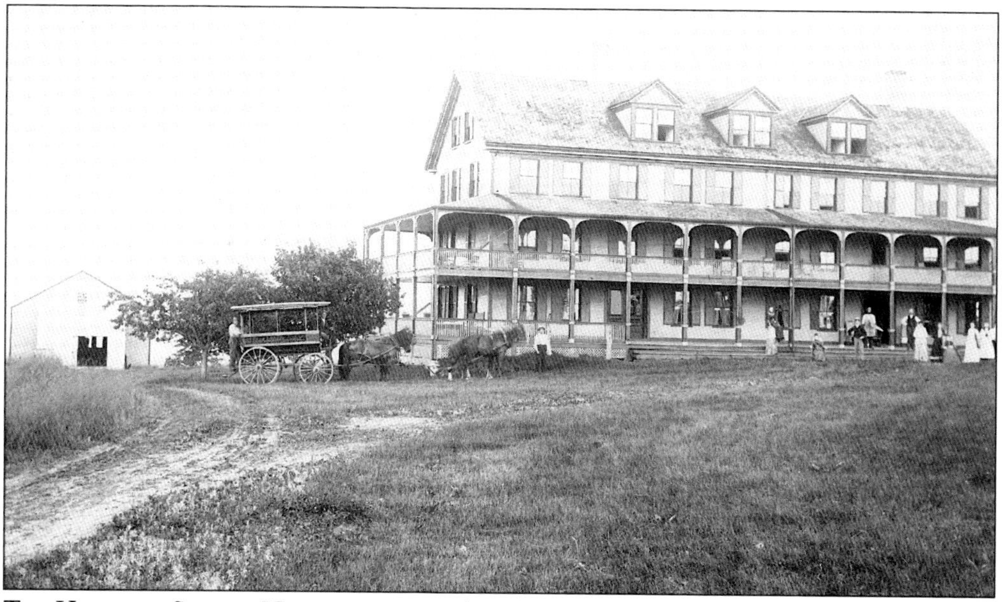

THE HOTEL AT SUMMIT HILL, C. 1910. Before the advent of the "summer boarder," inns and taverns remained open the year round to accommodate itinerant tradesmen, peddlers, teamsters, and passengers arriving by stagecoach. But shortly after the turn of the century, summer hotels such as the 55-room Summit Spring Hotel (built *c.* 1888) were opened to accommodate the increasing number of summer visitors arriving by steamboat and the narrow gauge railroad in quest of clear mountain air, country cooking, and a splendid view. Summit Spring Hotel had an additional attraction—pure, sparkling mineral water.

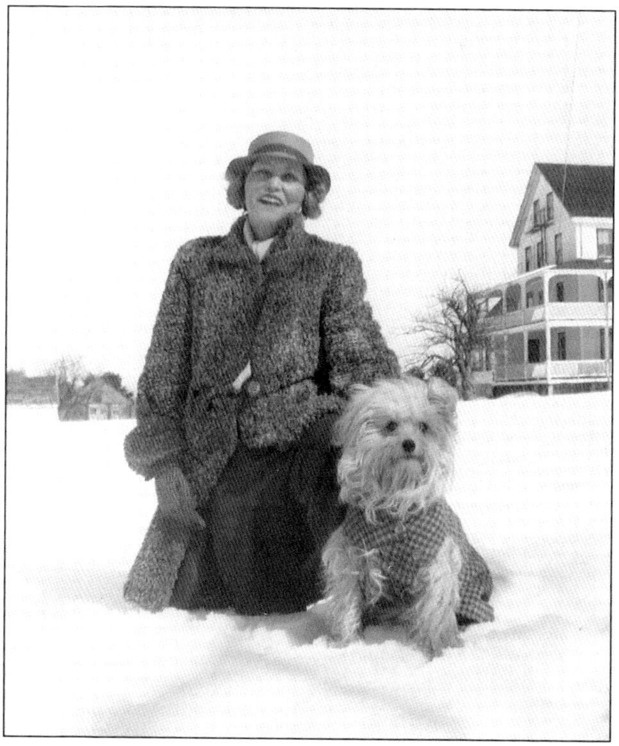

JANE MORRISON VAN ZELM (1888–1948), C. 1940. But the growing popularity of the automobile ushered in the tourist era, and overnight cabins, tenting areas, and housekeeping cottages became popular. By World War II, there were few hotels still operating.

Famed cartoonist Franklin Van Zelm purchased the Summit Spring House for a private residence in 1936 and constructed a stone springhouse here shortly thereafter. For two years he bottled carbonated water, which he then shipped from the railhead in South Paris to S.S. Pierce in Boston and the Holland-American shipping line. His wife, shown here, is enjoying a frolic in the snow with her dog.

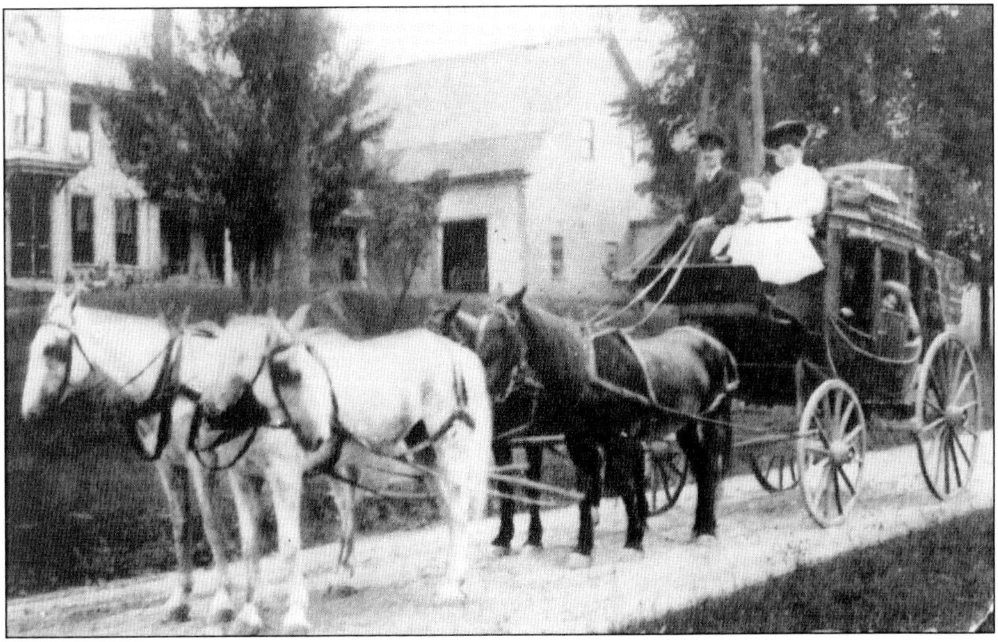

STAGECOACH DAYS, c. 1895. There are still those alive today who recall when stagecoaches plied the rutted, dusty roads, conveying passengers to the nearest railroads and the world beyond the Lake Region. Here the stagecoach Tally Ho, which travelled from Waterford to Harrison, pauses in front of the Philander Tolman house, known as the "Greenwood Villa."

Davis' Stage Notice.

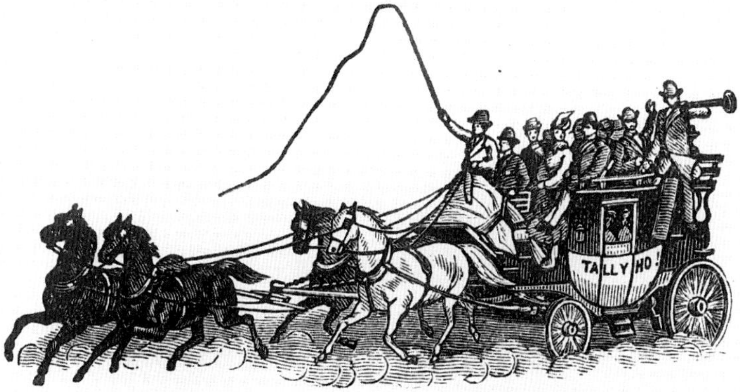

Our Stage leaves North Bridgton every morning at 7 o'clock, reaching Norway in season to connect with Portland and Boston trains. Leaves Harrison to connect with all trains on the Bridgton & Saco River R. R. Leaves Bridgton for North Bridgton, Harrison, Norway and Waterford. Leaves Norway on arrival of afternoon train for Harrison and Bridgton. Buy through tickets and save money.

HARRISON LIVERY STABLE.

THE HARRISON LIVERY STABLE, c. 1890. This copy of a flyer printed for the livery stable and stagecoach line owned by S.C. Davis of Harrison was taken from the 1890–1891 *Cumberland County Directory*. Davis's stage linked North Bridgton, Waterford, Norway, and outlying areas in Harrison with the Bridgton & Saco River Railroad and the Maine Central.

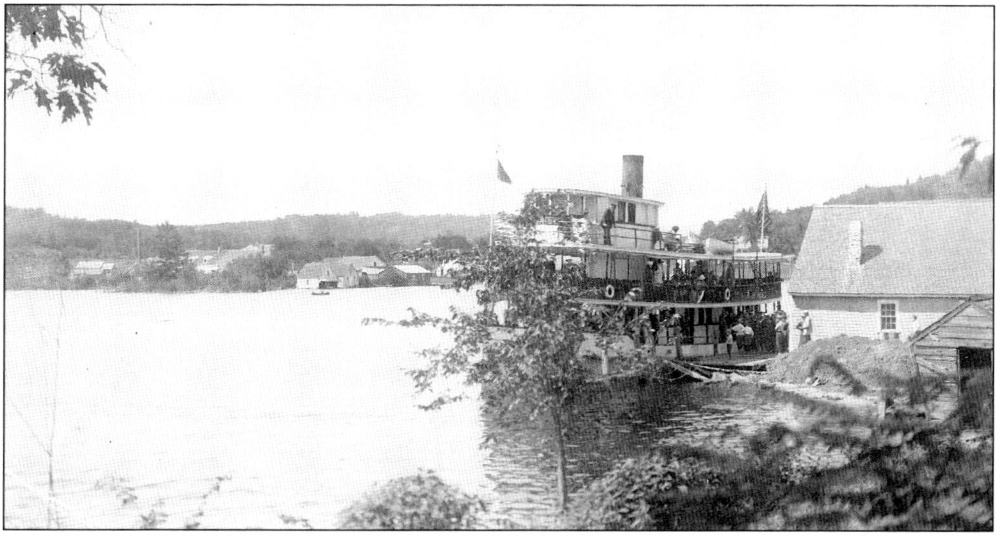

The Steamboat Landing, c. 1915. One of the most colorful and picturesque eras in the history of Sebago Lake and Long Lake and their environs was the steamboat era, which reached its zenith during the years between 1892 and 1917 (when the Bay of Naples Steamboat Company was owned by Charles L. Goodridge). Here the two largest steamships connecting Harrison with Sebago Lake Station, the *Goodridge* and the *Bay of Naples*, are docked at the Harrison Landing.

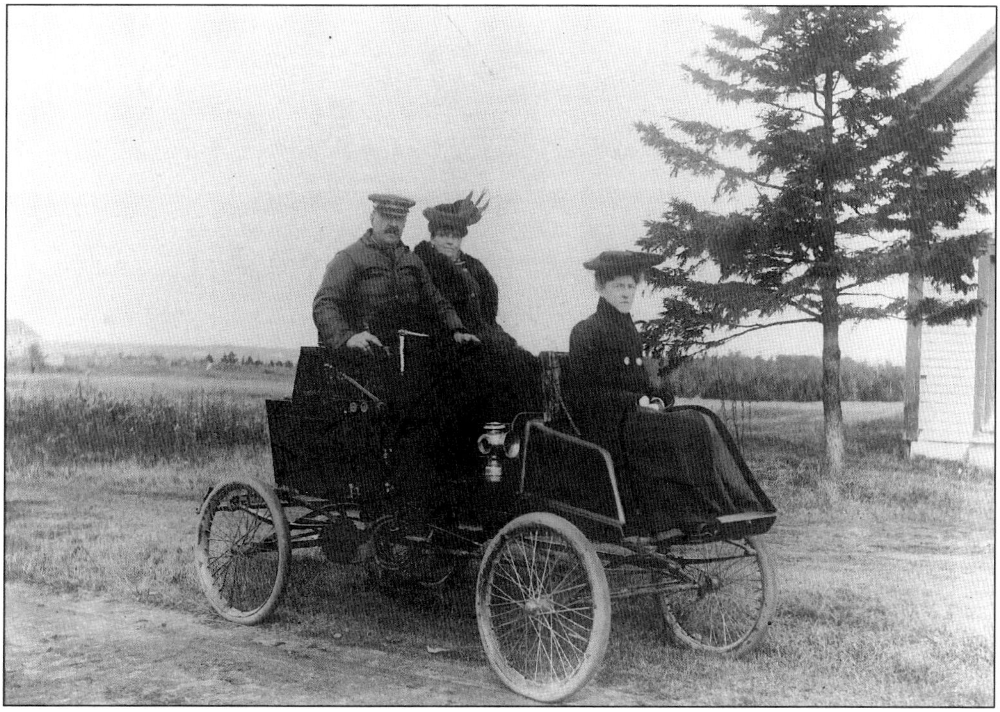

Going for a Jaunt in a Stanley Steamer, 1903. Lyman and Nellie Dawes (seated in the rear) and Nellie Sawyer are bundled up and enjoying perhaps their last jaunt in their Stanley Steamer before they store their vehicle away for the winter. Within a few years the automobile would bring about dynamic changes to the Lake Region and all of Maine.

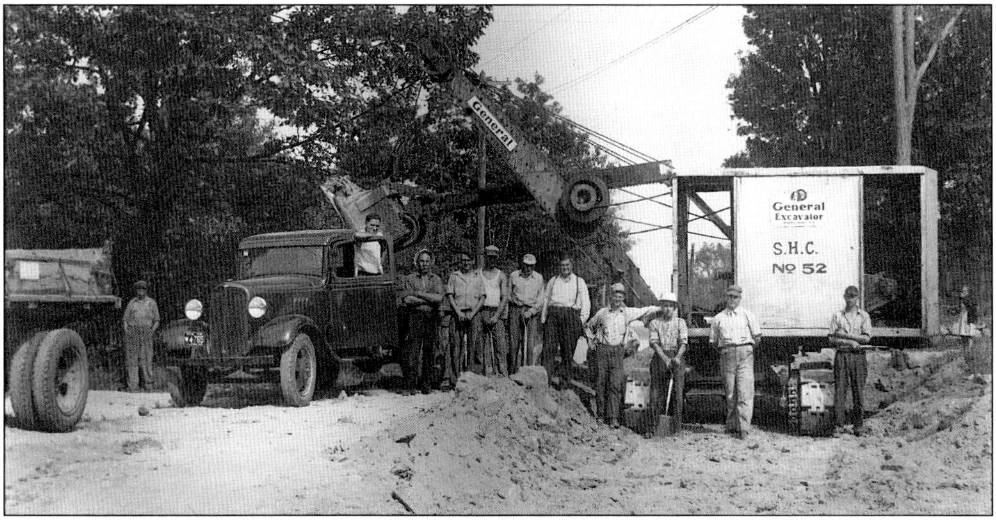

ROAD CONSTRUCTION, C. 1936. One of the dynamic changes that the automobile era brought about was that more and more carriage roads were widened and surfaced with tar. Although there were none in Harrison, many major highways were surfaced at this time with concrete. Harrison residents identifiable are Walter D. Chute (the state highway supervisor), Elmer Dingley (road commissioner), Hartley Little, and Stanley Nutting.

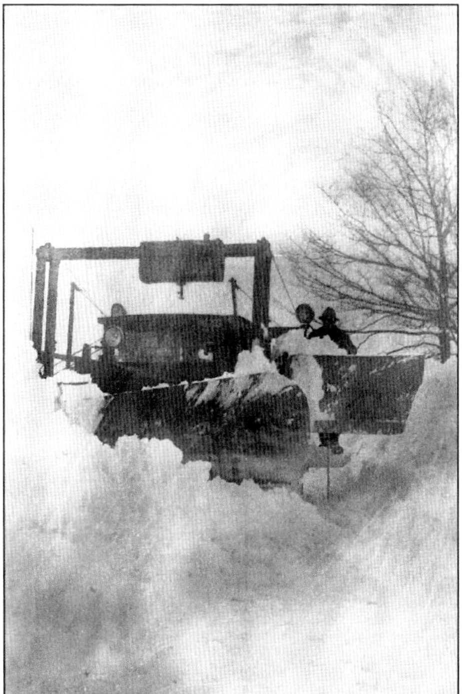

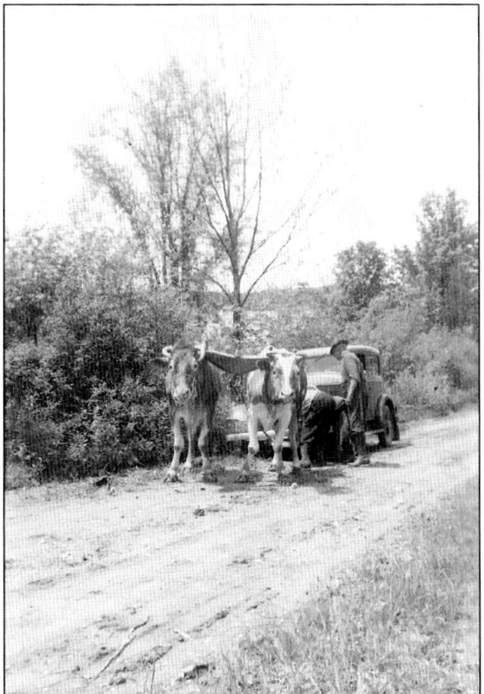

THE PERILS OF TRAVELLING IN NEW ENGLAND. By the 1920s powerful, slow-moving crawler tractors had replaced the horse- and oxen-drawn snow rollers, but there were still many back dirt roads in the 1940s that became quagmires of mud in the early spring. And even in May motorists sometimes had to hire a local farmer with his horses or oxen to pull their vehicle out of a muddy area.

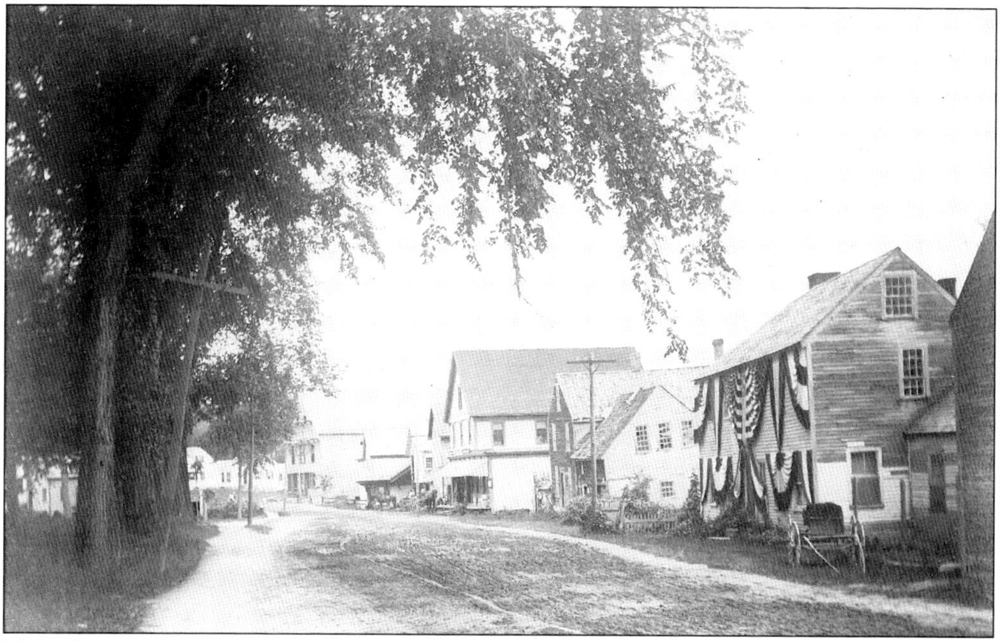

MAIN STREET LOOKING EAST, AUGUST 1905. As the buntings on the Haskell place indicate, this photograph, which includes the H.H. Caswell Store and the Grange, was taken either before or after the Harrison Centennial Celebration on August 23. It looks as though the nearly deserted Main Street had been recently wet down to settle the dust.

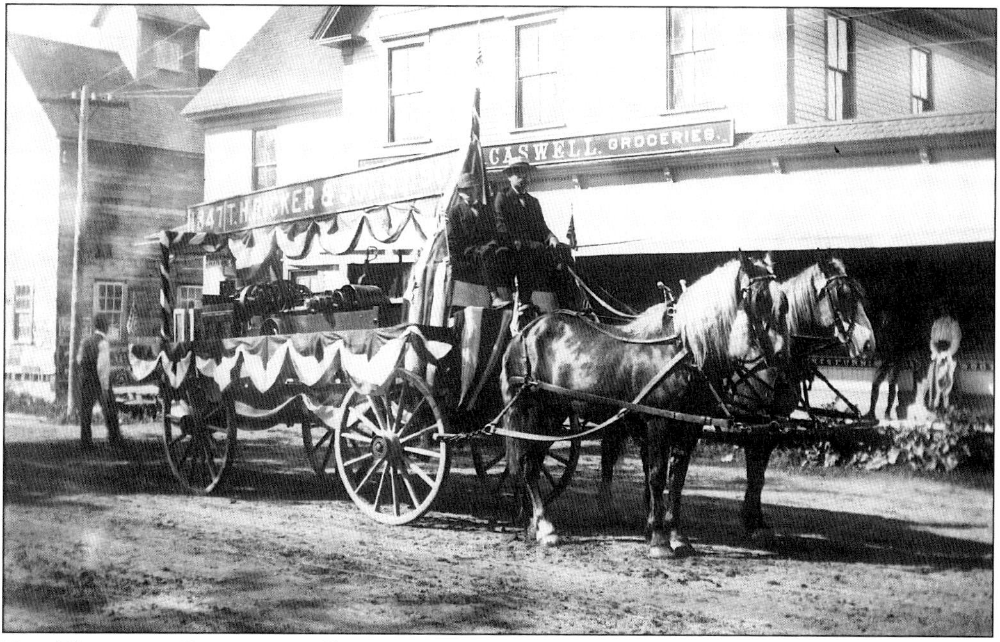

THE HARRISON CENTENNIAL CELEBRATION, AUGUST 23, 1905. The bedecked T.H. Ricker & Son wagon trundles by the H.H. Caswell Store on Main Street during the Harrison Centennial Parade. To the left of the store is Caswell's gristmill. This area would escape the 1907 conflagration that destroyed so much of Main Street; the Jordan and IOOF Blocks would not be so lucky.

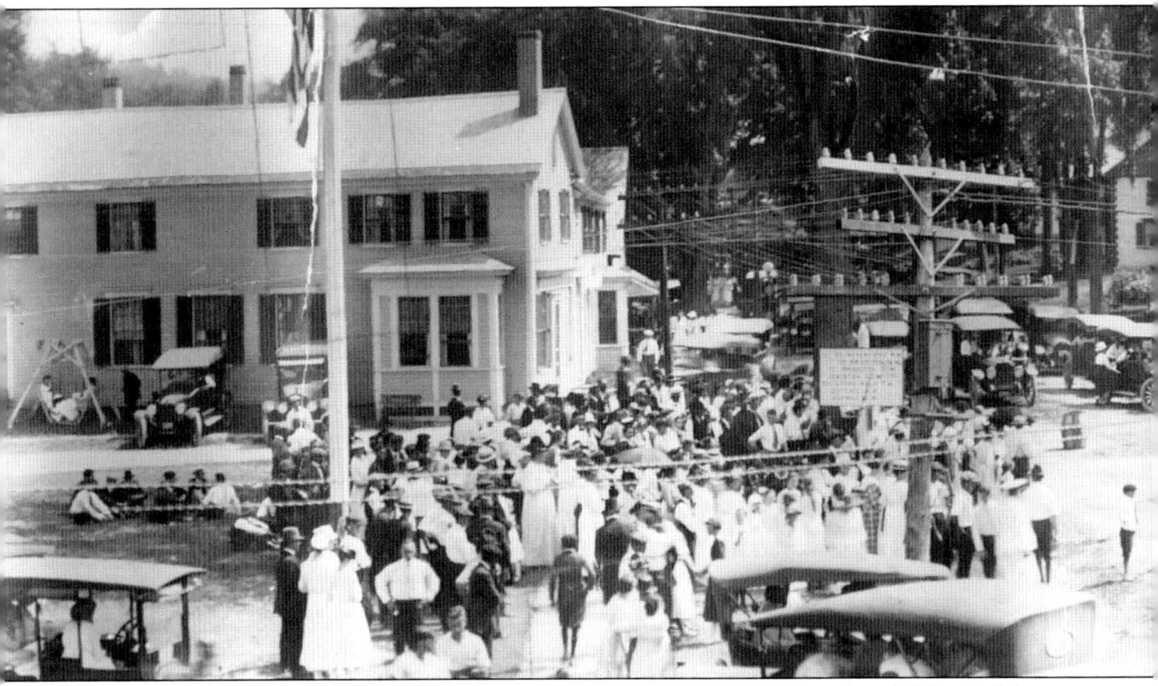

THE 1919 FOURTH OF JULY CELEBRATION. The gala 1919 Fourth of July Celebration, in contrast to the centennial celebration just a few years before, is a startling revelation of how dynamically lifestyles in Harrison and other Maine communities were altered by the automobile. People and automobiles seem to be swept up in a vortex of activity here in front of the large Bailey Block (behind the flagpole to the left of the Tavern Stand). The chain

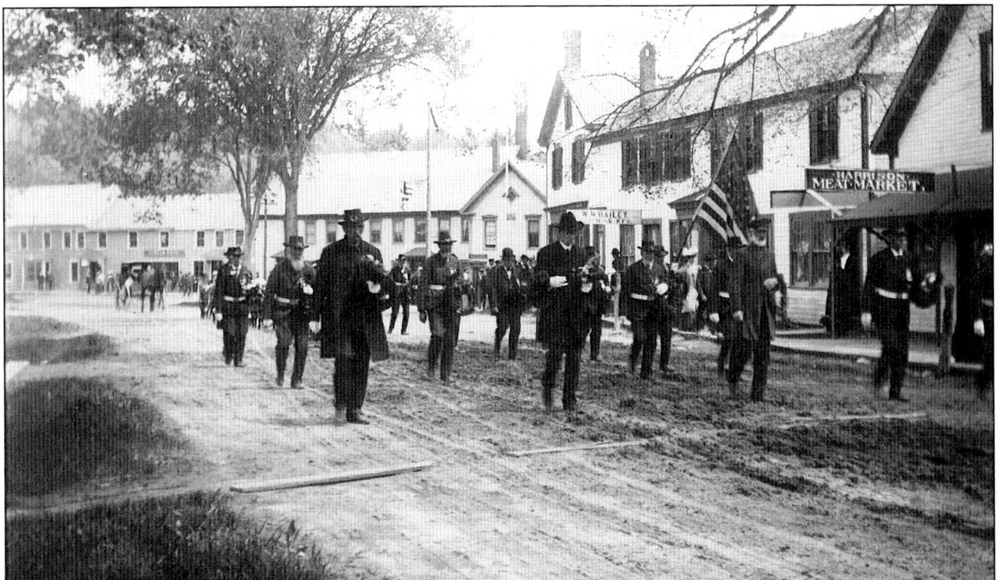

THE 1904 MEMORIAL DAY PARADE. GAR and Spanish-American War veterans parade with great dignity up Front Street toward the cemetery. Both the Jordan Block and GAR Hall were decimated by the conflagration of May 14, 1907.

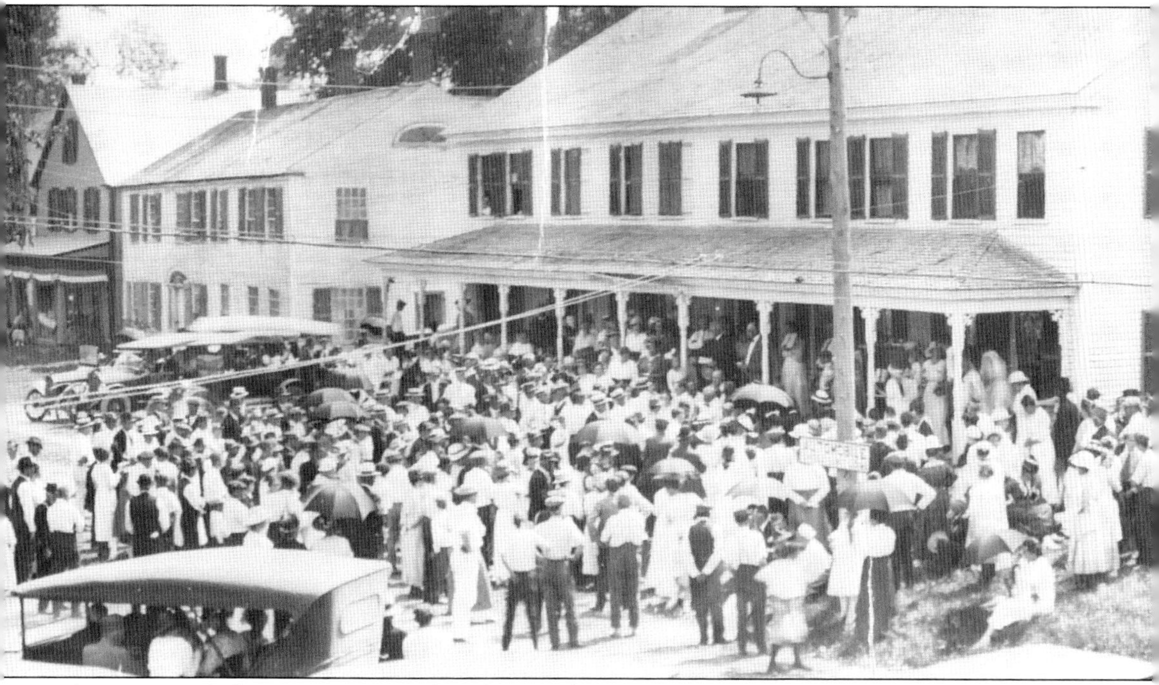

of waterways linking Harrison with Sebago Lake Station and Portland would continue to be an important channel for people to get to and from Harrison until 1932, but the automobile provided those who lived far away from the waterways and railroads real mobility for the first time.

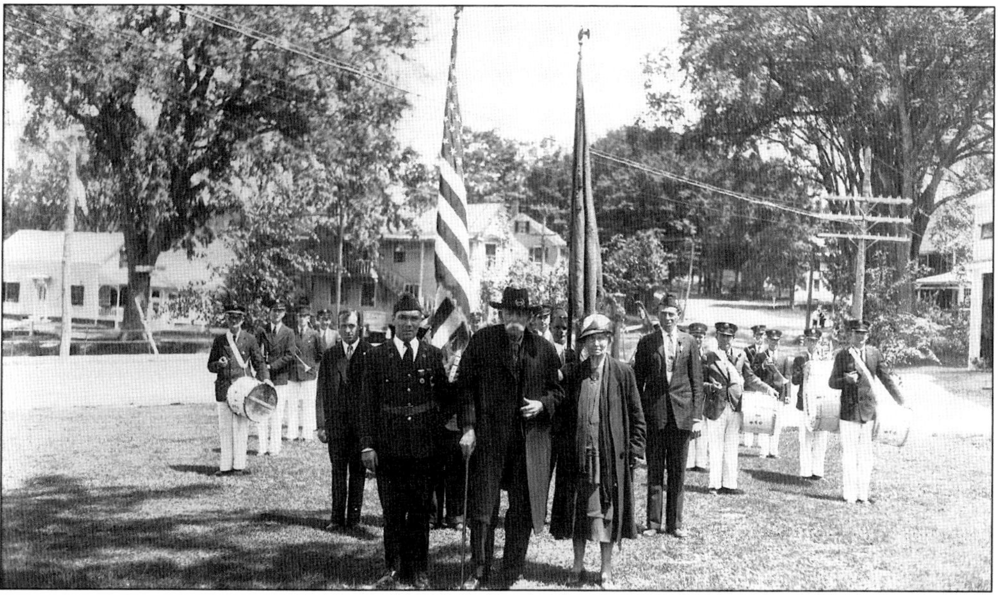

HARRISON'S LAST CIVIL WAR VETERAN, 1932. Seth M. Keene, who bravely served in the infantry of the 10th Maine and returned unscathed, was honored one last time here in the Common to the beat of the recently formed unique Harrison Drum and Bugle Corps before his death in 1933. He is being escorted by his wife, Nellie (Huntress) Keene, and by Maynard Burnell, legion commander and a veteran of World War I.

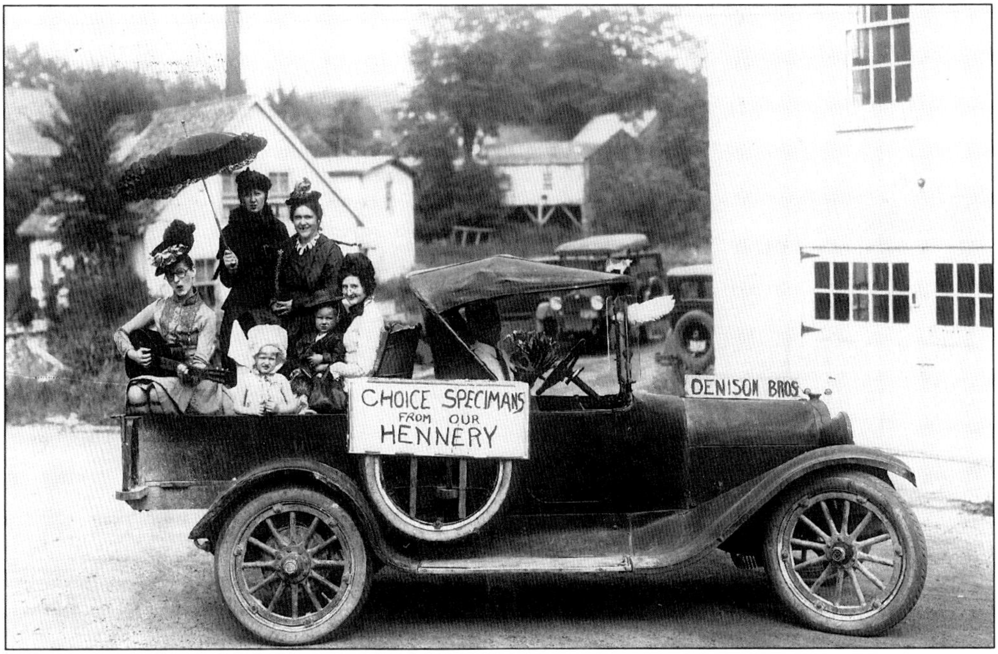

THE HENNERY, C. 1928. Hobart and Clifford Dennison, who operated an egg farm on Dawes Hill, were well represented in this annual Harrison Old Home Day parade by members of their family riding in a 1917 Dodge Brothers truck. Playing the guitar is Margaret Dennison. Holding the umbrella is one of two Perkins sisters. Standing next to her is Alice Dennison. Another Perkins sister is holding Jack Dennison, and the little girl is Carol Dennison.

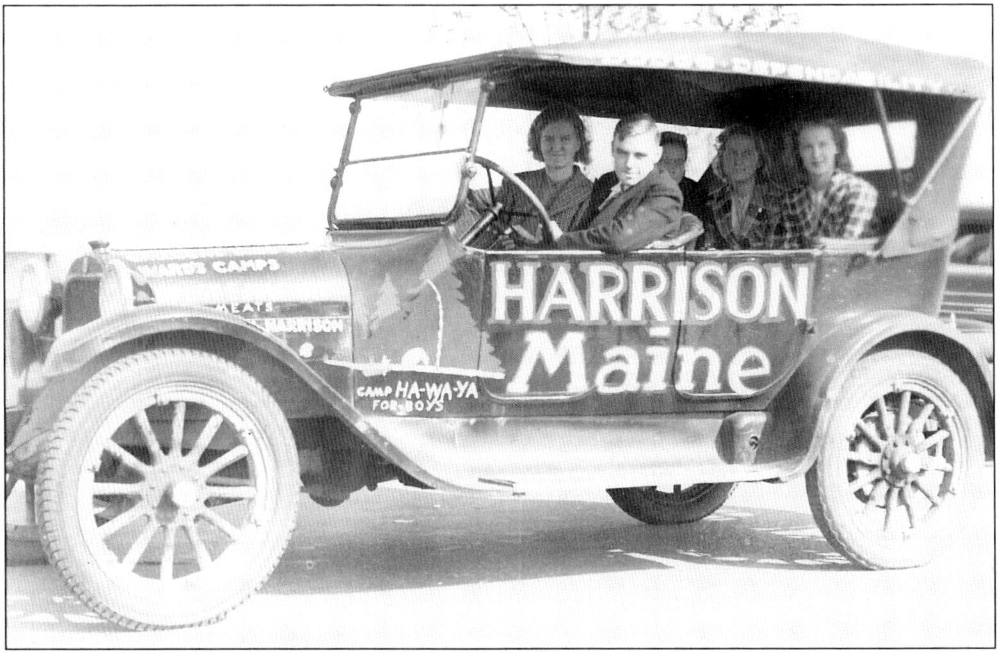

BOUND FOR THE NEW YORK WORLD'S FAIR, 1939. Harrison is getting a little publicity as Bill Culbert, Saima Pulkkinen, Viola Mattson, and two other unidentified ladies head out of Harrison for the 1939 New York World's Fair in a classy 1922 Dodge.

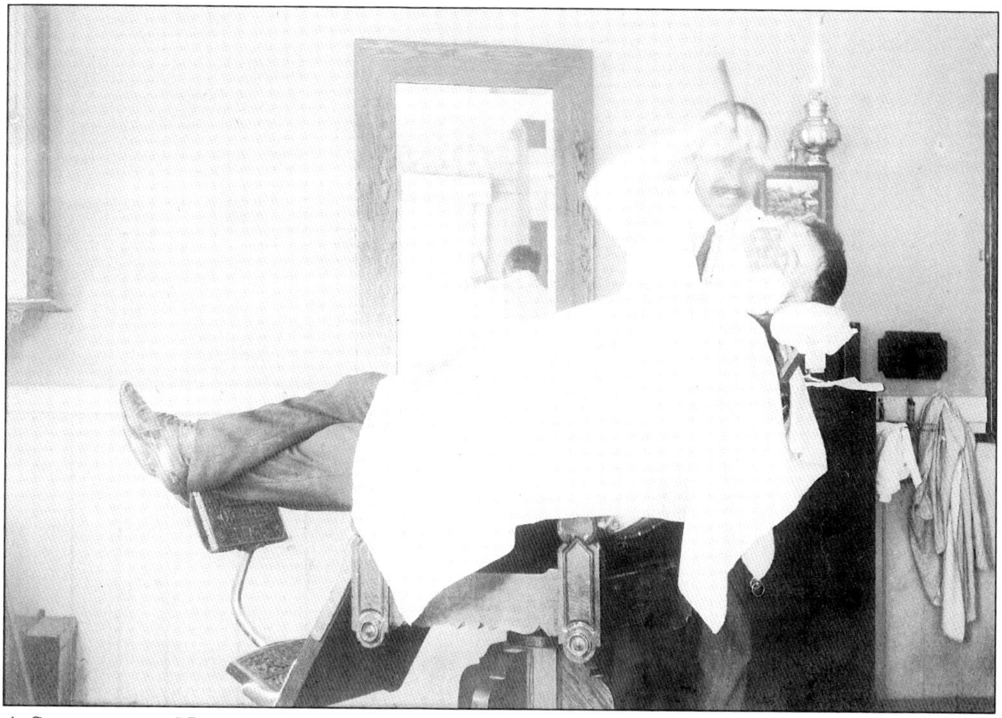

A Shave and a Haircut, c. 1925. Fred Lamb, who owned and operated the F.S. Lamb & Son Barber Shop in the Downing Building for many years, is poised with a straight-edged razor he has just sharpened on a leather razor strop ready to give a well-lathered customer a clean shave. In 1940 the shop was sold to Carl Day, who moved it to the IOOF Block. A haircut cost 25¢; a shave cost 15¢.

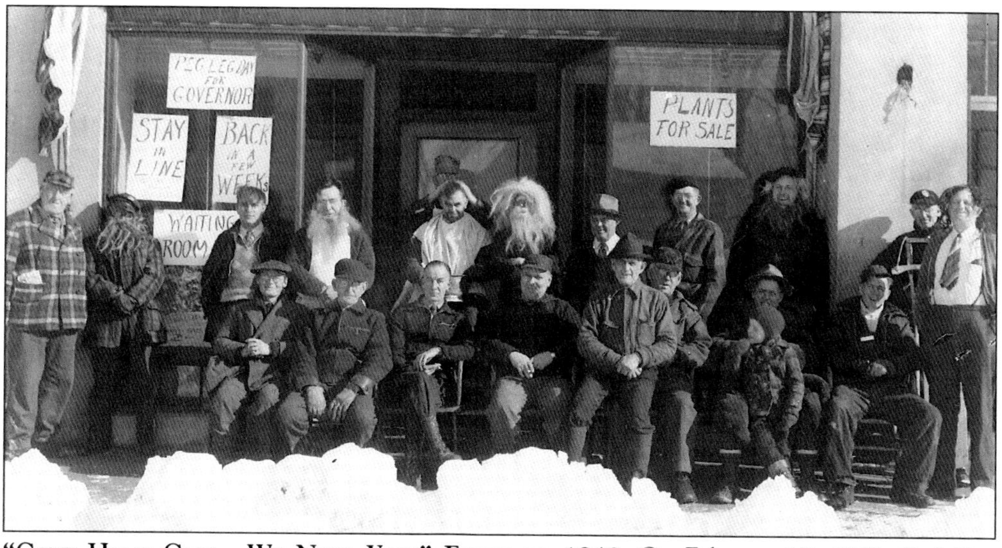

"Come Home Carl—We Need You," February 1940. On February 10, 1940, Carl Day broke his leg and was sent to the Osteopathic Hospital in Portland. He was thoroughly missed by his customers, who are posing here for a get-well photograph that was sent to him in the hospital. Carl recovered and continued to operate his barbershop until he leased it to Scott Briggs in 1965.

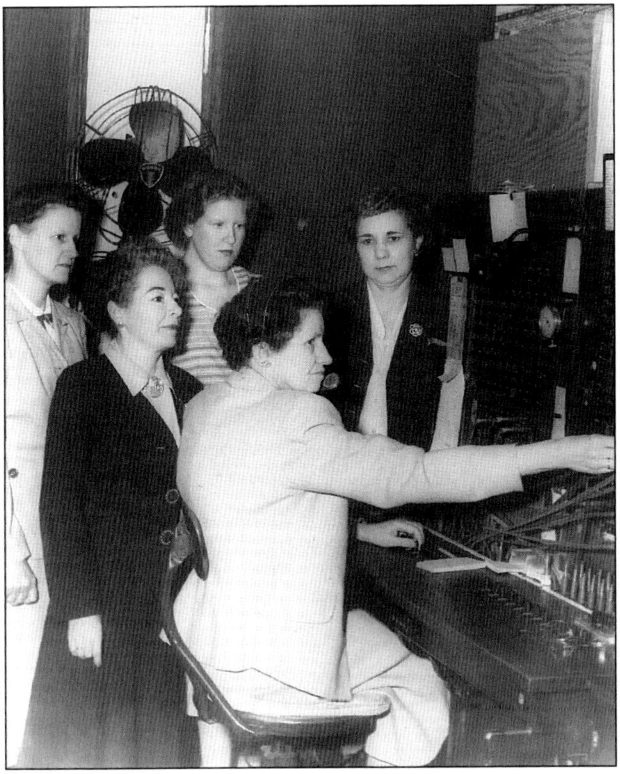

Elsie Spaulding Instructing Her Operators, c. 1940. Harrison was linked to the outside world on August 26, 1907, when the Maine Telephone Company set up the Harrison Exchange in the Grange Hall. Here Chief Operator Elsie Spaulding—who began working for the Maine Telephone Company in 1910—is giving her operators (from left to right are Freida Huwyler, Doris Little, Nellie Kilgore, and Dorothy Stuart) some pointers sometime after the office had been moved in 1922 to the IOOF Block. In 1930, the Maine Telephone Company became part of the New England Telephone & Telegraph Company. Elsie continued as chief operator and agent until she retired in 1955, when the office changed to the dial system.

The Telephone Girls, c. 1945. Elsie Spaulding and her telephone girls are enjoying a few pleasant hours away from the office on a picnic somewhere in a field in Harrison. Back in the days of the Harrison Exchange, the chief operator was paid the munificent sum of $8 for a 72-hour week. Relief operators were paid $3 a week. Night operators, who were usually boys and were permitted to sleep on a cot in the office between calls, received $3.46 per week.

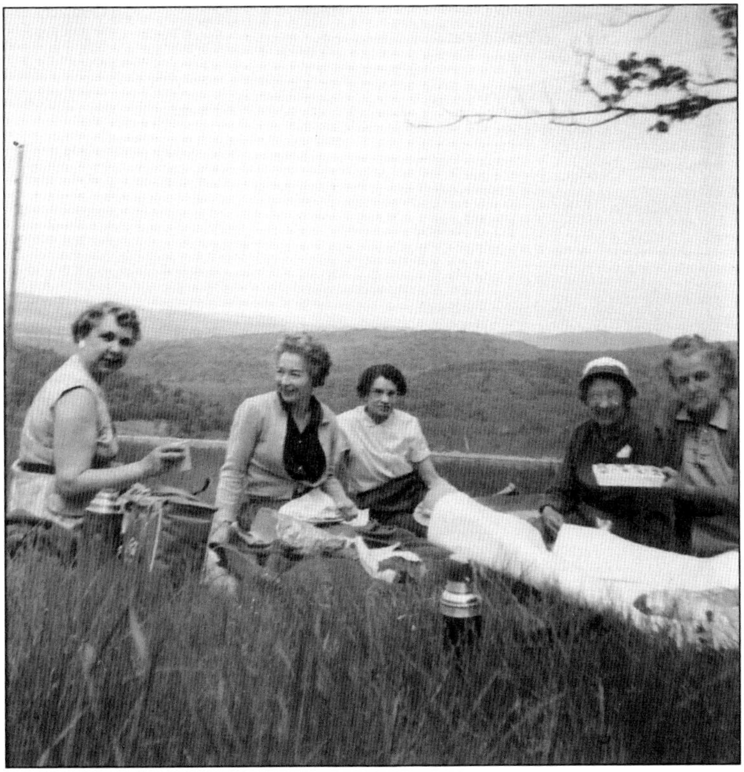

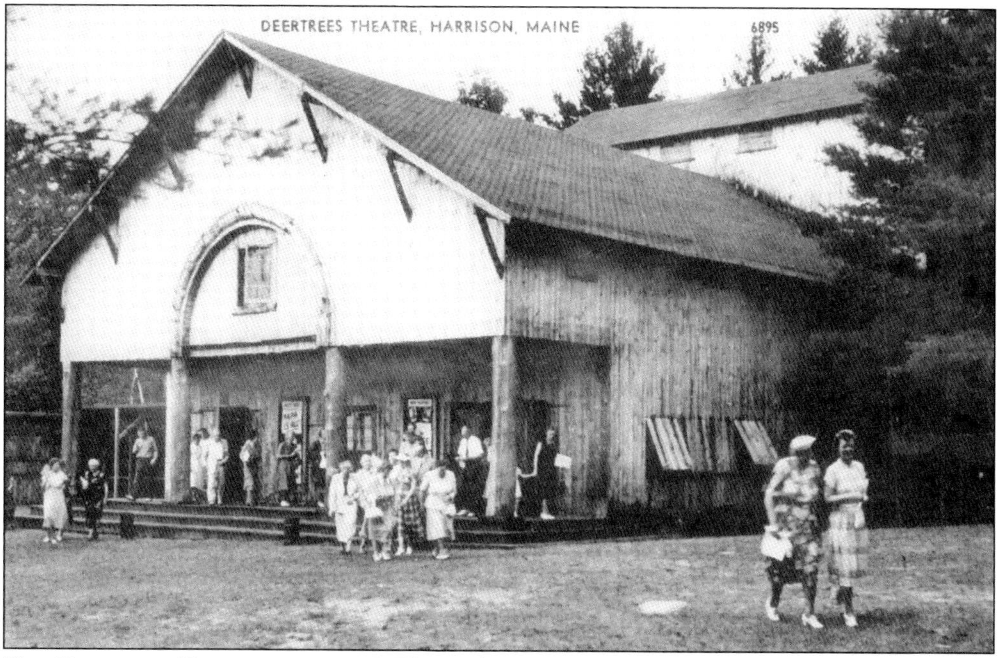

THE DEERTREES THEATER, c. 1945. The enduring Deertrees Theater, constructed in 1936 of rose hemlock cut on the Dawes Hill premises at a cost of $60,000, is symbolic of Harrison's fame as a summer playground and haven for artists, musicians, theatrical and Broadway celebrities, and opera stars. It was the dream child of opera teacher and director Enrica Clay Dillon of New York. The architect was Harrison G. Wiseman.

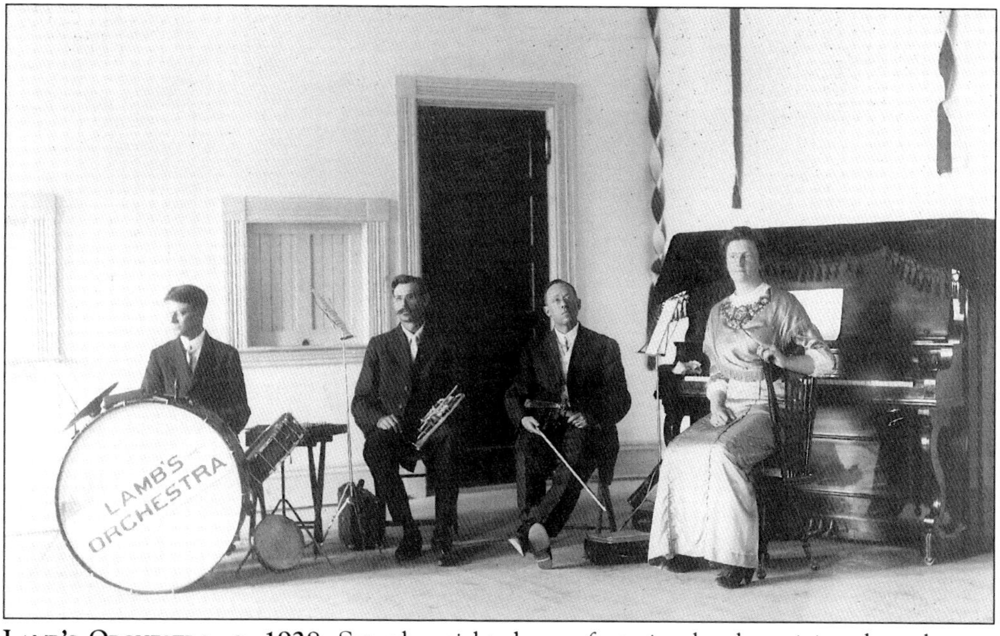

LAMB'S ORCHESTRA, c. 1928. Saturday night dances featuring local musicians have been a long-standing tradition in Harrison, and for many years dances were held upstairs in the IOOF building. These members of the orchestra are Harry Smith (on the drums), Ernest Davis (with the cornet), Fred Lamb (with the violin), and Vida Greene (at the piano).

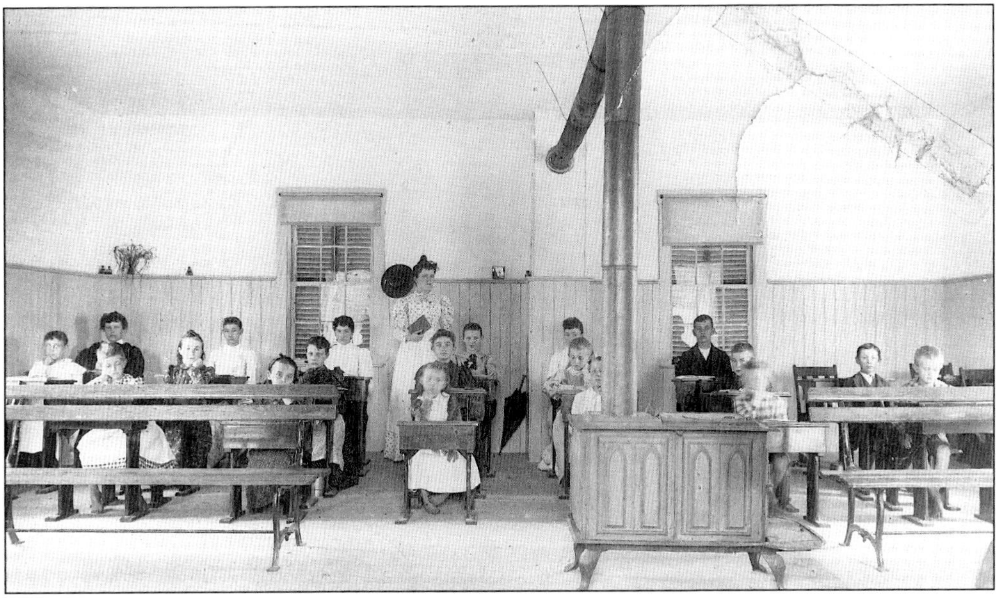

THE SOUTH HARRISON SCHOOL, C. 1895. Sara Milliken had the unenviable task of teaching grades subprimary through eight in this single room heated by wood in a cast-iron box stove and a long extended metal funnel or pipe suspended from the ceiling with wire to provide a maximum amount of heat. Except for Ella Thompson, Isabell Spaulding, and Geneva Merrow, all the other students are either Strouts, Bucks, Batchelders, Pendexters, or Foggs.

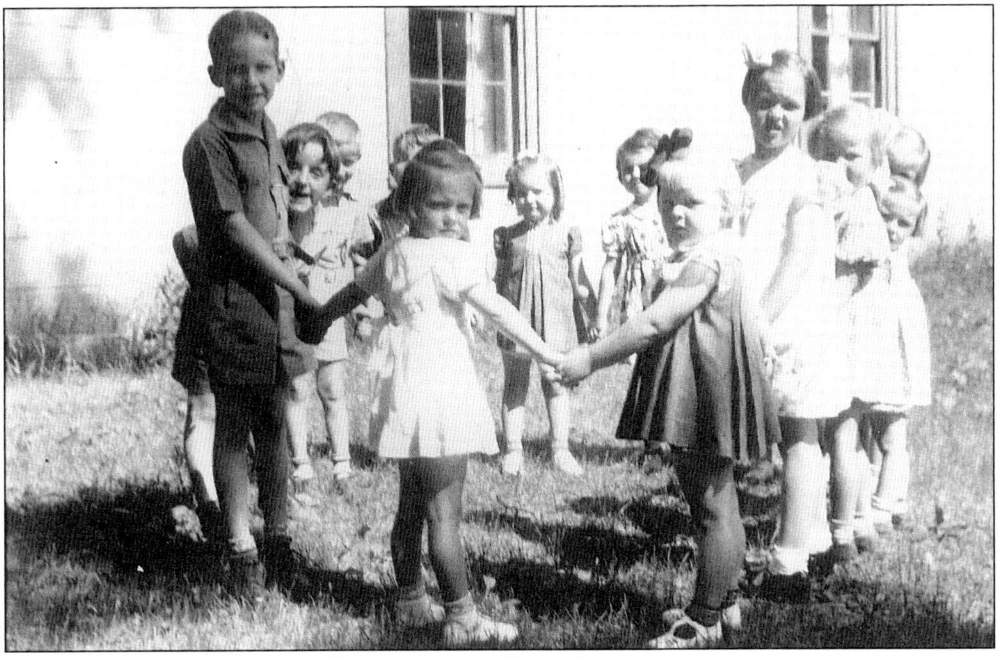

A HARRISON SUNDAY SCHOOL PICNIC, 1938. These Harrison youngsters are enjoying a game of Ring around the Roses on their annual Sunday school picnic. Clockwise, from left to right, are David Day, Joe Wentworth, Gray Sampson, David Morrison, Martha Day, Nancy Whitney, Carol Johnson, Madeline Johnson, Eva Lundstrum, Nola Skillings, Mary Helen Maxfield, and Winnie Merrill.

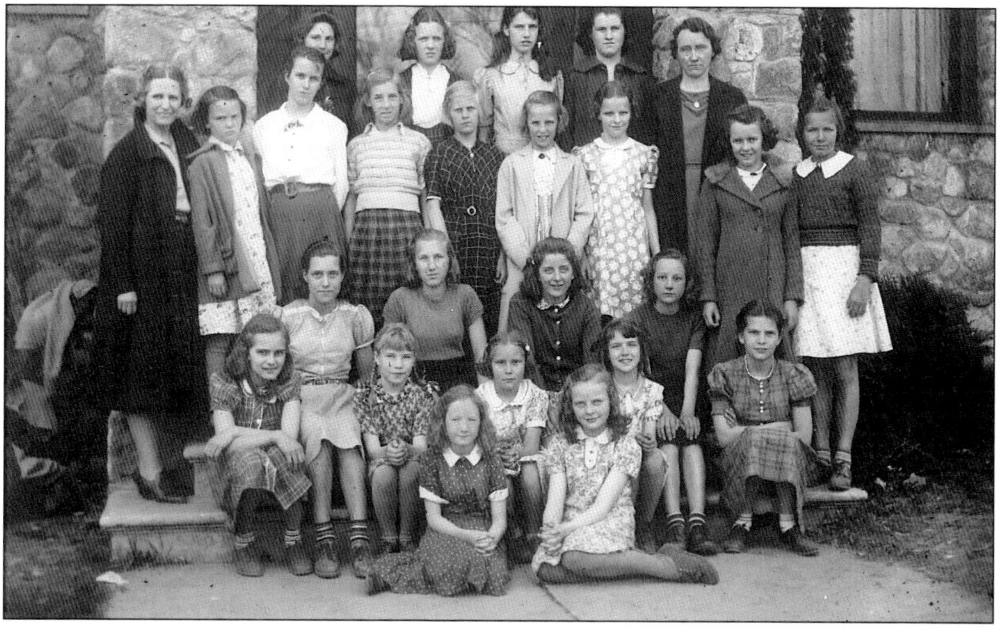

The Girls 4-H Club, 1937–38. Shown here are, from left to right, as follows: (front row) Margaret Butterfield and Marion Day; (second row) Virginia Purington, Aune Heino, Betty Carlson, Jacqueline Reilly, and Barbara Peary; (third row) Verna Martin, Pauline Allen, Margaret Wentworth, and Lillian Butterfield; (fourth row) Margaret Dennison (leader), Barbara Reilly, Sally Higgins, Phyllis Briggs, Vivian Ward, Patsy Merrill, Blanch Merrill, Arlene Merrill, and Ruth Lundstrom; (back row) Effie May Nisbet, Hilda Chapman, Dorothy Peary, Janet Higgins, and Edith Bradbury (assistant leader).

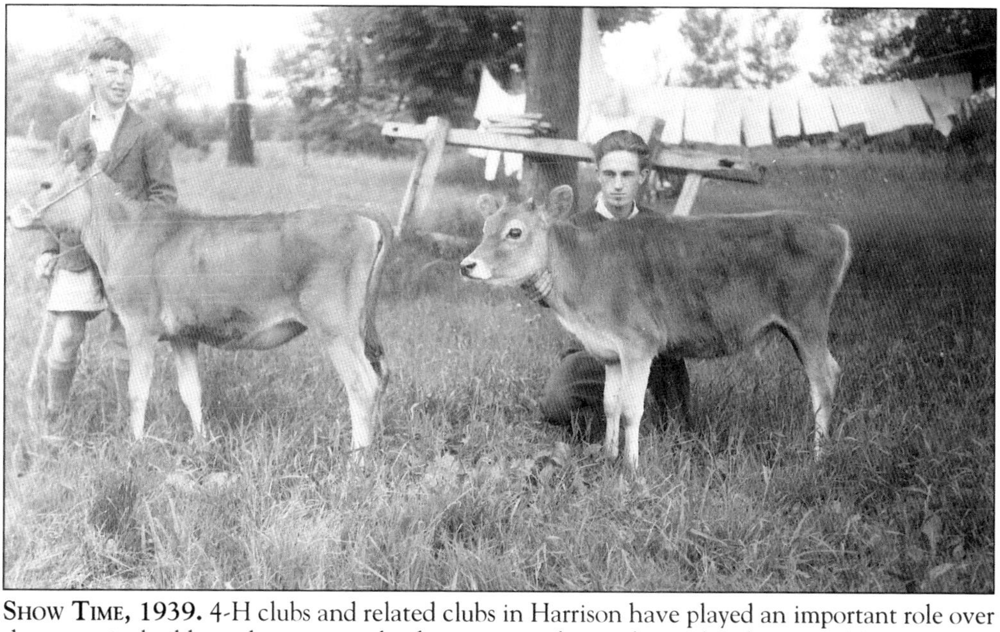

Show Time, 1939. 4-H clubs and related clubs in Harrison have played an important role over the years in building character and other noteworthy qualities that have enabled its young people to become successful in life. Here Dwight Sawin (left) and Wyman Dresser (right) are showing their Jersey heifers on the Dairy Club tour.

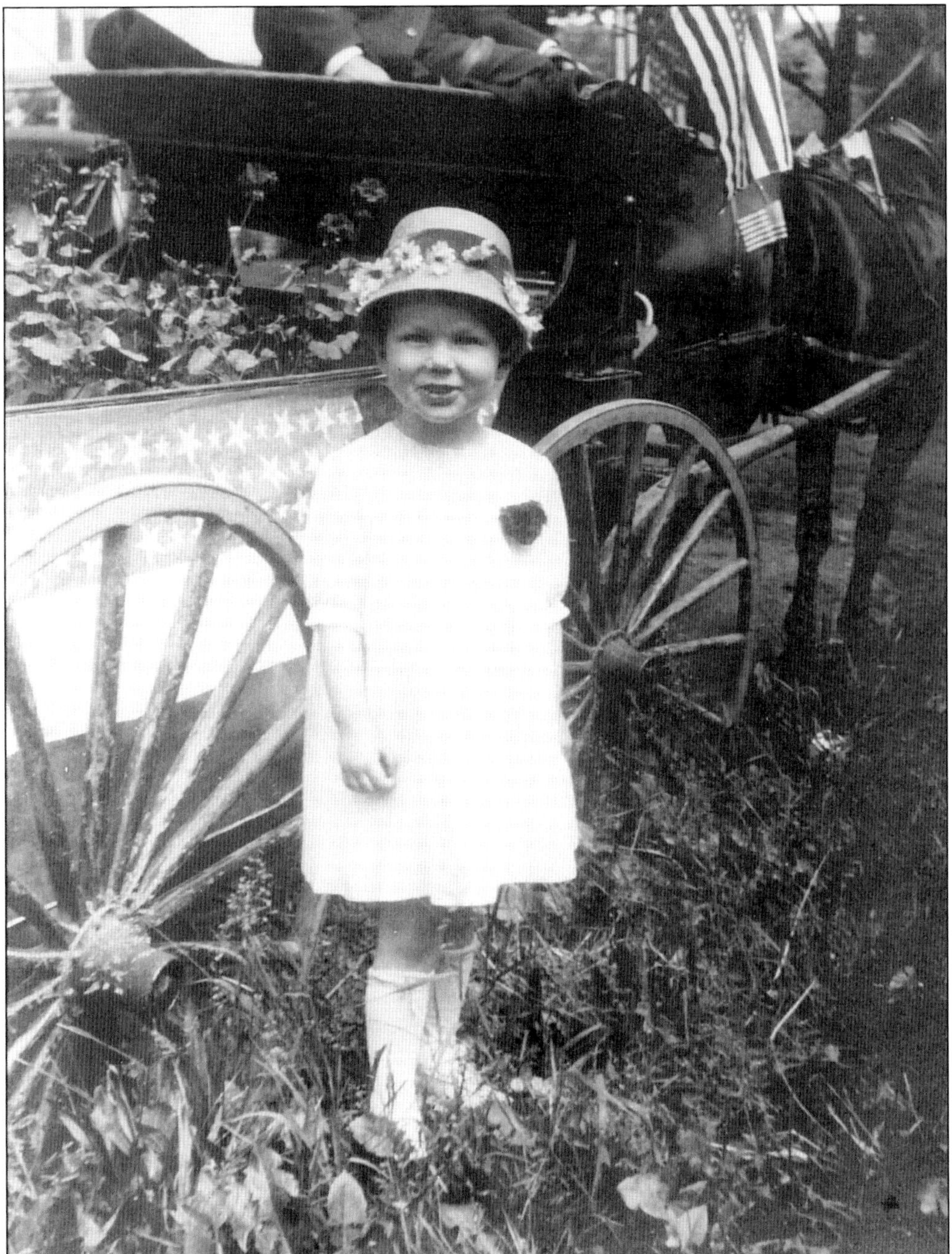

FLORENCE SPAULDING, C. 1920. Florence Spaulding, who was born June 20, 1917, in Springville, New York, is all dressed up for what appears to be either a Fourth of July celebration or an Old Home Day parade here in Harrison. Florence was the daughter of Edgar Otis and Ethel (Worthley) Spaulding. Edgar ran a photography and gift shop in Harrison, and Florence—their only child—attended the Harrison schools. During World War II she taught airplane identification courses. She married Robert Coe and lived in Naples, Florida, for many years until her death on November 28, 1970. This photograph was taken by her father.

Three

Otisfield

First Settled: 1776
Incorporated: 1797
Population: 1,136
Principal Settlements: East Otisfield, South Otisfield, Bolsters Mill, Spurrs Corner, Bell Hill

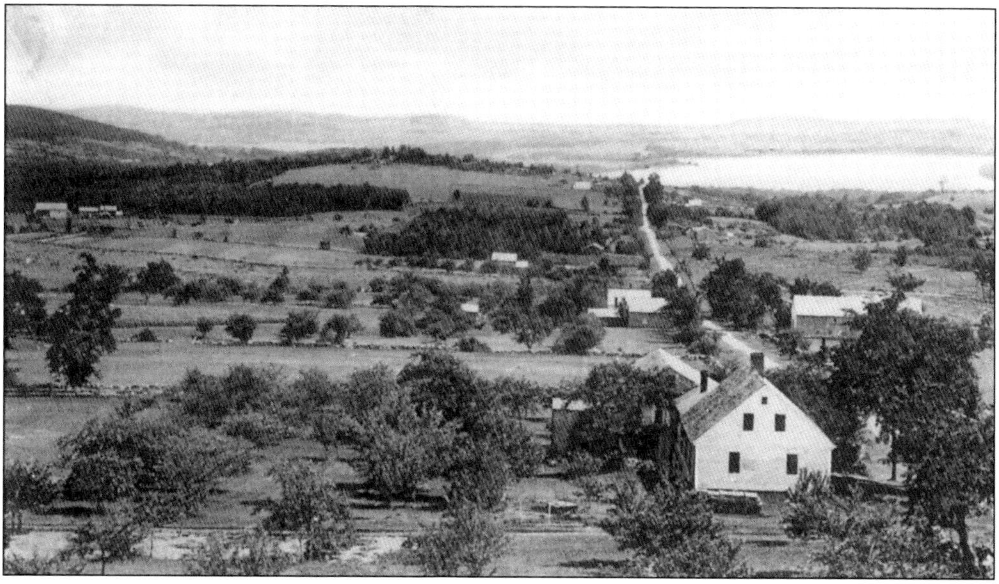

A VIEW FROM BELL HILL, 1936. Looking down from Bell Hill, one of Otisfield's most prominent vantage points, a portion of rural landscape unfolds to Pleasant Lake (Pond) and to the distant hills at a time when agriculture was still a viable part of the local economy in Otisfield. It was on the west side of Bell Hill that Benjamin Patch settled in 1779, began clearing land the following spring, and is said to have planted the first crop ever raised by a white settler in Otisfield. The farm in the left corner of this photograph was owned by Benjamin Dyer and the property remains in the Dyer family. The house in the foreground was built in 1798 by Major Jonathan Moore; it served as a tavern for 20 years.

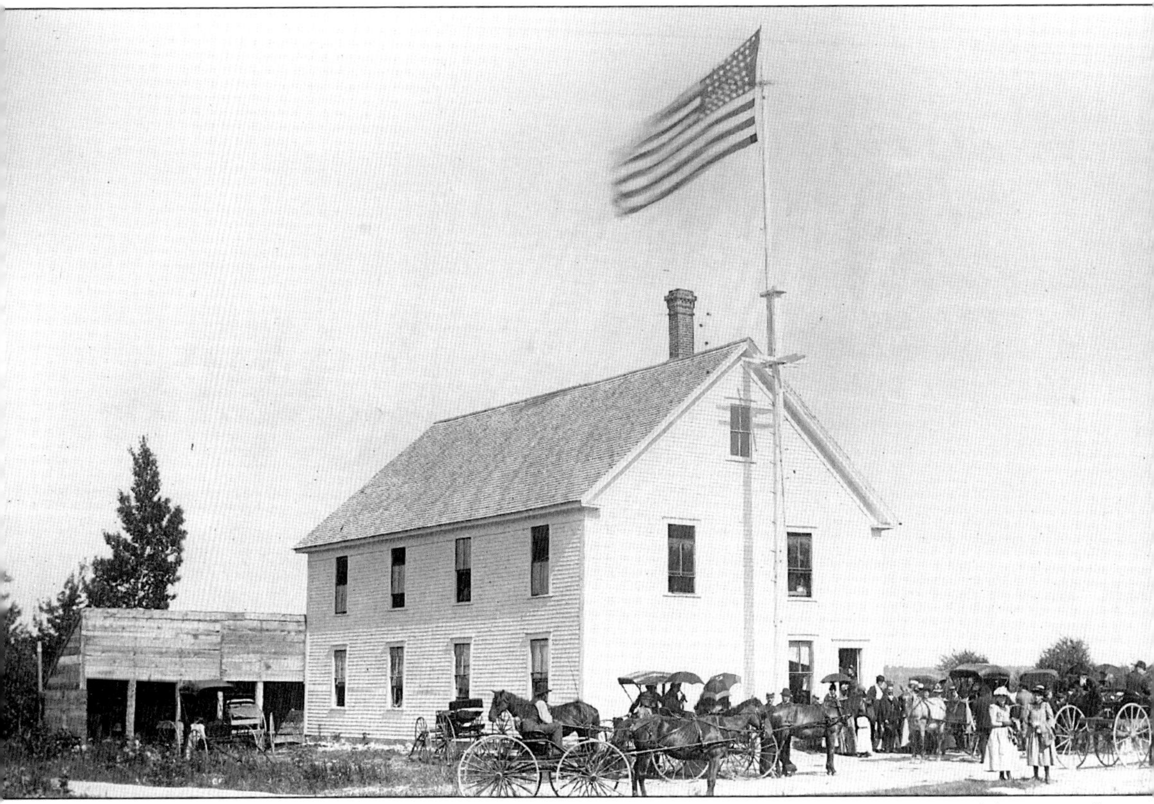

OXFORD COUNTY PAMONA GRANGE MEETING, C. 1900. No institution was more emblematic of the importance of agriculture until after World War II in Otisfield and other Maine communities than the grange. The Old Gore Grange (the Frederick Robie Grange), located at the Phillips Gore (annexed to Otisfield in 1803), is pictured here. It was one of two granges located in Otisfield (the other was at Spurrs Corner), and was a focal point on this day for members of the Oxford County Pamona Grange, many of whom must have rattled for miles over rutted, dusty country roads to gather here for an all-day meeting. A business meeting would have been held in the morning, followed by a noon meal commonly called dinner, and an afternoon program. Of course, most had to leave in time to return to their respective farms in order to do the evening chores and have supper. Each year more and more granges are being discontinued for lack of membership, and all too many of these prominent old structures have been torn down or remodeled for other purposes. The original structure here has been replaced by a concrete structure and remains the Frederick Robie Grange.

Whether Otisfield (Otis Field) in 1776 was named after Harrison Gray Otis (b. 1765), the son of Samuel Allyne Otis, or perhaps his grandfather—Col. James Otis (his oldest son was James Otis Jr., declared *non compos mentis* in 1769)—Otisfield is a proper name for this sparsely populated rural community. It was Col. James Otis, along with Nathaniel Gorham, who laid the groundwork beginning in 1768 for Otisfield being petitioned, surveyed, and settled. Harrison Gray Otis actually visited his property here September 1797, shortly before Otisfield was incorporated on February 19, 1798.

No one, however, played a more prominent role than George Peirce of Groton in surveying the area, laying out roads, setting up a sawmill and gristmill at Edes Falls on Crooked River (now Naples), and paving the way for Benjamin Patch (the town's first settler) and others to clear land and build their homes and a meetinghouse.

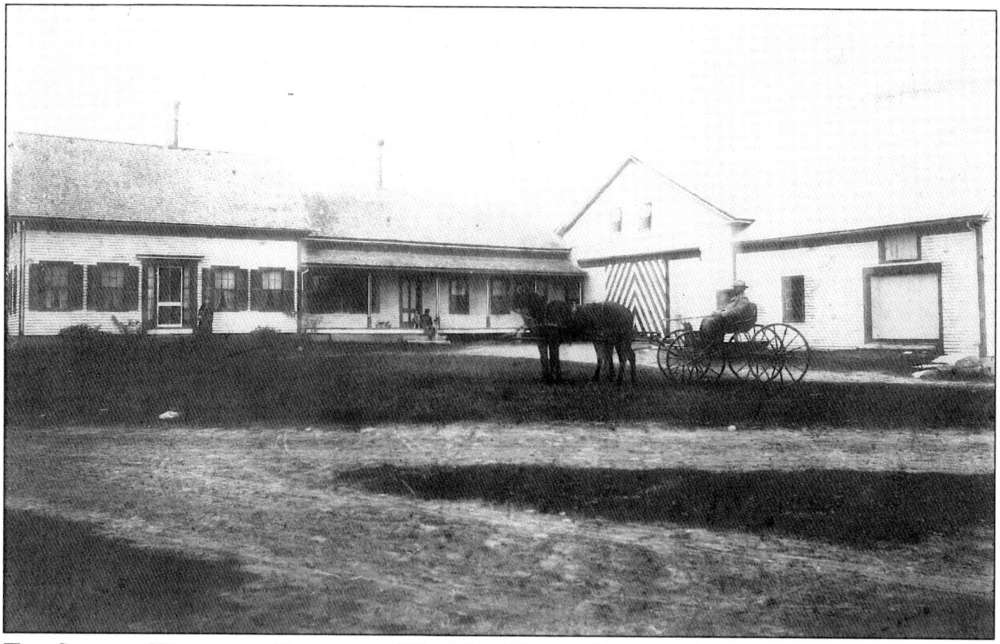

The Sumner Wardwell Farm, c. 1895. The Wardwell farm, where Amy Wardwell Nutting was born in 1882, was typical of the prosperous family farms that dominated the hills and valleys of Otisfield until several decades into the twentieth century. Sumner raised sheep and cattle and took cattle to the Bridgton market to be slaughtered for beef and veal.

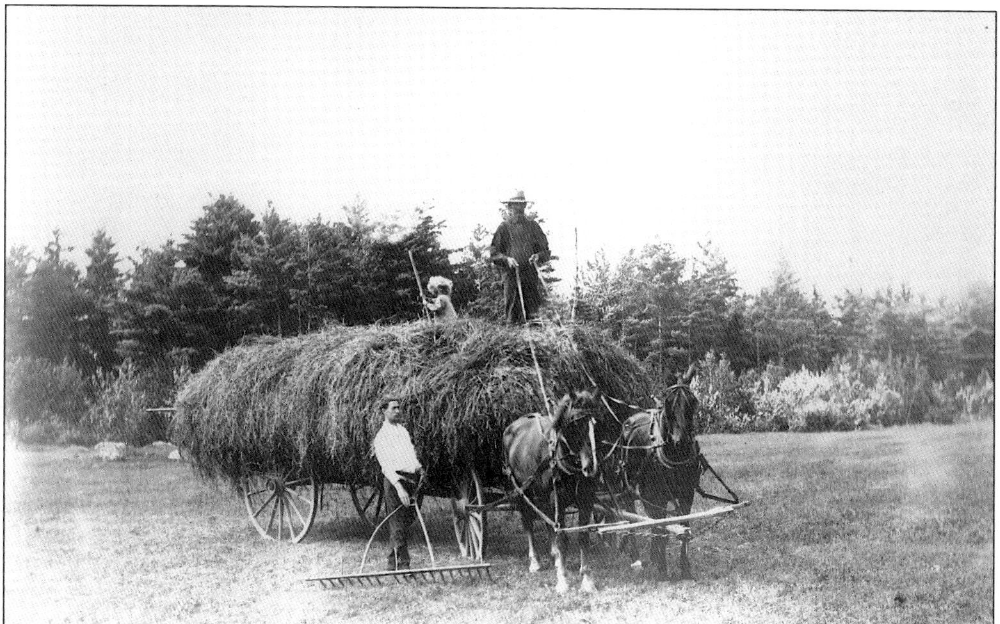

Haying Time, c. 1880. Haying season required the help of every able-bodied member of a farm family. A farmer (who may be Richard Bean of the Phillips Gore) is shown here holding his team of horses in check while a woman (who may be Richard's wife, Louisa) is making the load of hay. The person with the loafer rake gathering up the scatterings is thought to be Eastman Bean, who was killed on April 8, 1882, when he fell on a pitchfork in the barn.

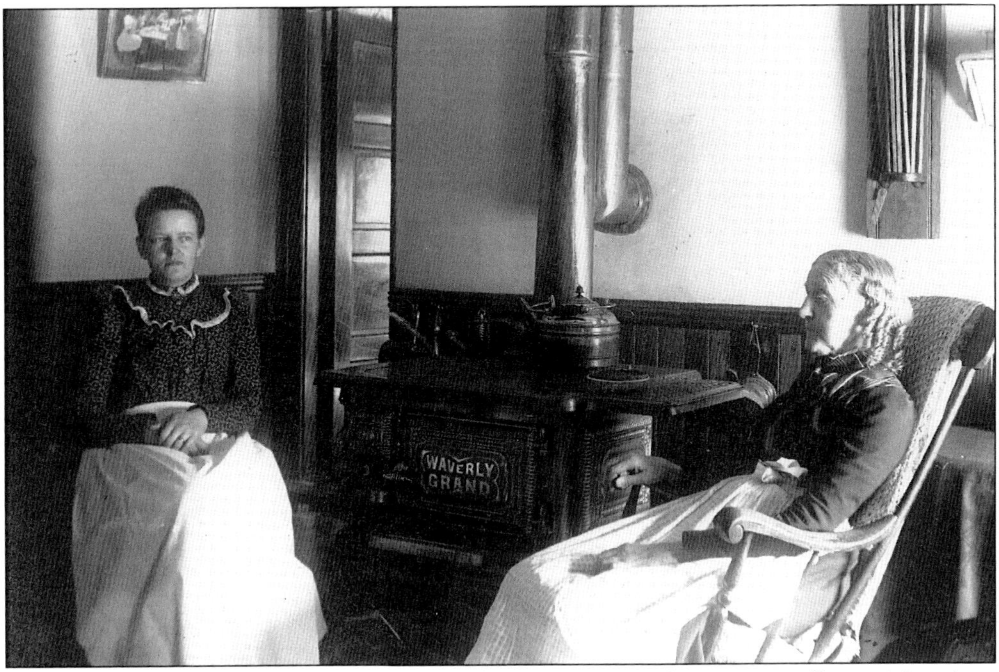

RELAXING IN THE KITCHEN, C. 1895. From late autumn to often times well into May, farm kitchens were the centers of social activities as well as a place of work. And the radiant heat from the iron stove was an immense improvement over the earlier huge kitchen fireplace that sent most of its heat up the great throat of the chimney. Note the lovely wainscoting in the kitchen of what is thought to be the Mark Knight farm on Bell Hill.

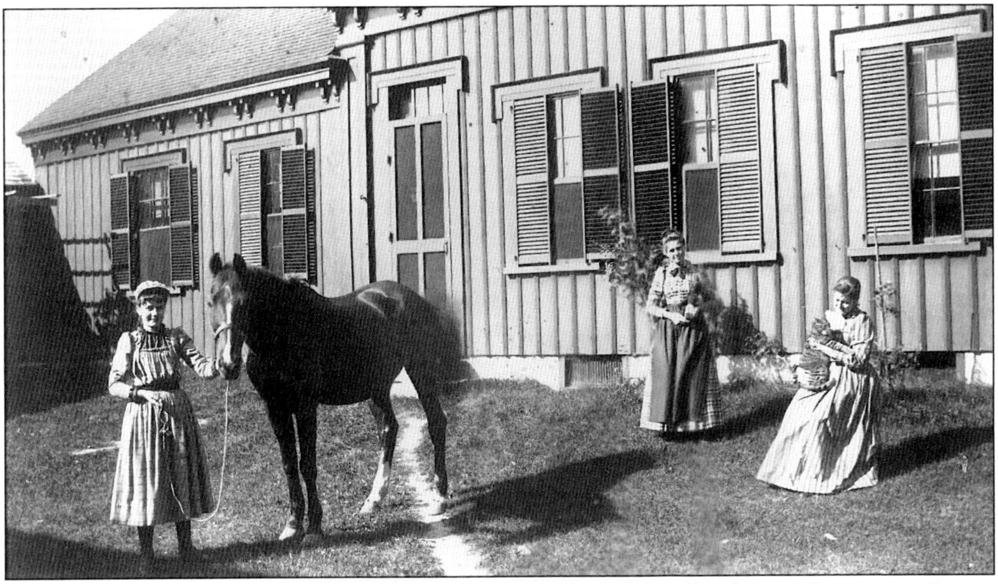

THE JOSEPH HANCOCK HOUSE, C. 1895. By the same token, the dooryard was a welcome respite from the hot cook stove in summer. The rather eclectic Joseph Hancock house in Hancockville, featuring brackets and board batten, was built in 1848. It presented an unusual combination of Italianate, Gothic, and Greek Revival architecture. Sadly, it has been recently demolished.

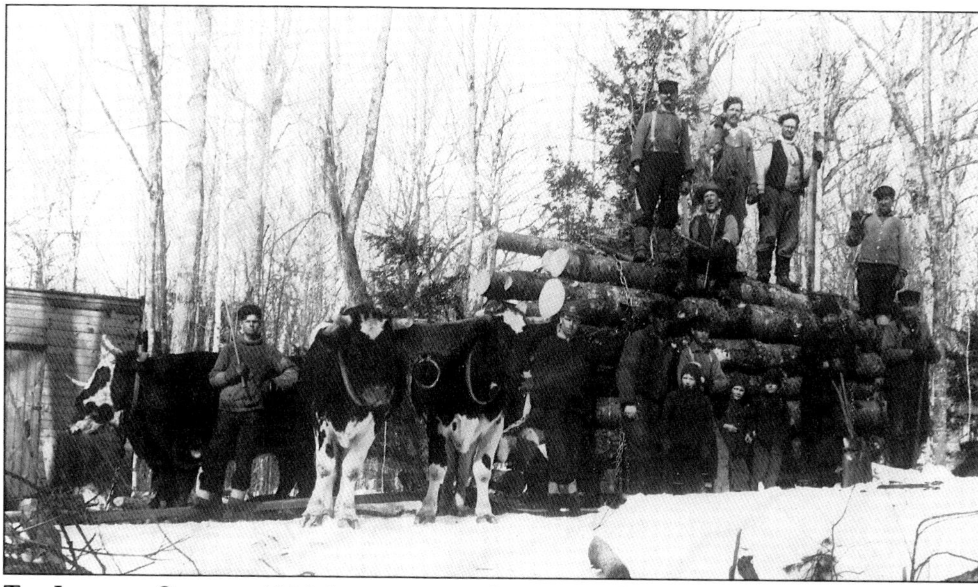

The Logging Crew, c. 1910. In winter most farmers supplemented their incomes by working in the woods. This logging operation, being carried out by Jim Thomes's logging crew in Otisfield, was a major commercial venture. The teamster posing beside the brockel-headed pair of oxen is Walter Mains of Harrison.

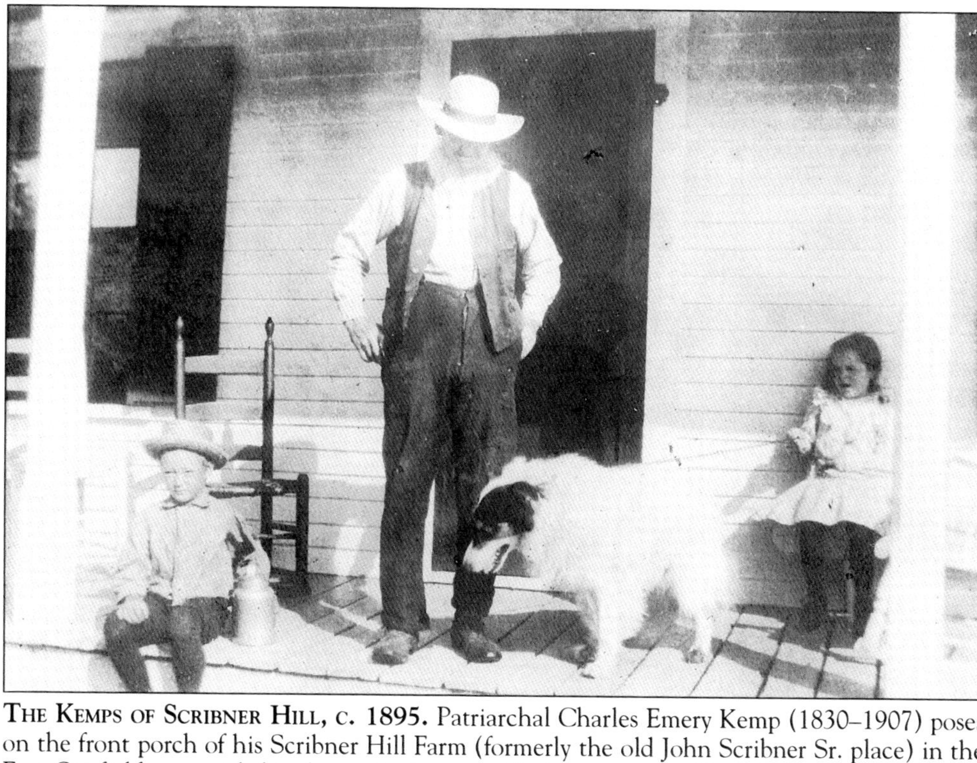

The Kemps of Scribner Hill, c. 1895. Patriarchal Charles Emery Kemp (1830–1907) poses on the front porch of his Scribner Hill Farm (formerly the old John Scribner Sr. place) in the East Otisfield area with his dog and what very likely were two of his grandchildren. Charles was the son of Jonathan and Martha Kemp. He purchased this farm from Edward Scribner after being married to Sibyl Jane Wardwell in 1856.

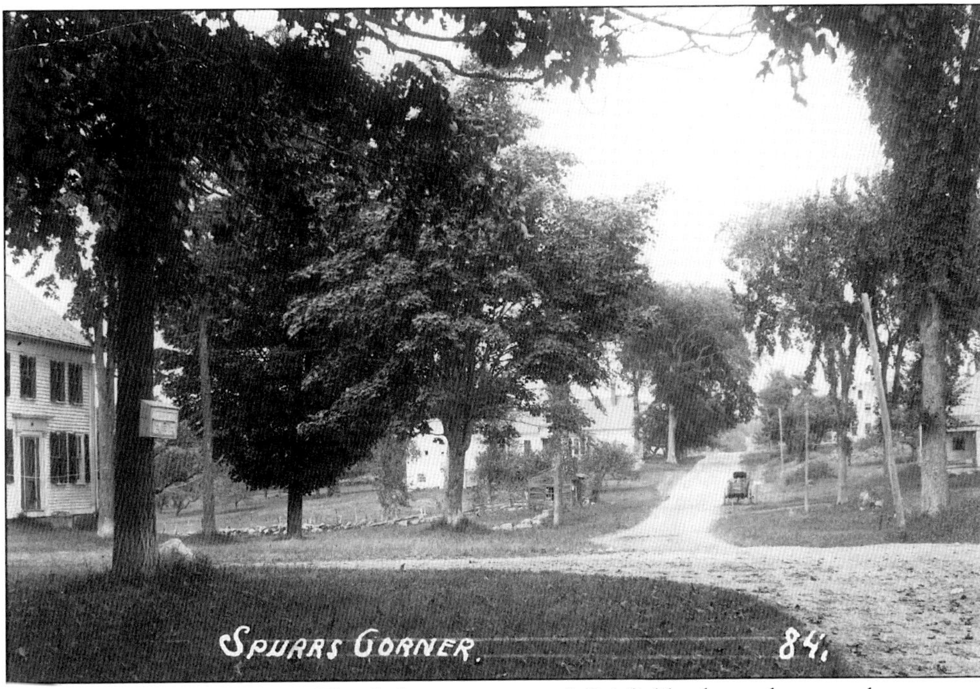

SPURRS CORNER, C. 1910. This halcyon corner of Otisfield where three roads converge was named after Enoch Spurr (1761–1843), who as a young man fought at Monmouth and Yorktown, and wintered at Valley Forge in the Revolutionary War. He was a progenitor of one of the town's most distinguished families, which included the historian William Samuel Spurr (1883–1977), author of *A History of Otisfield.*

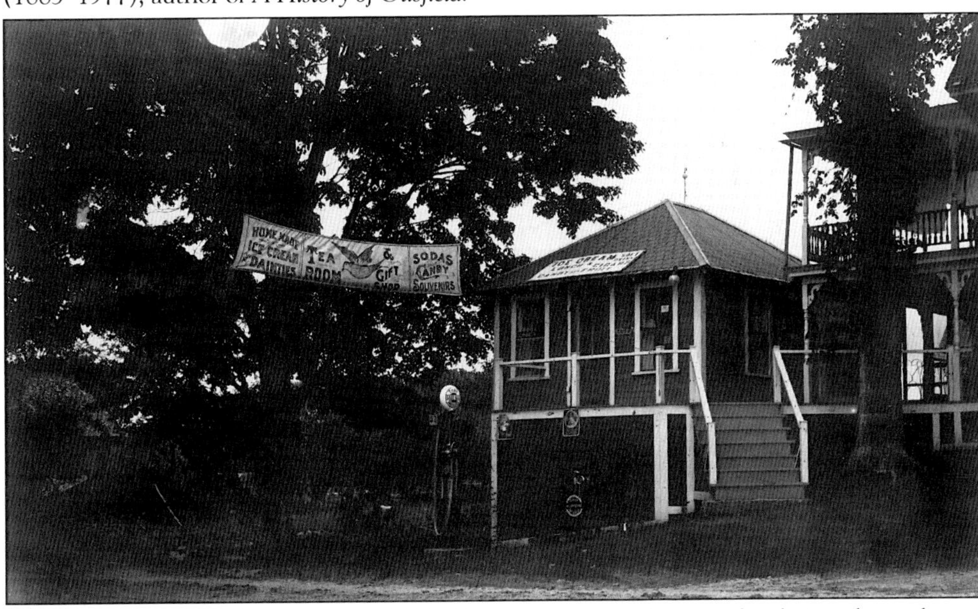

SARAH HANSCOME'S TEA ROOM, C. 1920. Tearooms were rather popular during the early part of the twentieth century in many Maine communities that attracted summer residents and tourists. Sarah Hanscome operated this tearoom at Spurrs Corner for a decade or so. She served homemade pastries, tea, coffee, ice cream, and soft drinks.

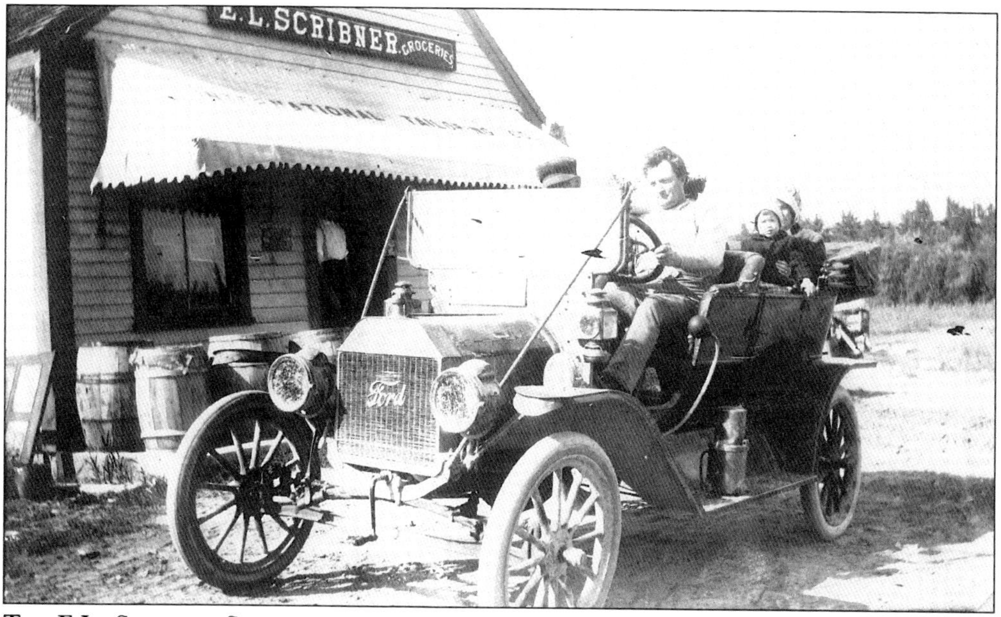

THE E.L. SCRIBNER STORE, c. 1912. Eugene Scribner ran this store, which was located on Route 121, and lived with his father, George, in the house now owned by Dorothy Lombard. The barrels containing sundry items in front of the store are a reminder of the important role many Maine communities ("barrel towns") played in manufacturing barrels and shooks for export as well as for domestic use. The unidentified motorist with his family is driving a c. 1912 Model-T Ford touring car with gas lights.

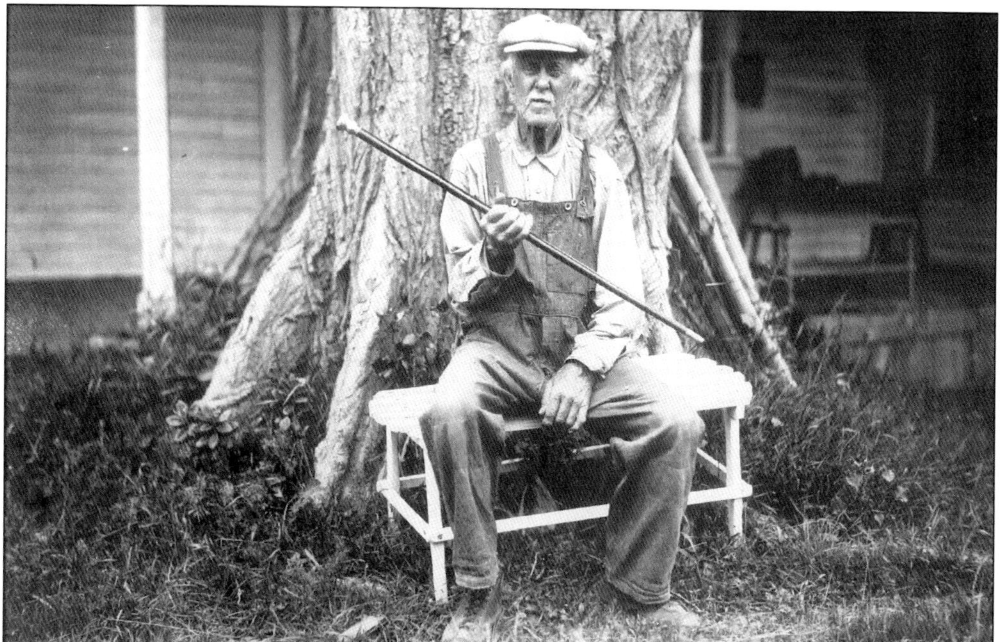

DANFORTH WINSHIP, c. 1936. Danforth Winship sits in front of his family home on Cobbs Hill proudly holding the Boston Post Cane, given to Otisfield's oldest citizen. He was born in 1846 and died at his granddaughter's home in Revere, Massachusetts, in 1938.

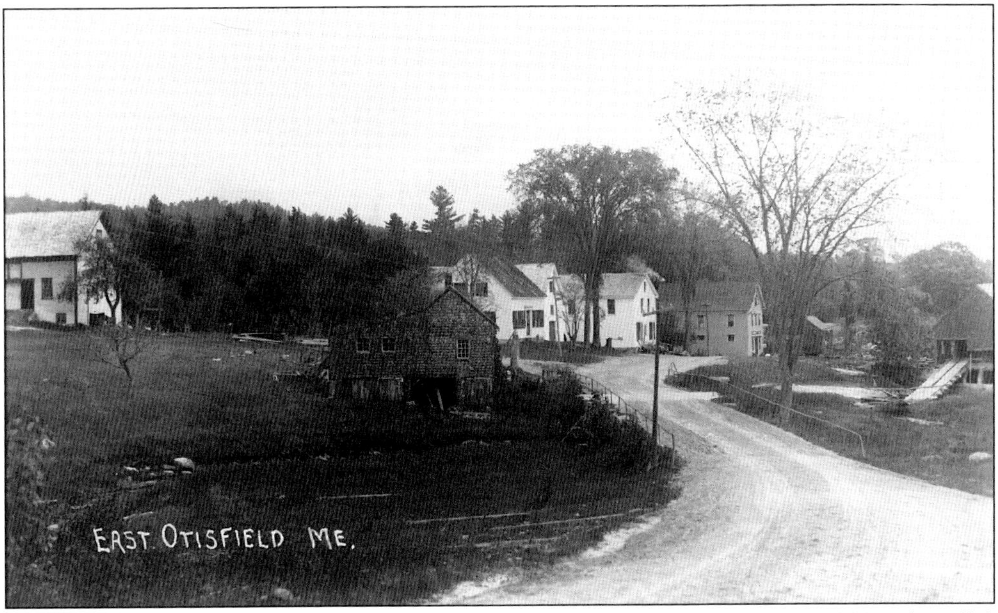

East Otisfield, c. 1895. The sinuous Old Gore Road passes through East Otisfield (Pugleyville) by the old blacksmith shop, Edwin Lamb's barn, and the Ellis R. Stone house (all on the left). To the right is a sawmill, owned by Stephen D. Jillson at the time this photograph was taken.

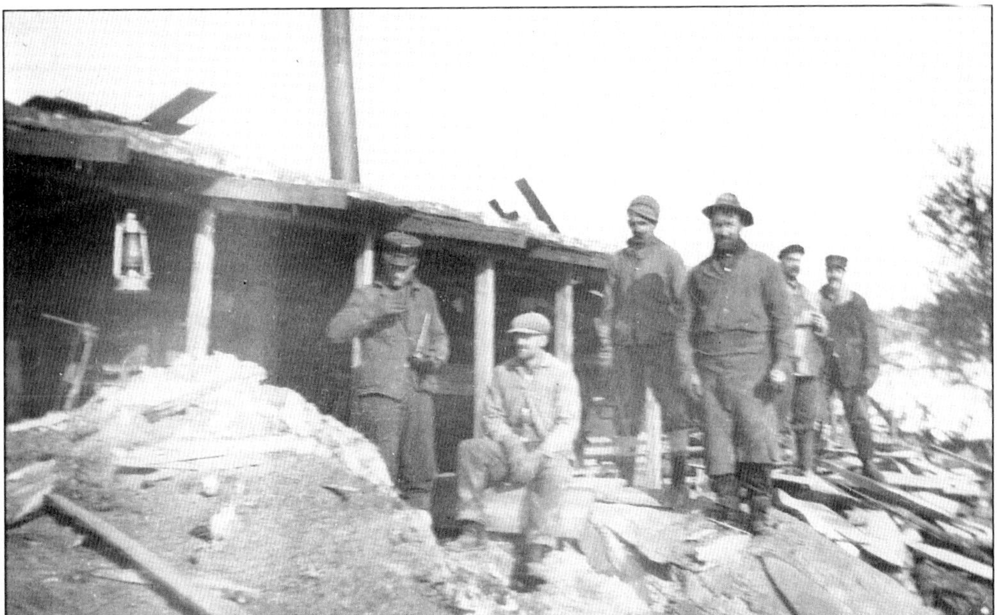

Kemps Mills, c. 1914. Jillson sold his mills in East Otisfield to John, Sidney, and Fred Kemp on December 3, 1900. About a year later the mills burned. The Kemp brothers promptly rebuilt and expanded the mill complex, which they operated until 1930. Beginning with Timothy Fernald in 1812, mills on this site had sawed logs and for more than a half century at least had ground grain into meal. The mills, which remained idle after the Kemps died out, were demolished in 1946.

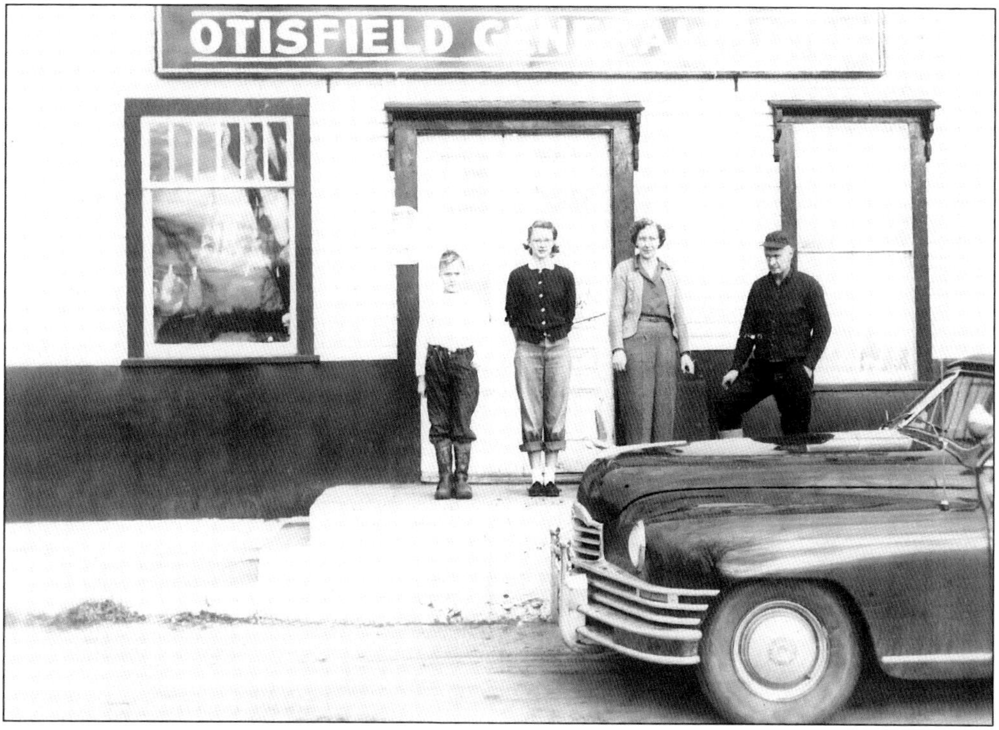

The Otisfield General Store, c. 1946. Like the mills, general stores have disappeared from the Otisfield hamlets. But until more recent years this general store, located in East Otisfield on Route 121 and owned at the time by David Bean (standing to the right of his wife, Resper, and their two children, Virginia and Norman), took care of the basic needs of its local citizenry as well as transients. The automobile is a 1946 Hudson.

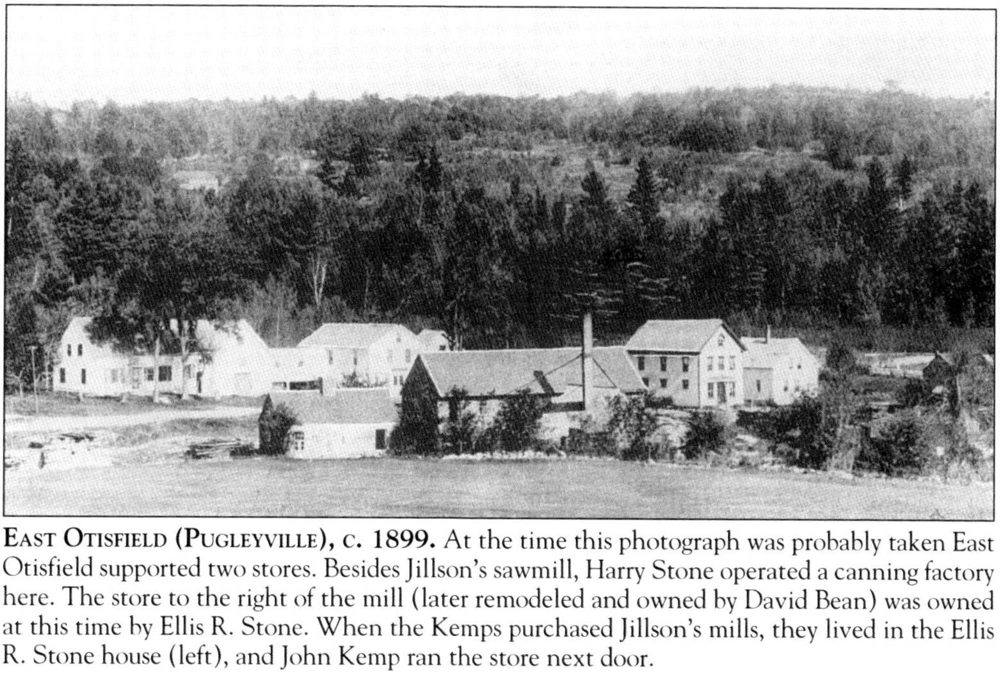

East Otisfield (Pugleyville), c. 1899. At the time this photograph was probably taken East Otisfield supported two stores. Besides Jillson's sawmill, Harry Stone operated a canning factory here. The store to the right of the mill (later remodeled and owned by David Bean) was owned at this time by Ellis R. Stone. When the Kemps purchased Jillson's mills, they lived in the Ellis R. Stone house (left), and John Kemp ran the store next door.

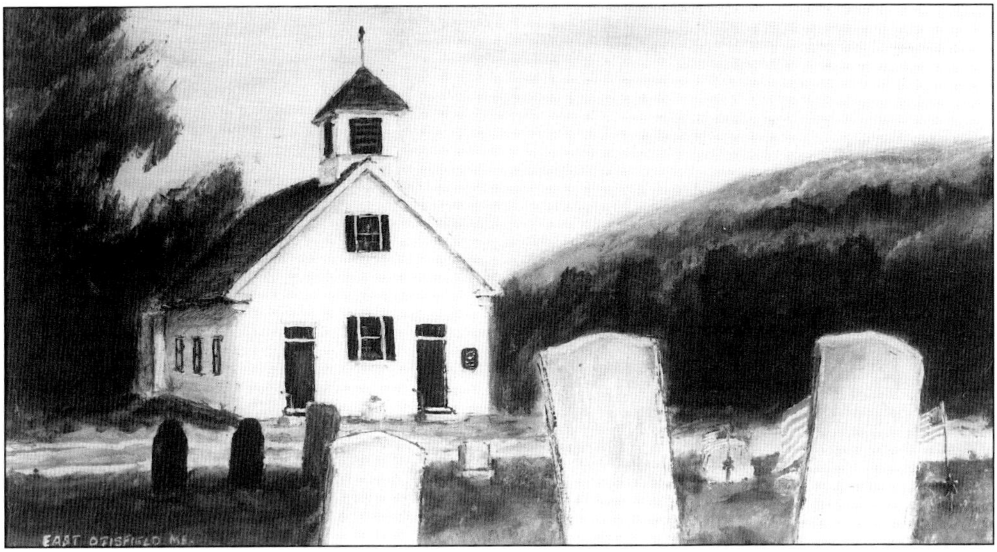

The Free Baptist Church at Rayville. The Baptists and Methodists united in 1828 to build this simplistic little Free Meeting or Union Church, located in Rayville within sight of Otisfield's earliest mill complex. In 1869 the church was taken over by the Freewill Baptist Society. It was remodeled (or possibly torn down and rebuilt) in 1870. (The photograph is of a painting by the Rev. William Morgan, pastor from 1964 to 1968.)

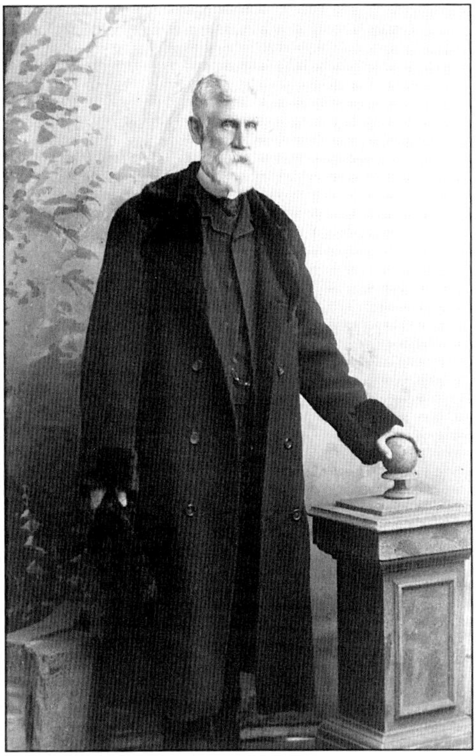

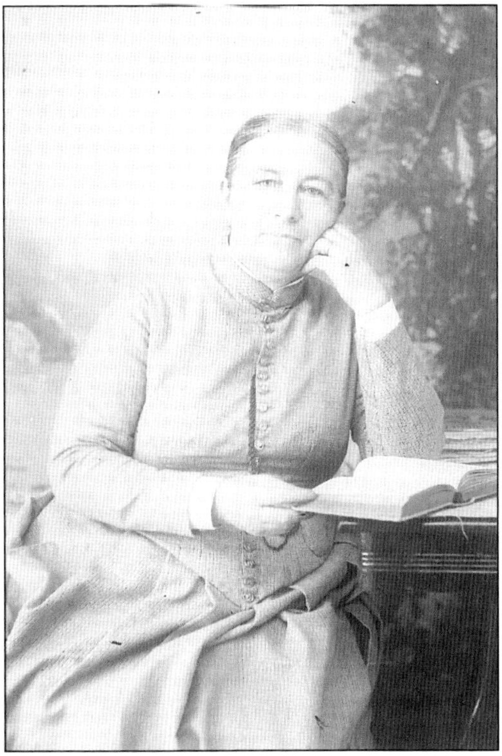

Church Pastors. Reverend Joseph Hutchinson became the first Baptist minister following the re-organization of the church in 1869 and apparently served the parish until 1872. Mrs. Towne was the wife of Reverend F.W. Towne, who served as pastor in 1885.

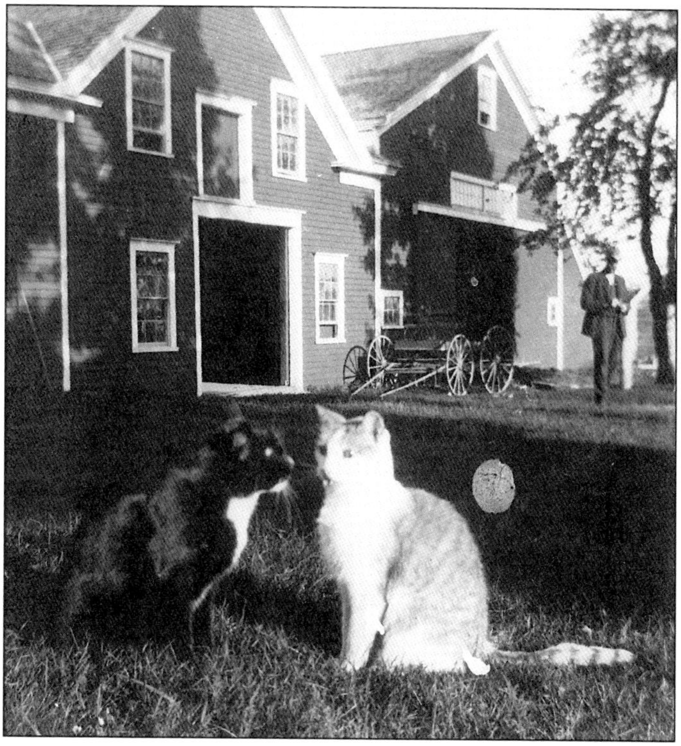

THE JILLSON PLACE, c. 1910. The Jillson farm, located in South Otisfield, was once the residence of Stevens Edwards. Ephraim B. Jillson (1847–1925), standing in front of the barn, owned and operated a corn shop near the farm and at one time ran a store in Dunkertown.

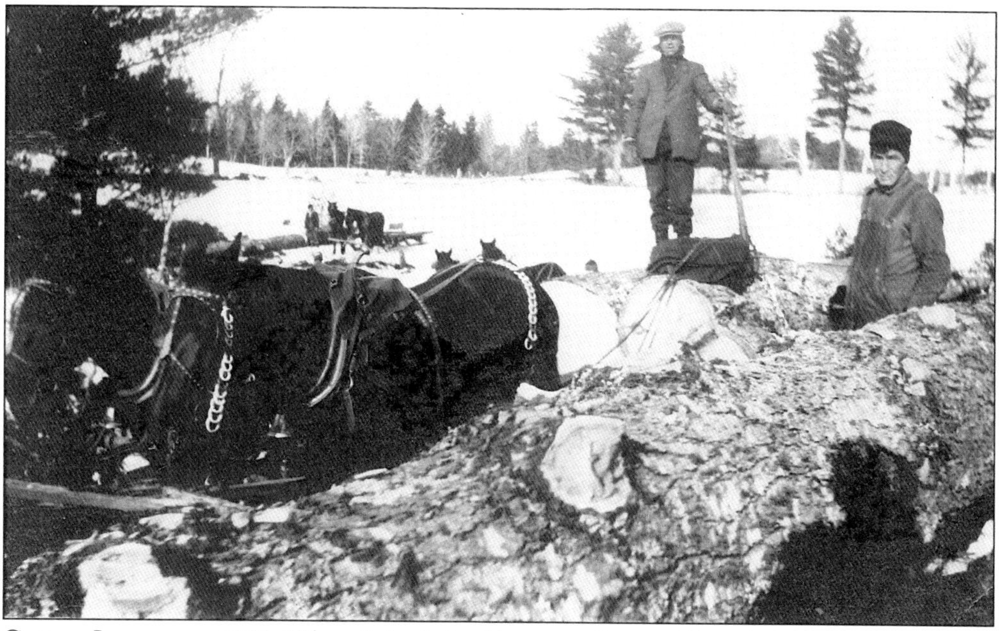

GEORGE JILLSON, c. 1920. When Ephraim's oldest son, George Jillson (who had studied law in Boston), married Esther E. Scott of Boston and moved back to Otisfield, Ephraim gave the farm to the newlyweds and moved to Oxford. George ran the corn shop, farmed, and logged until his untimely death from infantile paralysis November 14, 1924.

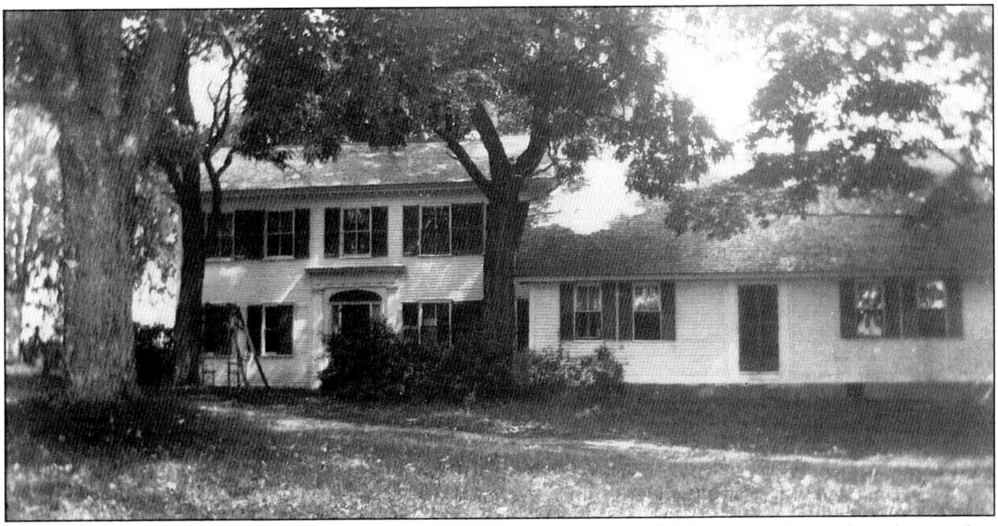

The Nutting Homestead, c. 1920. Five generations of Nuttings have lived on this vintage farm since Nathan Nutting Sr. and his brother Peter first cleared land and built a log cabin. Somewhere around 1796 Nathan and his wife were living in the cape part of the house. The lovely two-story Federal style portion, embellished with a "Venetian" entrance doorway, was designed and built around 1825 by their son, Nathan Nutting Jr. (his first known commission) for his brother Lyman and his wife, Charlotte. Lyman helped his father with the farming and logging.

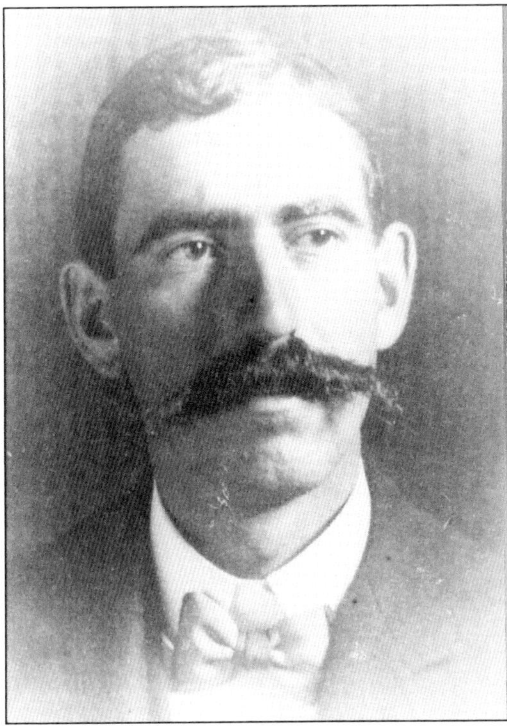

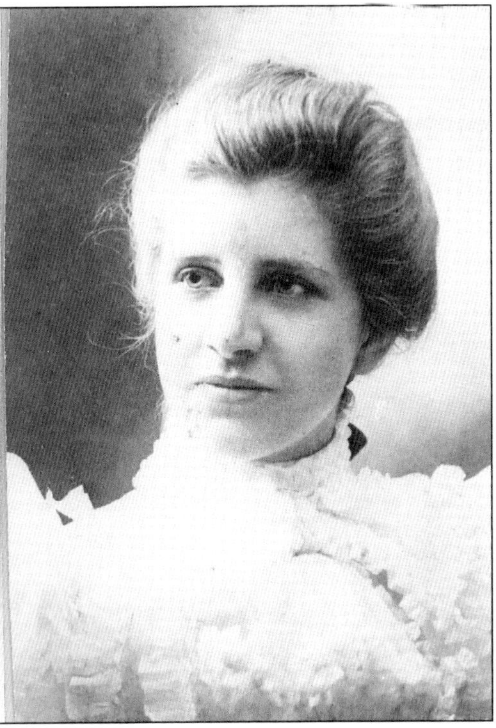

Silas Dexter (1875–1957) and Amy Wardwell Nutting (1882–1960). This couple lived and worked at the Nutting farm and reared five children, all of whom they put through college.

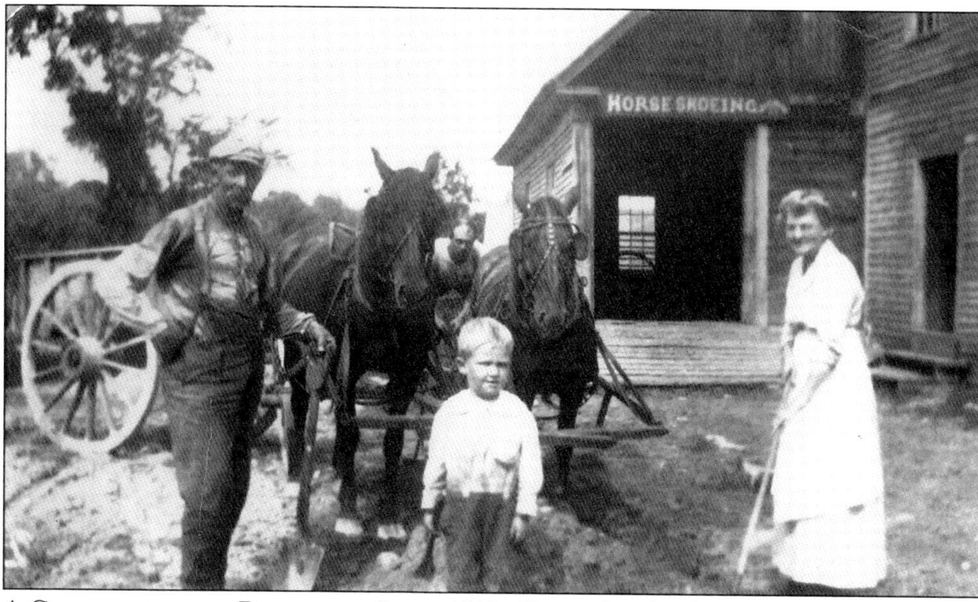

A GATHERING AT THE BLACKSMITH SHOP, 1918. Chester Lombard ran a blacksmith shop here at his farm (formerly the Sawyer place) in Hancockville. Standing with the spade is William Smith. Between the team of horses hitched to the dumpcart is Charles Mayberry. Sarah Sawyer is raking the yard. The little boy is Donald Lombard, the son of Chester and Maud Sawyer Lombard. Only the watering tub remains.

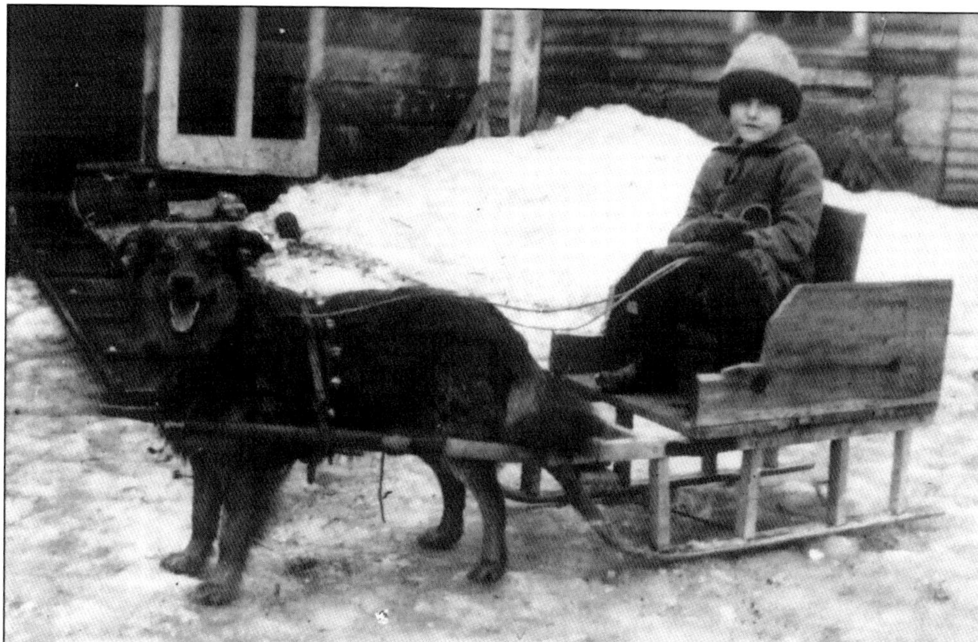

GOING FOR A RIDE, 1924. Five-year-old Dorothy Dyer Lombard (now living at Spurrs Corner) is enjoying a ride in her sled being pulled by her dog Teddy. Her father, Benjamin Dyer, operated this farm on Dyer Hill in East Otisfield. He rebuilt much of the farm after a disastrous fire in 1936. Garry Dyer, Dorothy's nephew, represents the fifth generation of Dyers to live here.

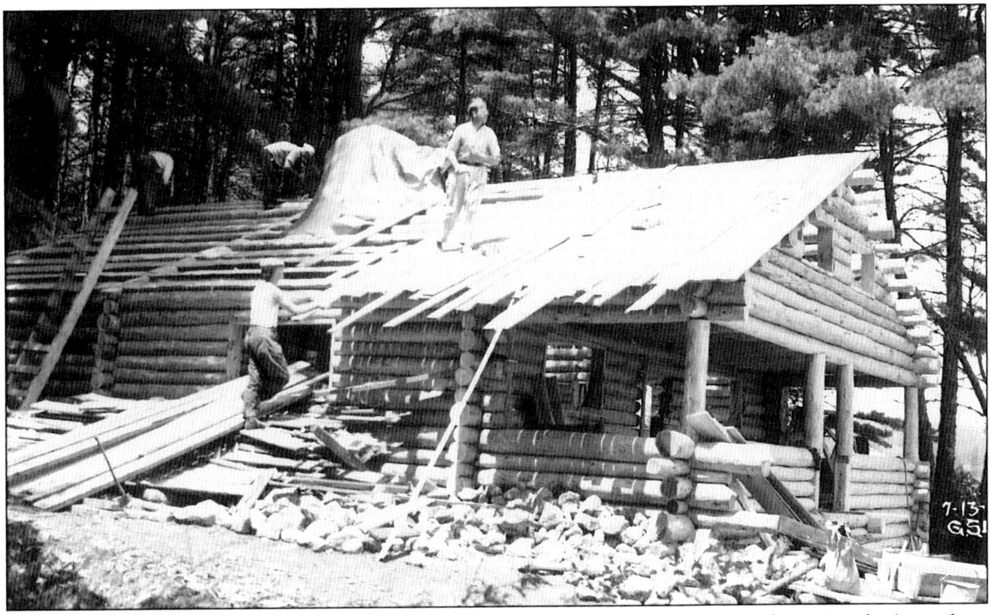

THE CONSTRUCTION OF CAMP LOSEEKUM, 1937. John Kemp Pottle, Moulton Pottle (standing on the roof), and other members of the family are in the process of building an impressive log cabin at Otisfield Cove, located on the west shore of Thompson Lake. The property, which originally belonged to the Kemp Brothers of East Otisfield, included the Scribner Hill Farm (where Jean and David Hankins currently live). Many of these stately cathedral pines were uprooted in the hurricane the following autumn (1938), but the Pottle family camp has stood the test of time and continues to be shared by a fifth generation.

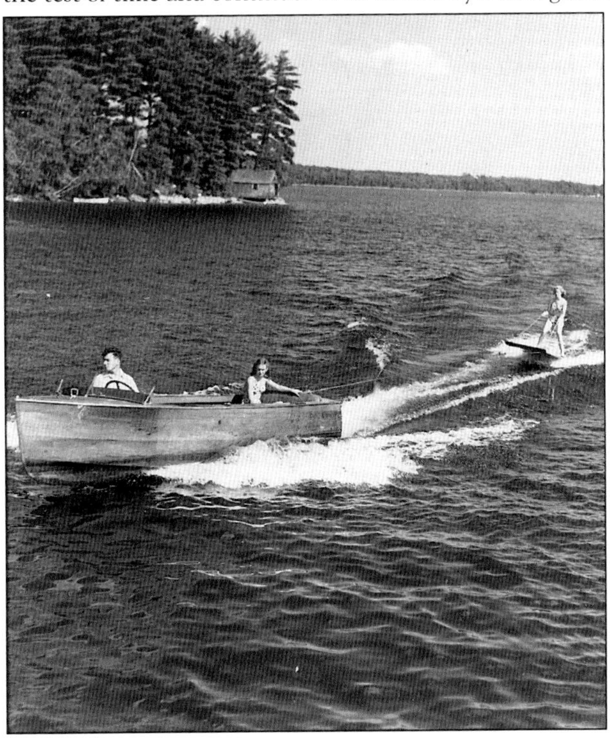

FUN ON THE WATER, 1946. Before water skis were invented, aquaplaning behind a speedboat such as the Chris Craft was a popular sport on Maine lakes and ponds. Shown here on the west shore of Thompson Lake (known as The Cape), Frank Bean; his daughter, Janet Bean Swinchatt; and his niece, Patricia Bean Bourque, are taking full advantage of an opulent summer's day at the lake.

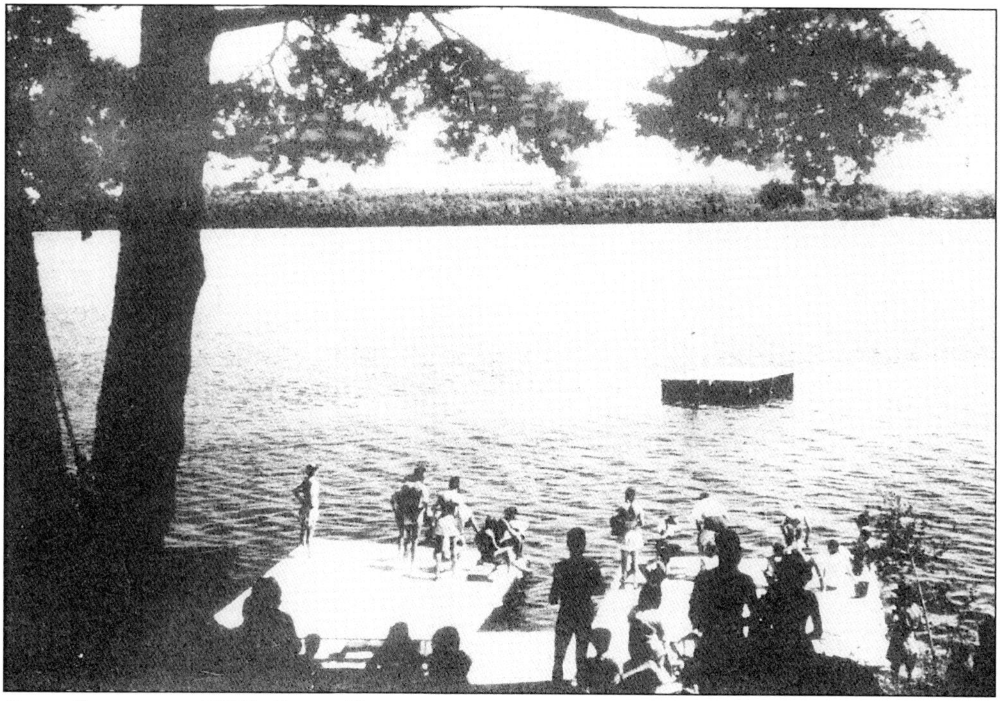

CAMP OHUIVO, C. 1925. Camp Ohuivo was founded in 1913 on the west side of Thompson Lake as a camp for girls by Mary North, a high school history teacher from Montclair, New Jersey (her nephew is Richard North, a retired teacher presently residing on family property on Cobbs Hill near the this site). Since there was no road leading to the camp property for a number of years after it was founded, the campers, mostly from New Jersey, came up from Portland on the Grand Trunk Railroad to the Oxford Station and then were transported by boat to the camp. In the early 1930s Camp Ohuivo ceased to be a girls camp and for a number of years was operated as a family camp. The property has since been divided into individual cottage lots.

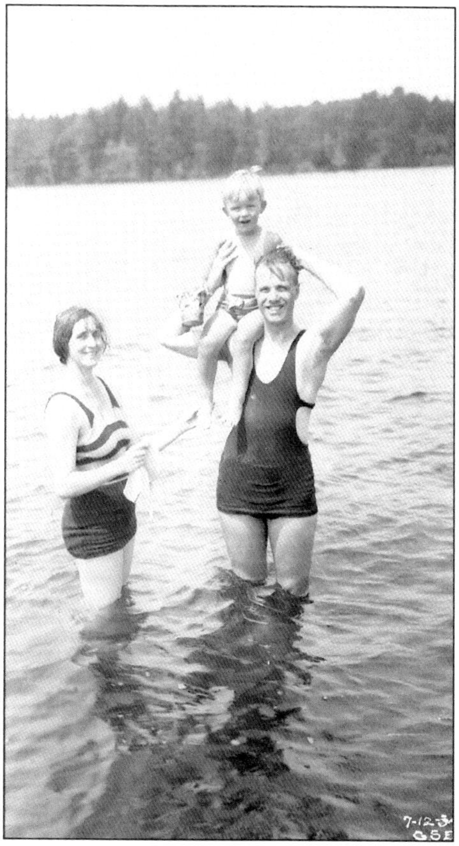

A FAMILY SWIM, JULY 12, 1934. Marian and Frederick Pottle and their son Christopher are enjoying a swim in Thompson Lake in front of Camp Loseekum, the Pottle family camp.

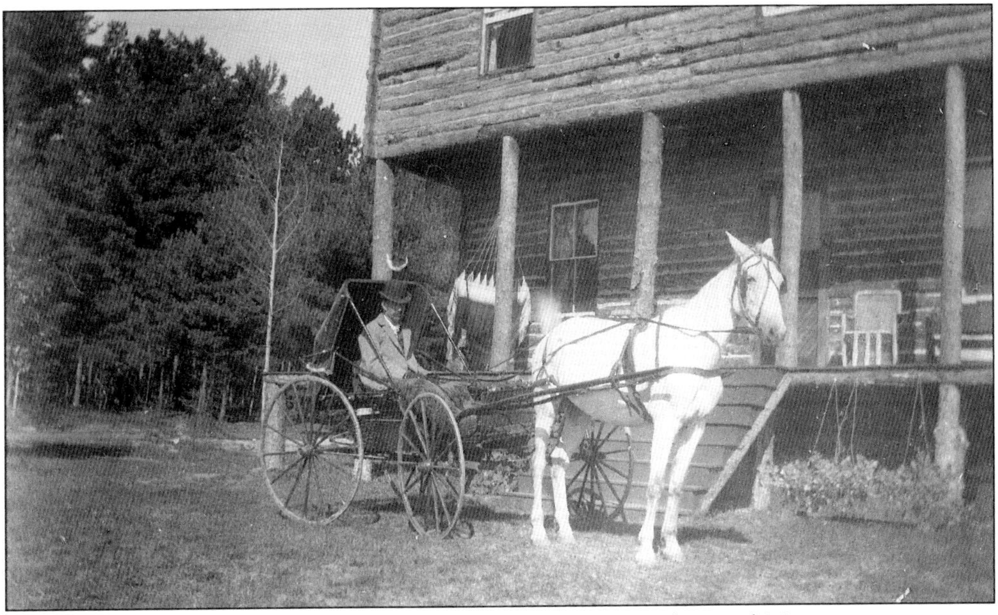

Arthur "Pop" Bean and Maggie, c. 1895. It is likely that Arthur and Maggie are waiting in front of Pemoacwa Lodge to take their employers, Dr. George Thompson Elliot and his wife, Eva, or guests of Dr. Elliot for a joy ride or to the Grand Trunk Railroad station in Oxford. Dr. Elliot, a world-famous dermatologist from New York City as well as an avid sportsman, first came to Thompson Lake in the early 1890s. He became enamored of its beauty and purchased the entire Cape, where he first built this rustic lodge as a sportsmen's rendezvous.

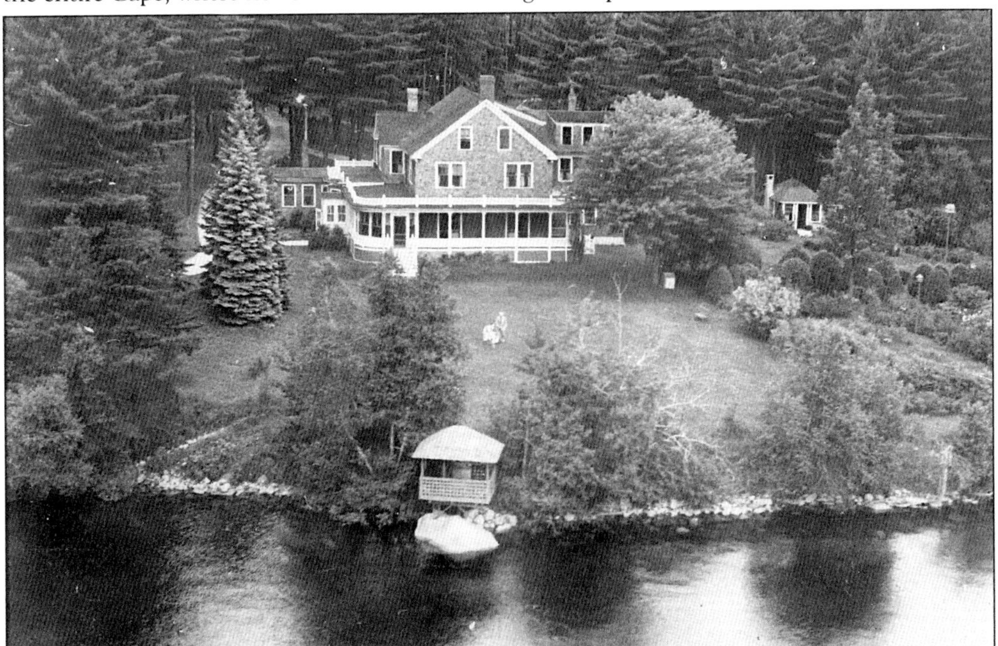

The Cape, c. 1930. In 1906 this expansive main house was built at the tip of The Cape, and Frank "Cy" Bean became the proprietor. The lodge and cottages are presently owned and operated by his daughter-in-law, Ethel Bean Turner.

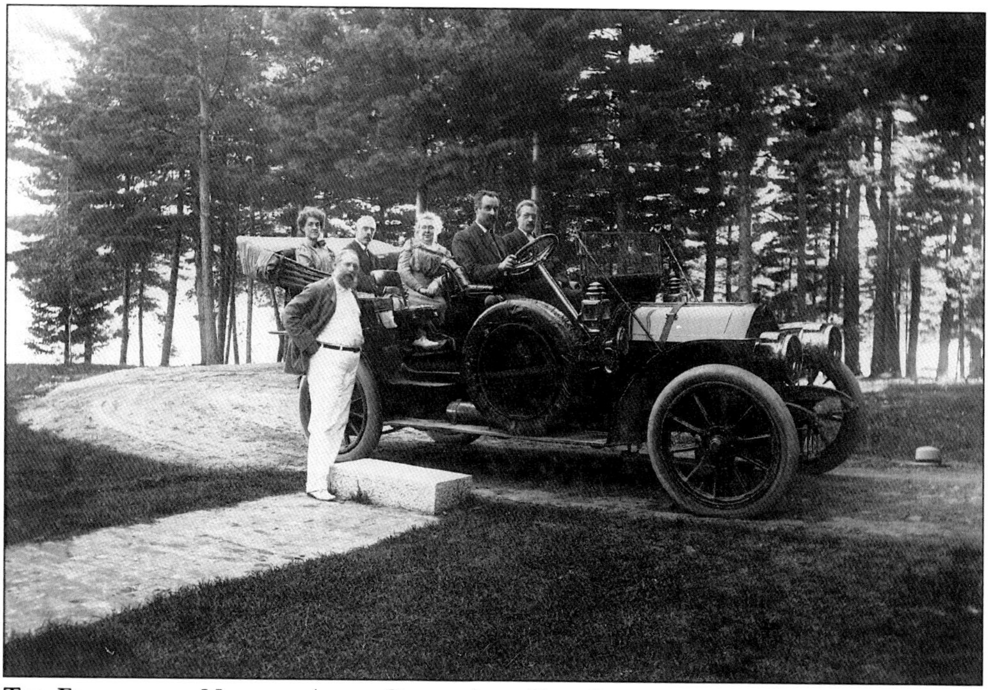

THE ELLIOTS AND NESBITTS (FROM CANADA) AT THE CAPE, C. 1910. Dr. Elliot is standing beside this jewel of a 1909 Thomas Flyer, said to be the first automobile to appear in Otisfield. Arthur Bean, seated next to the chauffeur, is driving. The Elliots eventually became permanent residents here at The Cape; Dr. Elliot wrote in the *Fiftieth Anniversary Record* of the Class of 1877 from Yale College that "I just quit New York without any trumpets and fire works and came down here and did not go back." Dr. Elliot, who was born in New Orleans in 1855, died in 1931. Eva Elliot, remembered for her generosity to Otisfield, died in 1946.

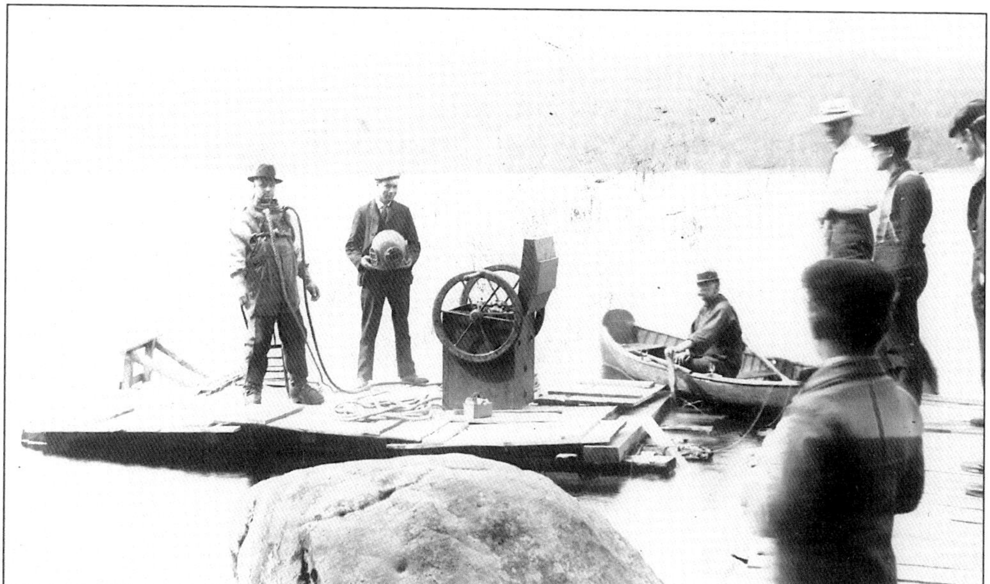

A TRAGEDY AT THE CAPE, 1906. During a lunch break, one of the 14-member crew erecting the main lodge at The Cape drowned. His body was recovered by a diver and assistants.

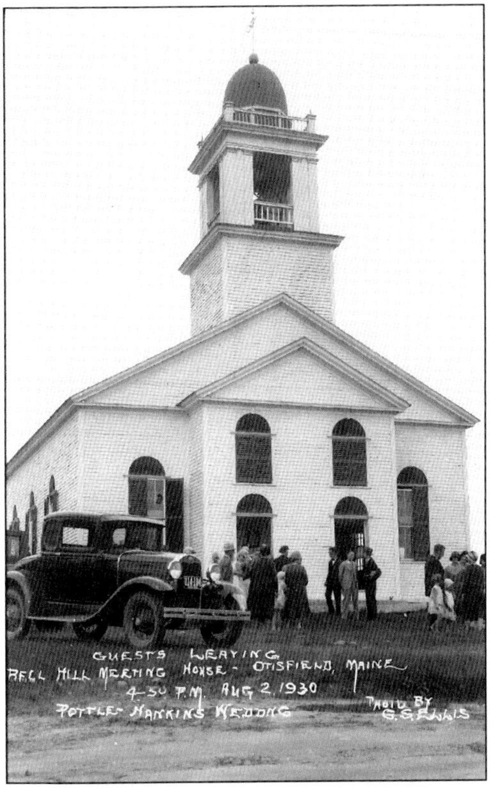

THE BELL HILL MEETING HOUSE, AUGUST 2, 1930. Nathan Nutting Jr., Otisfield's native son and one of Maine's most distinguished early-nineteenth-century architects, designed and built what originally was the Congregational church on Bell Hill in 1839. This structure replaced the much simpler meetinghouse built in 1794 by David Ray (Ray's building typified the earlier meetinghouses in the nascent communities in the area). The rectilinear form of the tower and belfry signifies an effort on Nutting's part to juxtapose the more ornate Federalist style in the building itself with simpler lines and heavier trim associated with the impending Greek Revival movement.

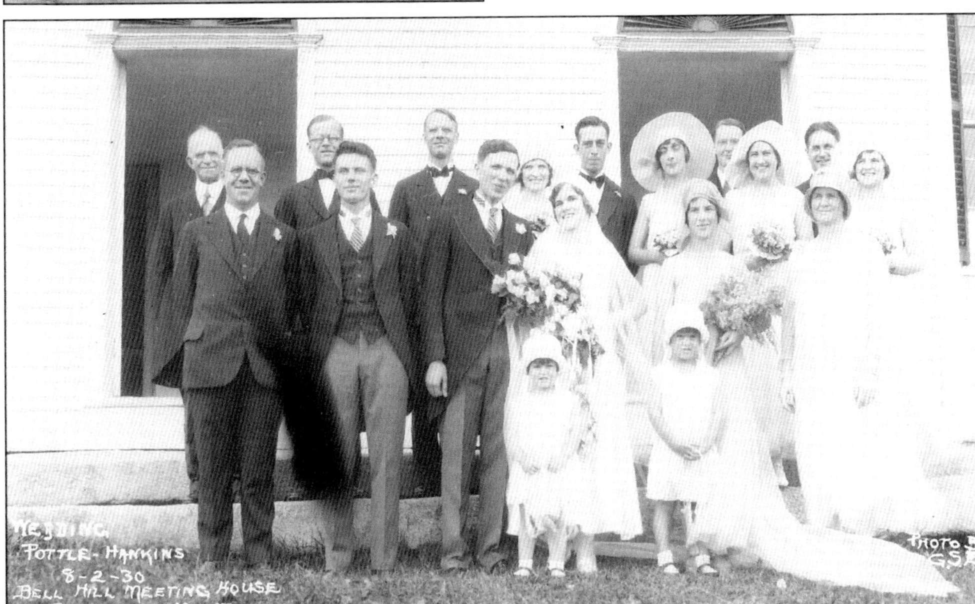

THE POTTLE-HANKINS WEDDING, AUGUST 2, 1930. John E. Hankins and Nellie E. Pottle were united in marriage on this August afternoon at the Bell Hill Meeting House, said to have been the first marriage performed in this church. In the front row, to the left of the groom, are James M. Hankins and John K. Pottle; also in the front row, to the right of the bride, are Estelle Pottle and Annette Kemp Pottle. The two little girls are Jane and Miriam Pottle.

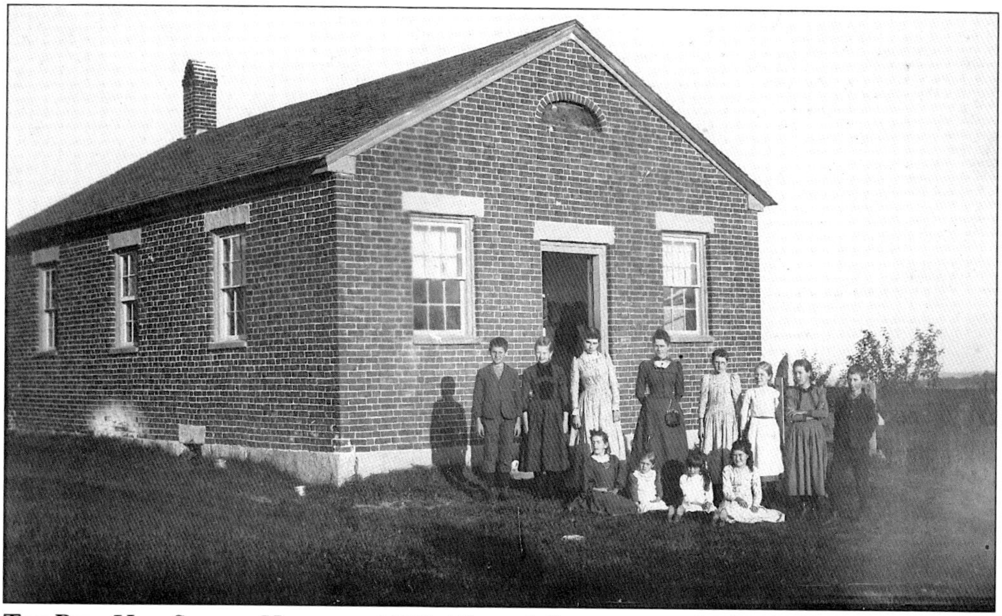

The Bell Hill School House, c. 1899. This solidly constructed school of brick with a split-stone foundation and framework over the windows and doorway could have been built by Samuel Knight, known as "Mason Sam," whose 1835 brick house still stands on Bell Hill. Four school districts in Otisfield, including one here on Bell Hill, were created in 1798–99.

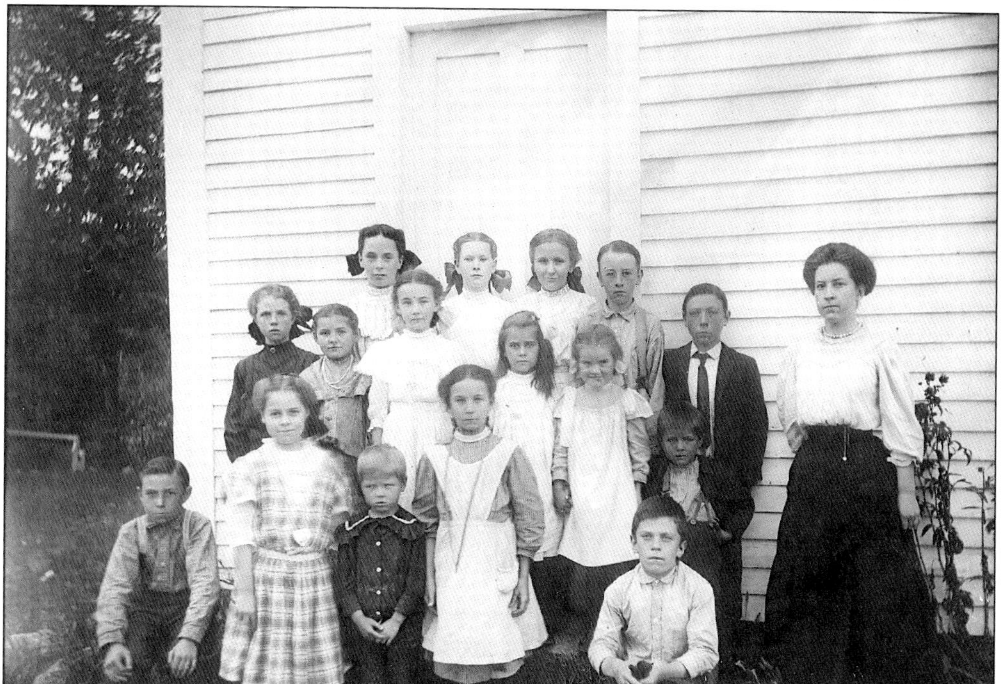

The Pugleyville (East Otisfield) School, c. 1910. The children in the photograph include Ruth Lamb, Elvira Edwards, Cynthia Mayberry, Earl Spiller, Margelia Dyer, Nellie Pottle, David Jillson, Eddie Wood, Lena Kemp, Edith Macaulay, and Carl Lamb. The teacher is Blanche Smith.

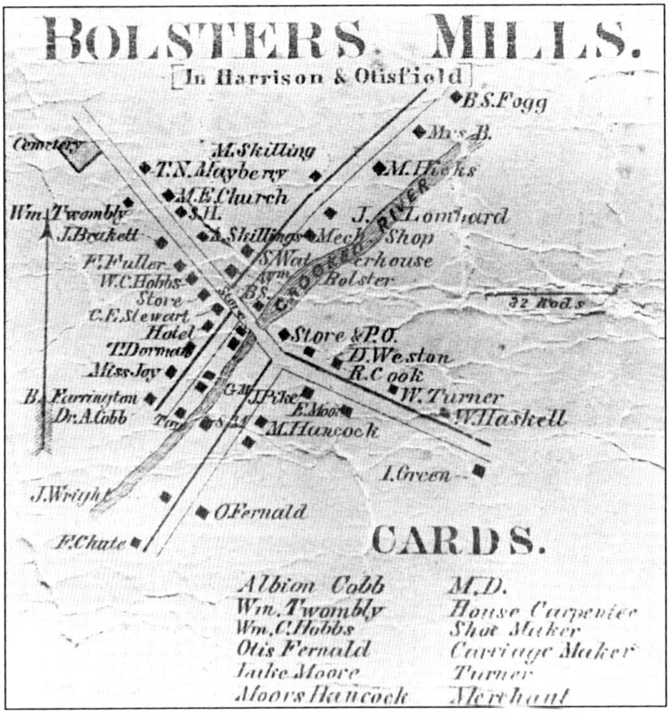

Bolsters Mills, 1857. Daniel Scribner is reputed to have built the first house in Bolsters Mills—a simple log cabin located on the Otisfield side of Crooked River (both sides were in Otisfield until Harrison was incorporated in 1805). The area was named for Isaac Bolster Jr., whose father was one of the Minute Men at Lexington and Concord. Isaac, who built the first store at Bolsters Mills, constructed a dam and sawmill (1819) and a gristmill (1820) in the area. He was joined in 1826 by his brother William, who built a fulling and carding mill on the Harrison side.

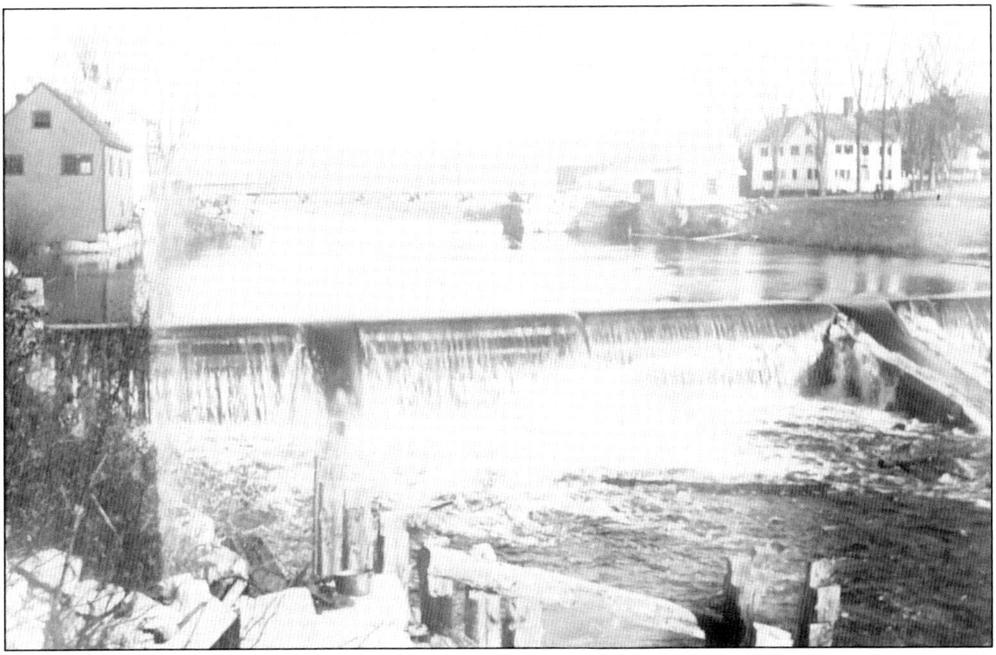

Bolsters Mills, c. 1890. The imposing house and barn at the iron bridge on the Otisfield side (right) was built by Daniel Weston (1805–1884), who ran a store here with Wyatt Turner before selling out to him in 1838. Together they bought and sold cattle, which they drove all the way to market in Brighton, Massachusetts. He also farmed and operated a grist and sawmill for a number of years before selling out in 1868 and moving to Wisconsin. He later returned to Otisfield, where he died. The building on the Harrison side above the dam was a blacksmith shop.

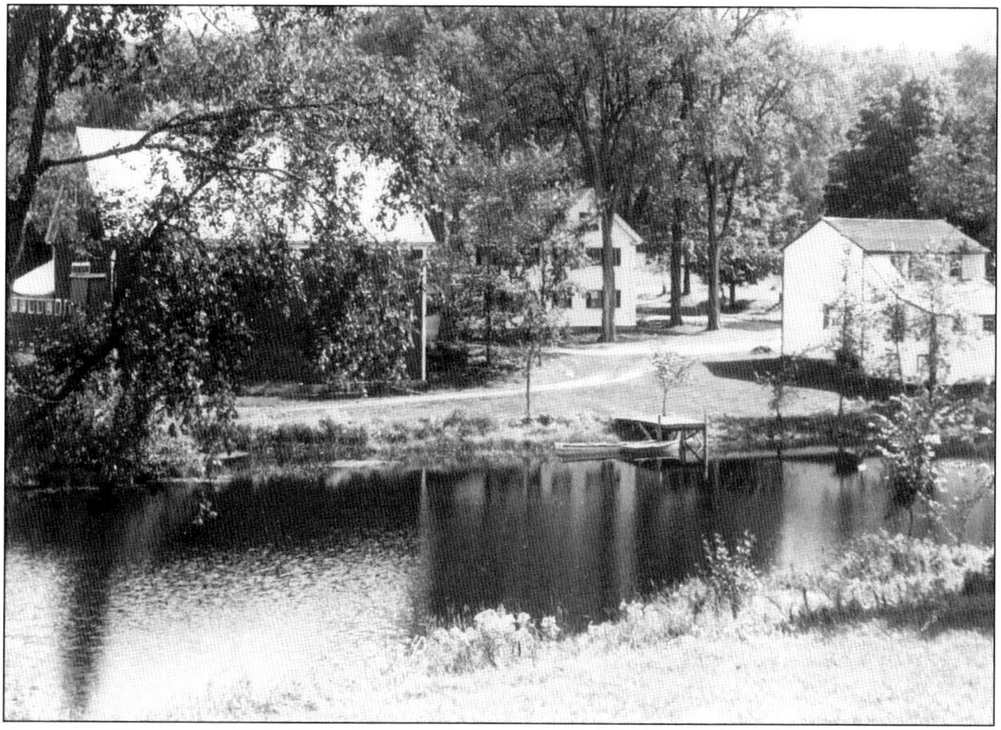

Bolsters Mills, c. 1920. This close-up of the Daniel Weston house, barn, and store near the bank of the Crooked River in Otisfield was taken from the Harrison side of the river. At the time this photograph was taken, the property belonged to Fred Clinton Weston (1864–1950), a nephew to Daniel Weston.

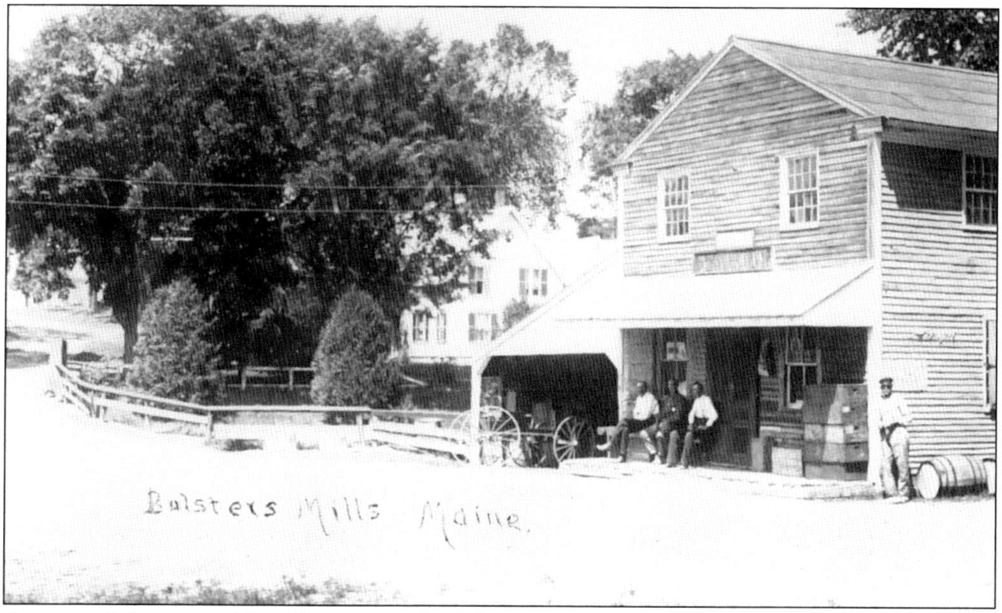

Bolsters Mills, c. 1895. This store, which for many years was operated by Wyatt Turner, was probably owned by Issac Skillings when this photograph was taken. The carriage shed is gone, but the store continues to operate.

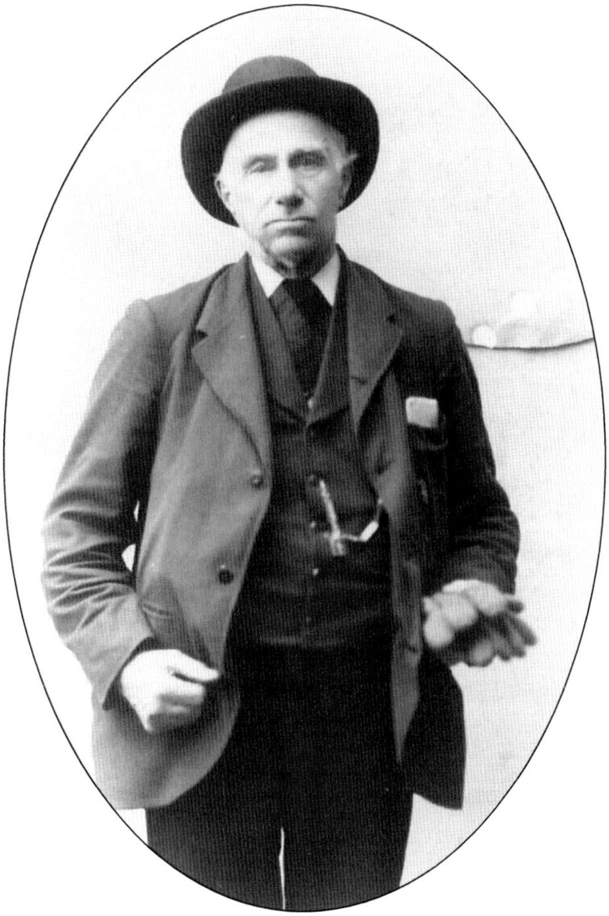

Joseph W. Holden, Otisfield's Eccentric, c. 1885. Joseph White Holden, better known as "Uncle Joe," heads the list of Otisfield eccentrics. He claimed he could prove the earth was flat! He lived in Rayville, named after Dr. David Ray—an ancestor who was Otisfield's first physician—and operated sawmills and a gristmill for most of his life. He never married. He took advantage of every opportunity he had, which included the Maine State Fair in Lewiston in 1892, the Chicago World's Fair in 1893, and Bowdoin College when he was 80, to expound on his favorite theory—"Why the World is Flat." On his grave opposite the Rayville Baptist Church, his Italian marble gravestone (provided for in his will) reads: "Prof. Joseph W. Holden—Born Otisfield, Me.—Aug. 24, 1816: March 30, 1900—discovered that the Earth—is flat and stationary and—that the sun and moon do move." He also left money to provide lemonade and ice cream for each child in Pugleyville during an annual picnic at Saturday Pond for a half century. (William Spurr, wishing to continue this tradition, left money in his will for each Otisfield child to enjoy strawberry ice cream, popcorn, and lemonade at the annual summer festival, which is still held at the Rayville Free Baptist Church the last Sunday in August. The tradition of Holden and Spurr lives on.)

Four

Waterford

First Settled: 1775
Incorporated: 1797
Population: 1,300
Principal Settlements: South Waterford, Waterford Flat, North Waterford, and East Waterford

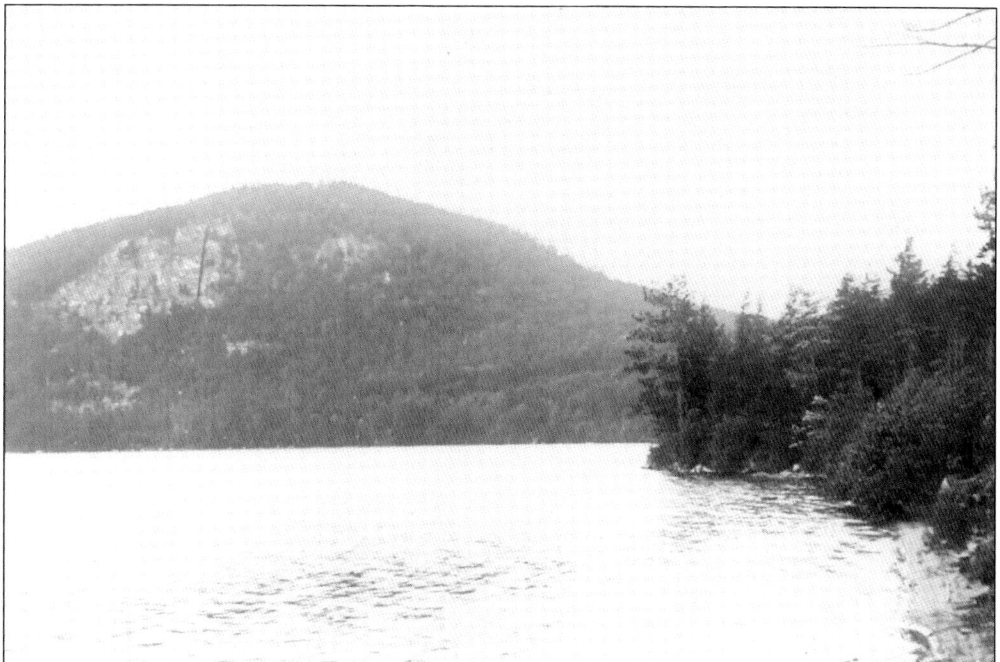

BEAR POND IN SOUTH WATERFORD, C. 1910. The dimpled waters of Bear Pond, rimmed by virgin conifers and the megalithic outcropping known as Flag Rock on the west side of Bear Mountain, greeted early settlers as they made their way up Bear River (Brook) from Long Pond (Long Lake). The shoreline, lapped by wavelets, seems to have remained unscathed when this photograph was taken, and motorists heading north will easily recognize the natural beauty of both the pond and the mountain as they approach South Waterford on either Route 35 from Harrison or Route 37 from North Bridgton.

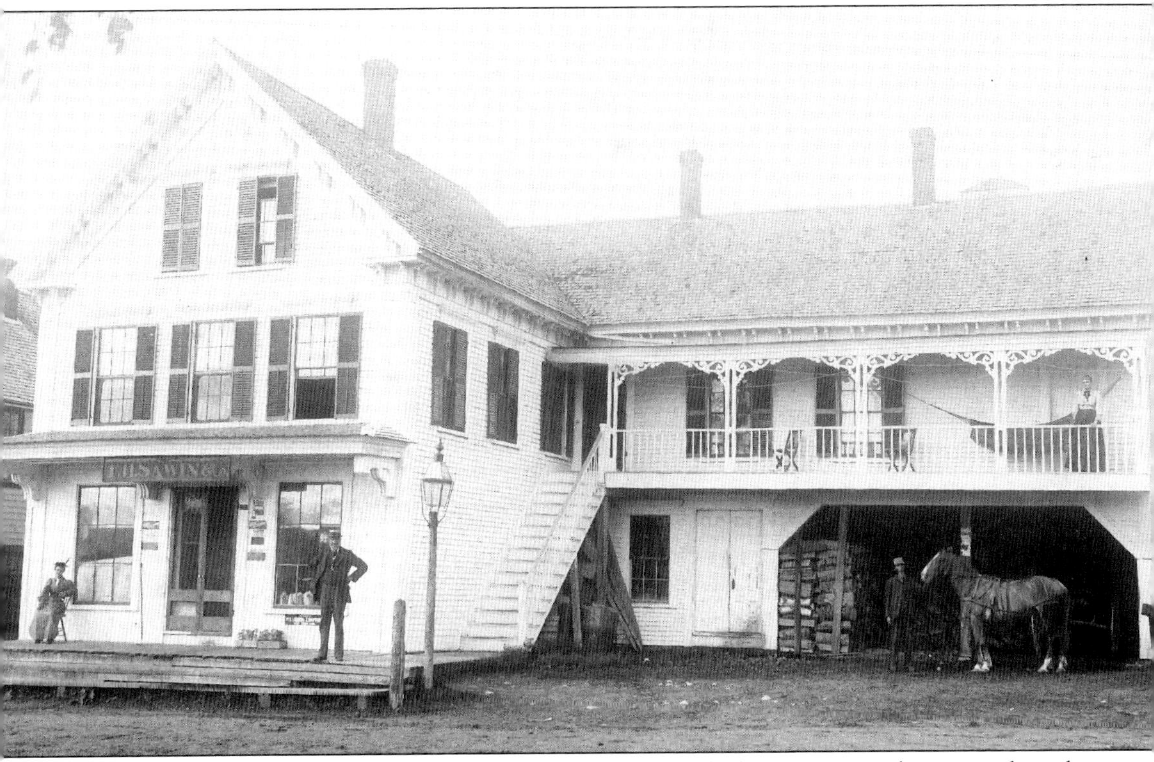

The Thomas H. Sawin Store, c. 1885. At least one and often two general stores such as this one, owned and operated by Thomas H. Sawin (1835–1909) and his brother Henry in North Waterford, did a thriving business in the villages and hamlets throughout Waterford. Thomas is standing on the platform next to the gas lamp. His brother Henry is leading the horse out of the shed. Thomas's wife, Cloe, is standing on the balcony next to the hammock. The woman sitting in the rocking chair in front of the store could be Emily Knight, a seamstress.

Many Maine townships owe their existence to the descendants of veterans who fought in the French and Indian wars—particularly those from eastern Massachusetts who participated in Sir William Phipps's ill-fated attempt to capture Quebec from France. Since the Province of Massachusetts Bay was rich in land but beggared of money, veterans and their heirs were compensated by land grants. But in a dispute between Massachusetts and New Hampshire, 28 of these townships were awarded to the latter in 1738 by King George II, acting as arbiter. Consequently, these townships were lost to the proprietors, many of whom in 1774 petitioned to Massachusetts Bay for compensation, including those of Toddstown, the progenitor of the town of Waterford, surveyed in 1774 and incorporated on March 2, 1797. David McWain of Bolton, Massachusetts, became the first settler in Waterford. In 1775 he arrived at the Stevens Brook mill site (Bridgton) and then, carrying the bare essentials, made his way up Bear River and over to his lots in what is today East Waterford. McWain Pond, Falls, and Hill bear his name. He never returned to Bolton after 1777. He died in 1825. McWain, who never married, left his farm to his nephew and namesake.

It was not until 1783 that further permanent settlers arrived in Waterford, most of them coming from Bolton, Harvard, and Rowley. Some of these early settlers were America, Africa, Eleazer Jr., and Hannibal Hamlin; Daniel Barker; Johnathan Robbins; Aseph Brown; and Philip Hor. (Ephraim Hapgood was the first boy and Clarissa Johnson the first girl to be born in Waterford.) Many of these early settlers very likely would not have survived the terrible cold years of 1814–16 had not McWain supplied them with corn at below the market price from his 800-acre farm.

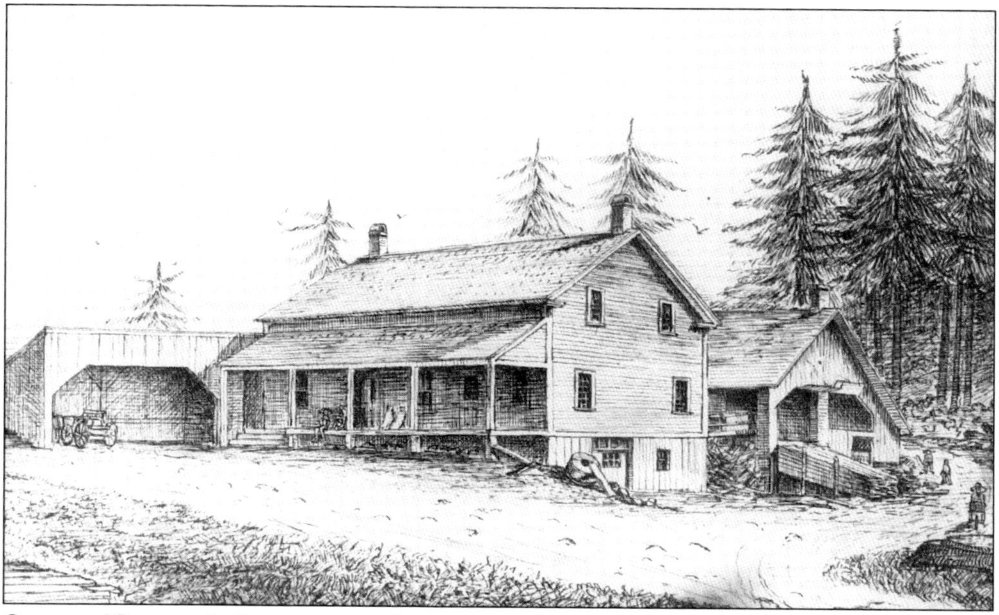

Captain Hapgood's Sawmill and Gristmill, c. 1830. Before 1790, when Ezra Jewell built the first saw and gristmill in Waterford, the nearest saw and gristmill was at Stevens Brook, 12 long miles away. Because of its location at Mill Brook (where there is a fall of 119 feet), South Waterford or Waterford City became a beehive of industrial activity. The Thomas Hapgood mills shown here were built around 1810 by Abram Whitney at the foot of Tom Pond.

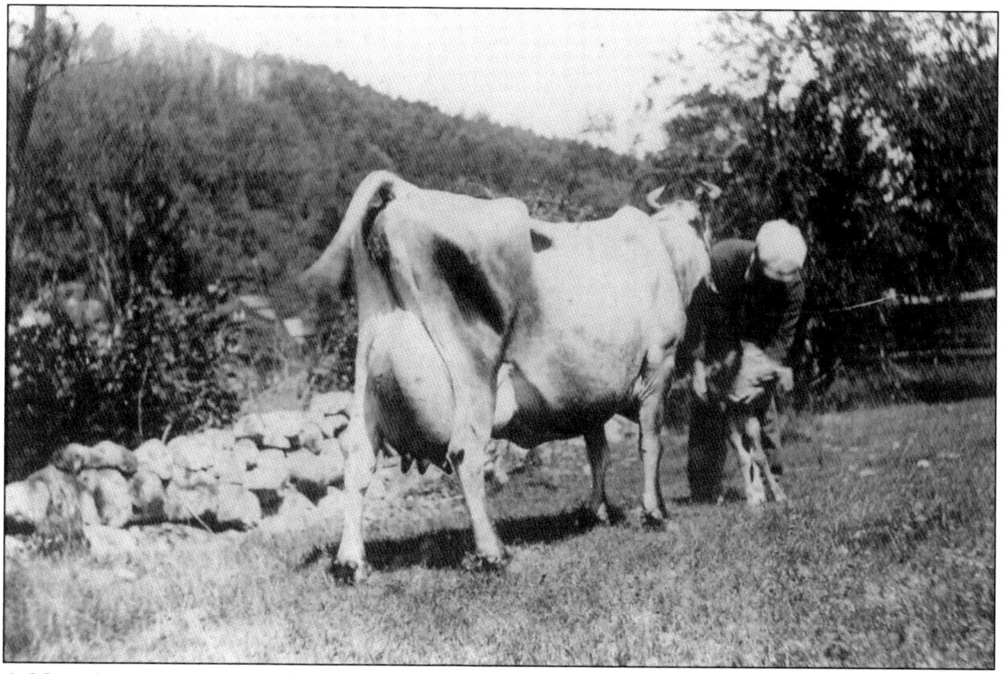

A New Addition to the Abbott Herd, c. 1920. Willard W. Abbott, president of the Jersey Breeder's Association (formed in South Waterford in 1909), is holding the newest addition to his registered Jersey herd. His wife, Flora, was treasurer and secretary of the Waterford Creamery until it burned in 1970.

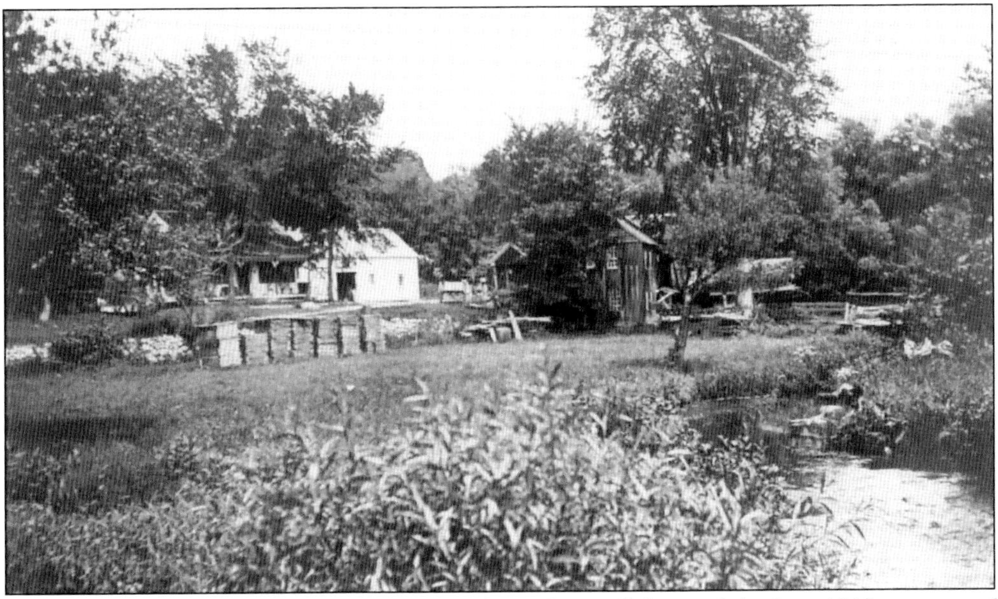

The Carding Mill, c. 1930. Oliver Hapgood's carding mill (center), built in 1810, was one of at least 14 power mills that operated at one time along Mill Brook in Waterford City. The mill passed through several ownerships until Walter K. Hamlin (who also operated a box factory, a wagon and carriage wheel factory, and, for a time, the Waterford Creamery) purchased the mill in 1887.

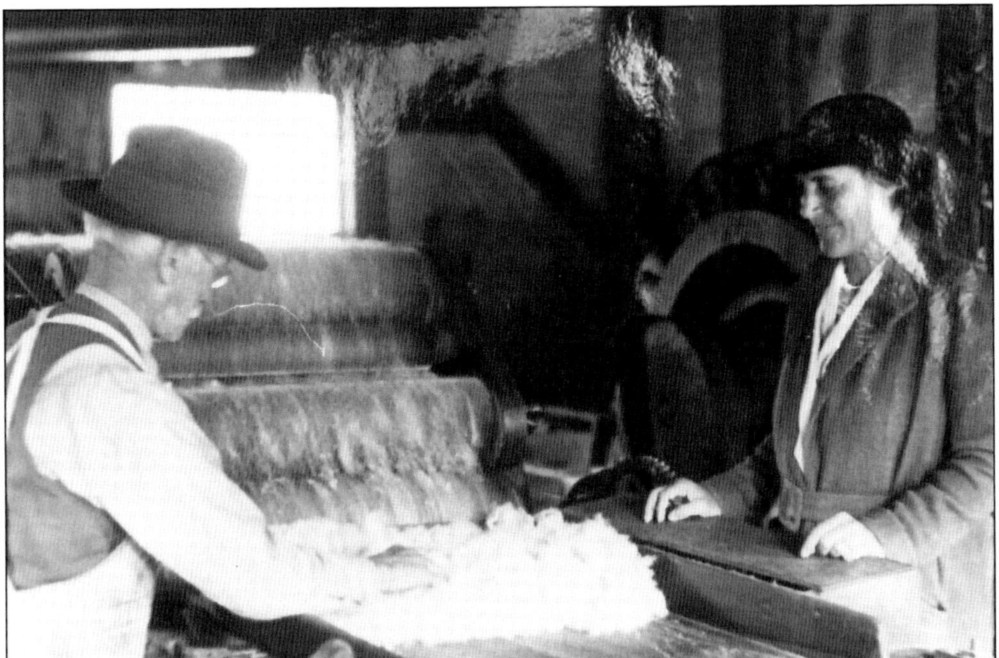

Carding Wool, c. 1940. W.K. Hamlin has an admiring audience as he processes wool from a carding machine. After his death, the mill continued to be run by his son, Albert Hamlin Sr., who carded batts for puffs rather than rolls of yarn into the 1950s. In 1963 this fine old Waterford landmark was moved to Sturbridge Village, where it continues to operate.

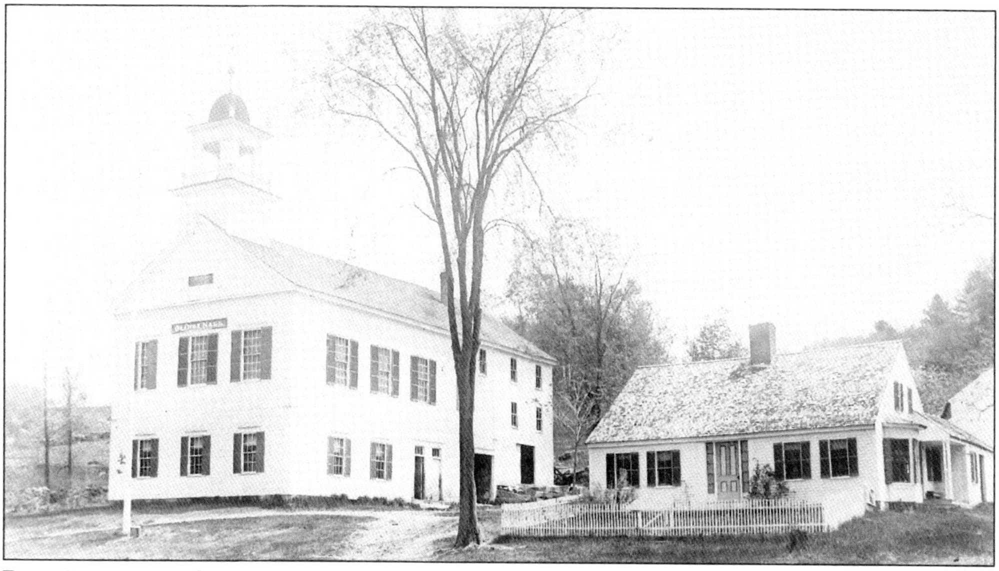

Bear Mountain Grange No. 62, c. 1895. This prominent landmark at the foot of Mill Hill in South Waterford was erected in 1844 and served as the Universalist church for a number of years. In 1874 the Patrons of Husbandry was organized in South Waterford, and soon thereafter the building was purchased by the Bear Mountain Grange.

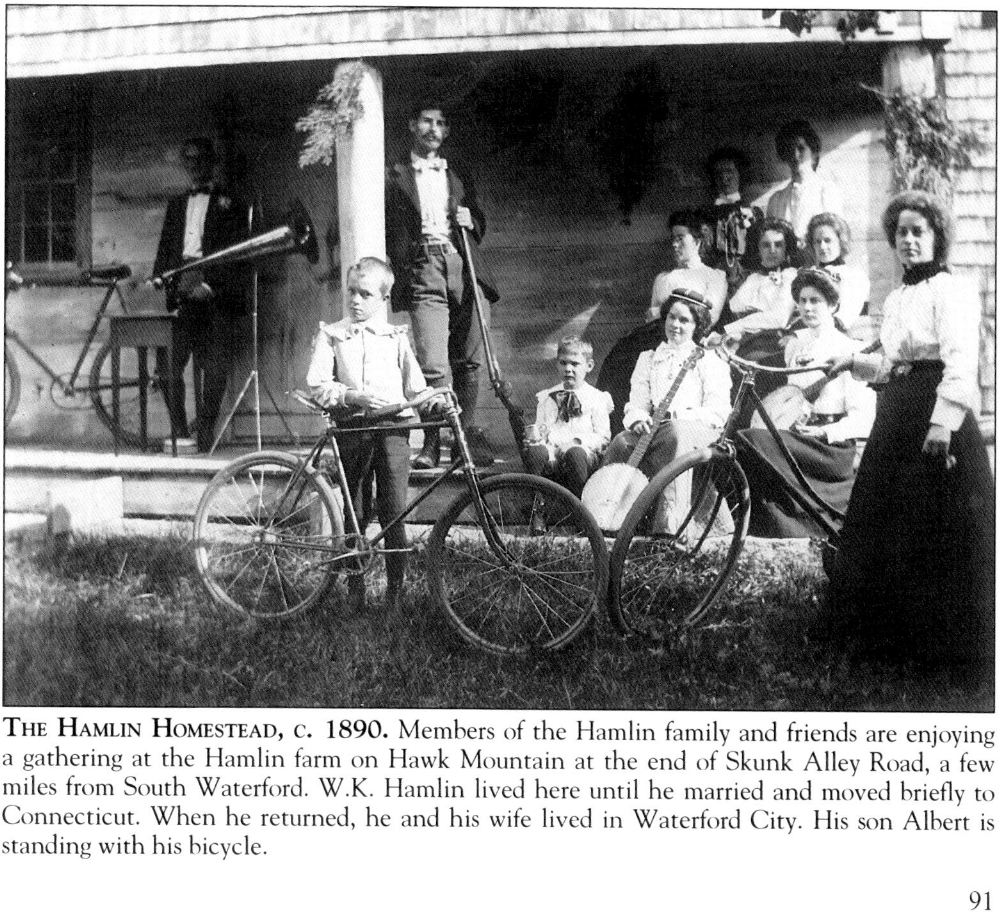

The Hamlin Homestead, c. 1890. Members of the Hamlin family and friends are enjoying a gathering at the Hamlin farm on Hawk Mountain at the end of Skunk Alley Road, a few miles from South Waterford. W.K. Hamlin lived here until he married and moved briefly to Connecticut. When he returned, he and his wife lived in Waterford City. His son Albert is standing with his bicycle.

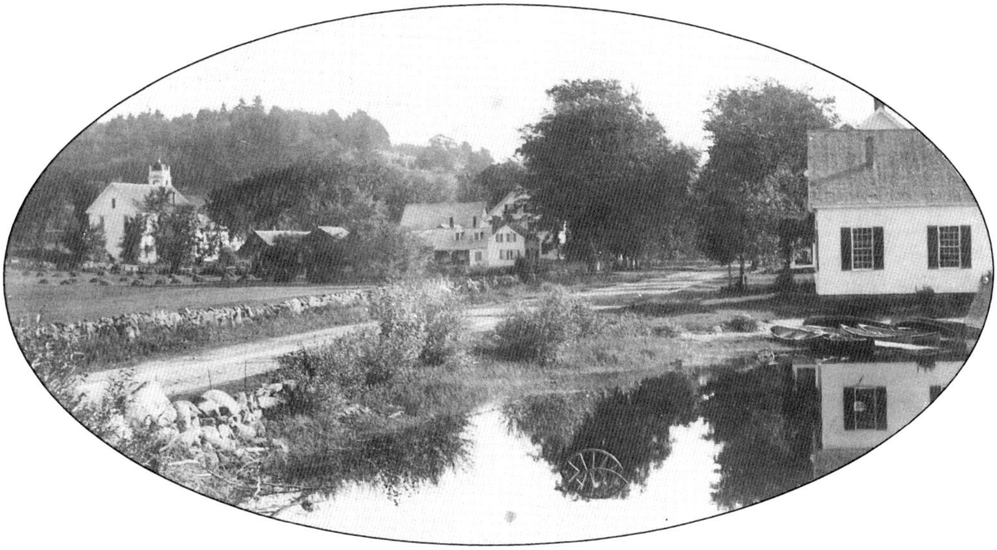

WATERFORD FLAT, C. 1885. The old Town House casts its reflection into the mirror-like waters of Thomas Pond (Keoka Lake) as one approaches the "Flat" from South Waterford. Originally, the Town House, Waterford's little house of democracy, was located on Plummer Hill, but in the early 1840s it was disassembled and reconstructed at the foot of Thomas Pond.

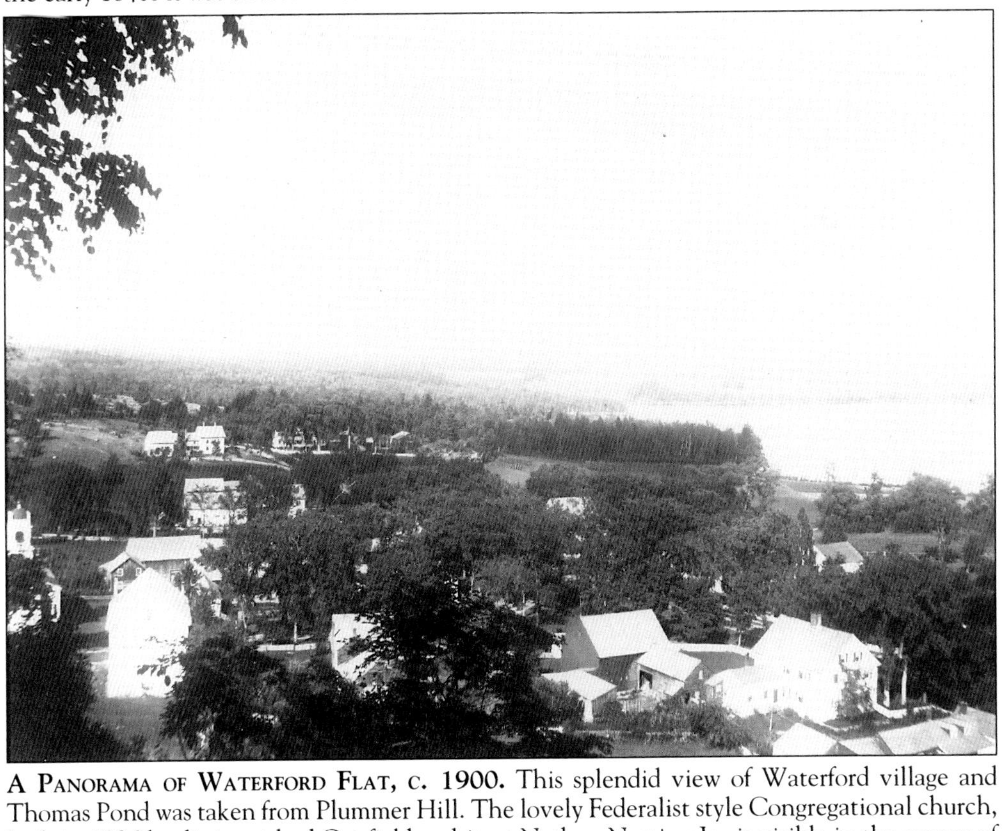

A PANORAMA OF WATERFORD FLAT, C. 1900. This splendid view of Waterford village and Thomas Pond was taken from Plummer Hill. The lovely Federalist style Congregational church, built in 1836 by distinguished Otisfield architect Nathan Nutting Jr., is visible in the corner of the photograph. Tragically, the structure was destroyed by fire on May 3, 1928.

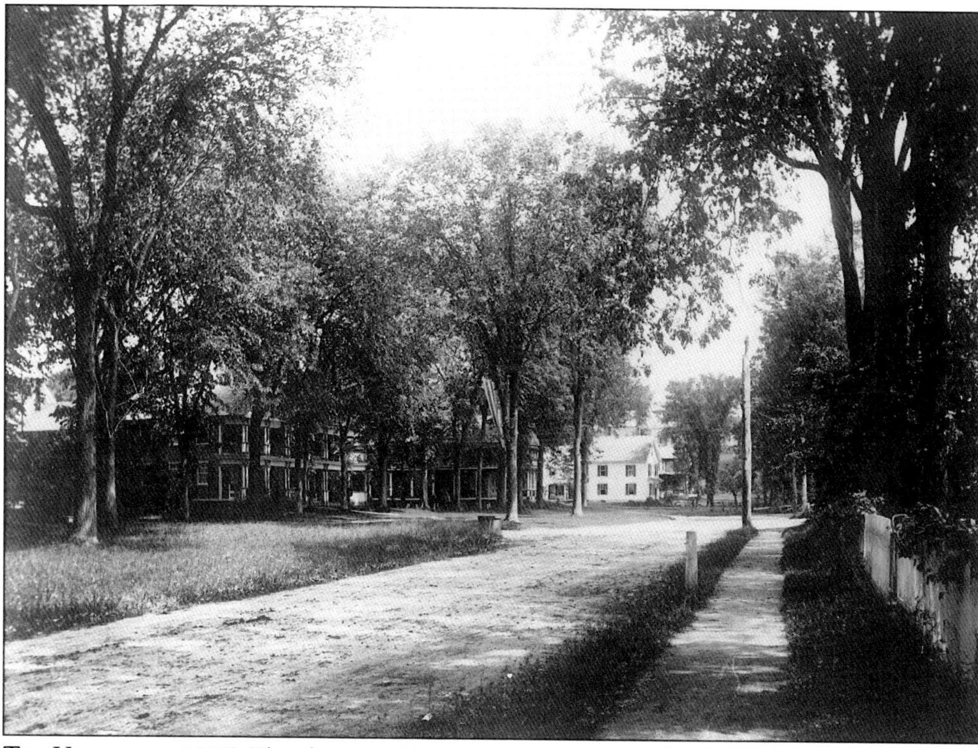

THE VILLAGE, C. 1895. The charm and beauty that so enchanted Ralph Waldo Emerson on the numerous occasions when he visited his three aunts here in the village has fortunately been little altered by time (except that the road is now paved). Partially visible behind the white picket fence is the Artemus Ward house. Opposite is the Lake House, when it still had porches on the front and side. As early as 1797 it was Longley's Tavern; in the nineteenth century, because of its spas in the backyard, it became Dr. Shattuk's Maine Hygienic Institute for ladies.

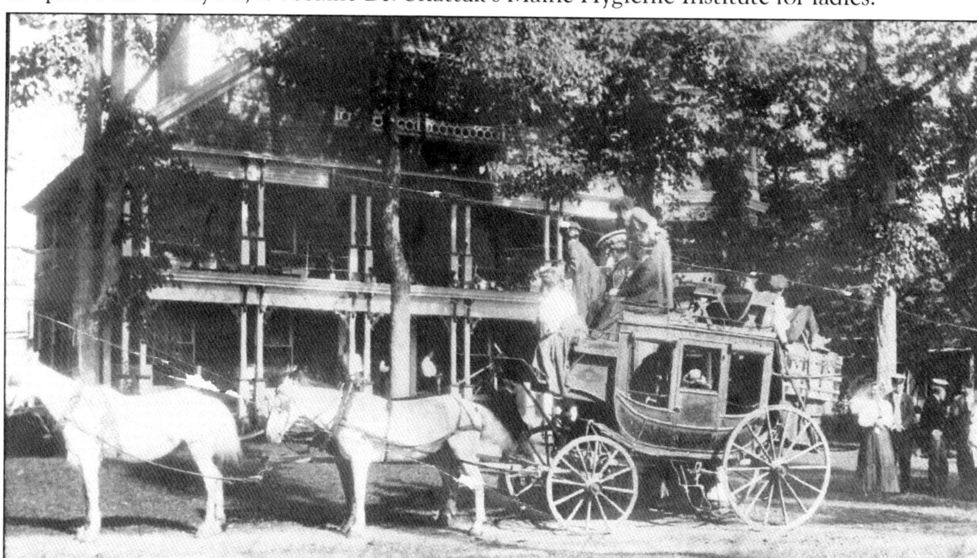

DISCHARGING PASSENGERS AT THE LAKE HOUSE, C. 1905. Guests and their luggage are being unloaded from Maxfield's Bridgton and Harrison stagecoach at the popular Lake House.

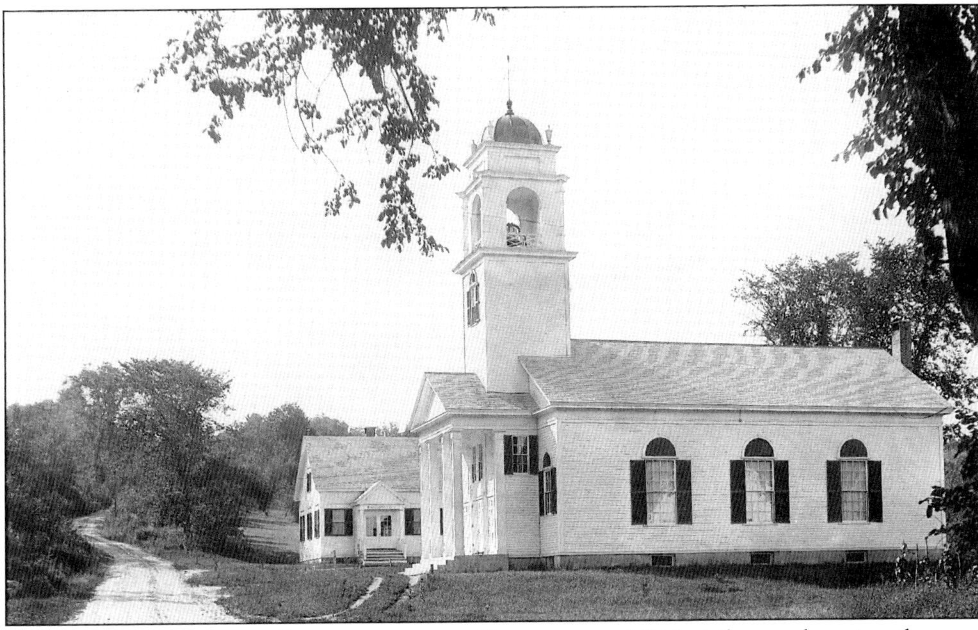

The New Waterford Congregational Church, c. 1940. Like a phoenix, the new Congregational church rose from the ashes of the original church and was dedicated on December 22, 1929. Except for the Greek Revival portico, it resembles closely Nathan Nutting's 1837 masterpiece. The Wilkins Community House, dedicated to Miss Susan Hamlin Wilkins—a Waterford native who taught here for a number of years before moving to New York to teach (she returned after her retirement)—was added primarily as a recreational place for Waterford's youth.

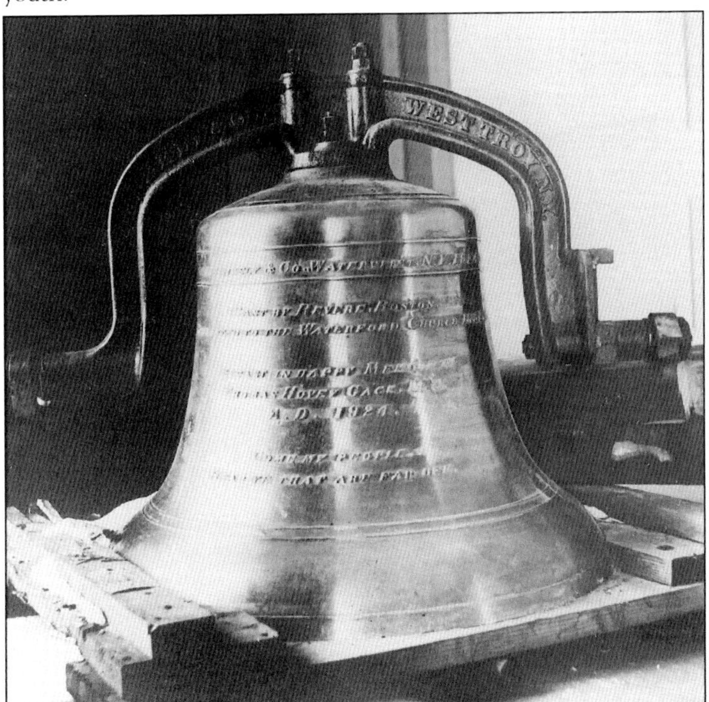

The Revere Bell in the New Congregational Church, c. 1929. This irreplaceable Paul Revere bell, weighing 840 pounds when it hung from the belfry of the old church, plummeted to earth during the 1928 fire and was recast to weigh 360 pounds. Earlier in 1925 the bell had cracked and was recast, thanks to the generosity of Mabel Gage.

THE REVEREND JOHN ABBOT DOUGLASS, c. 1877. The Reverend John Abbot Douglass, born in Portland on February 4, 1792, posed with his golden cane shortly before his death on August 7, 1878. Rev. Douglass graduated from Bowdoin College in 1814 and afterward studied theology under the tutelage of Rev. Dr. Abiel Abbott of Beverly, Massachusetts. In 1821 he became the minister in Waterford, replacing Rev. Lincoln Ripley, who was married to Phoebe Emerson—whose nephew was Ralph Waldo Emerson. At the time of his death, he was the oldest settled Congregational minister in the state of Maine and served as pastor of the First Church in Waterford for 56 years. In 1884 the Home School in Waterford was renamed Douglass Seminary in honor of this highly respected clergyman who devoted most of his life to the church and to serving many of the people of Waterford.

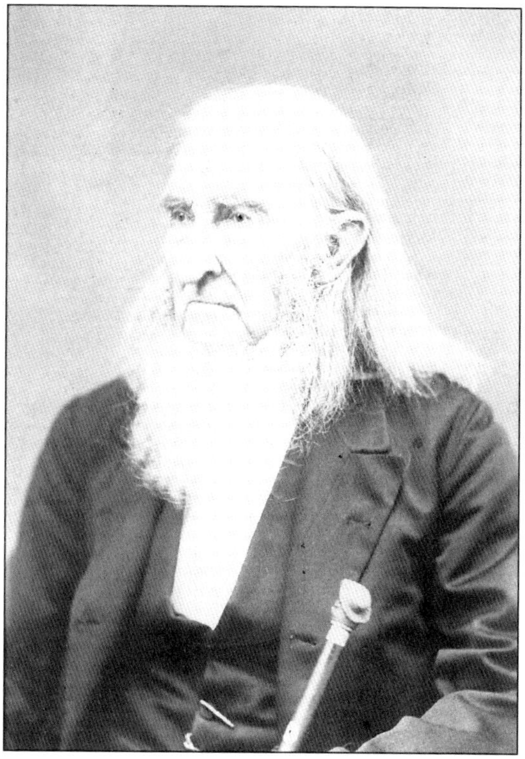

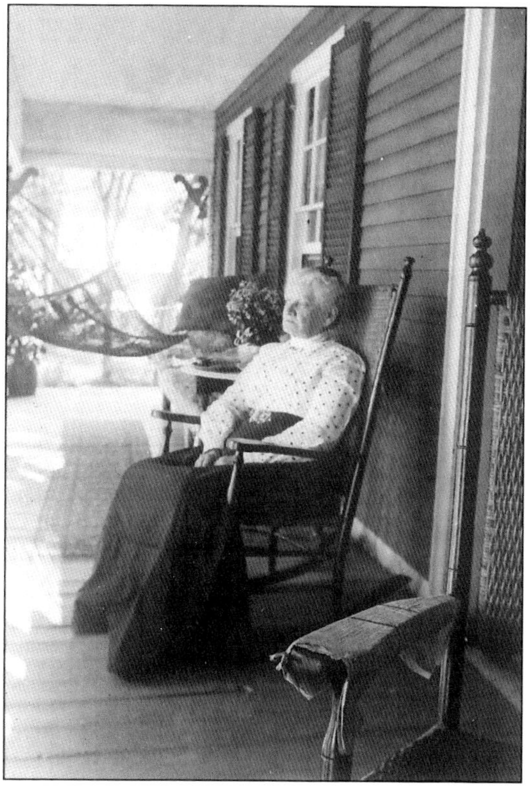

HARRIET KNIGHT, c. 1900. Harriet Knight, one of the Knight sisters, is seen here relaxing on the veranda of the Lake House. The best known of the Knight sisters were Carrie and Sarah Knight, who were prominent in the organization of "The Ladies Library Association of Waterford" in 1899, with Sarah acting as the first librarian. Prior to that, the local Ladies Sewing Circle for a number of years had maintained a small lending library in the Ambrose Knight Store (formerly the Increase Robinson Law Office) which the two sisters ran after their father's death. But as the number of patrons increased, it soon became evident to the Knight sisters that a larger library was needed. It was in 1911 that the sisters began the construction of the present stone structure named in their honor on the site of an earlier Ambrose Knight store. Unfortunately, the two sisters took leave of this earth a few months apart in 1911, shortly before the library was opened in 1912.

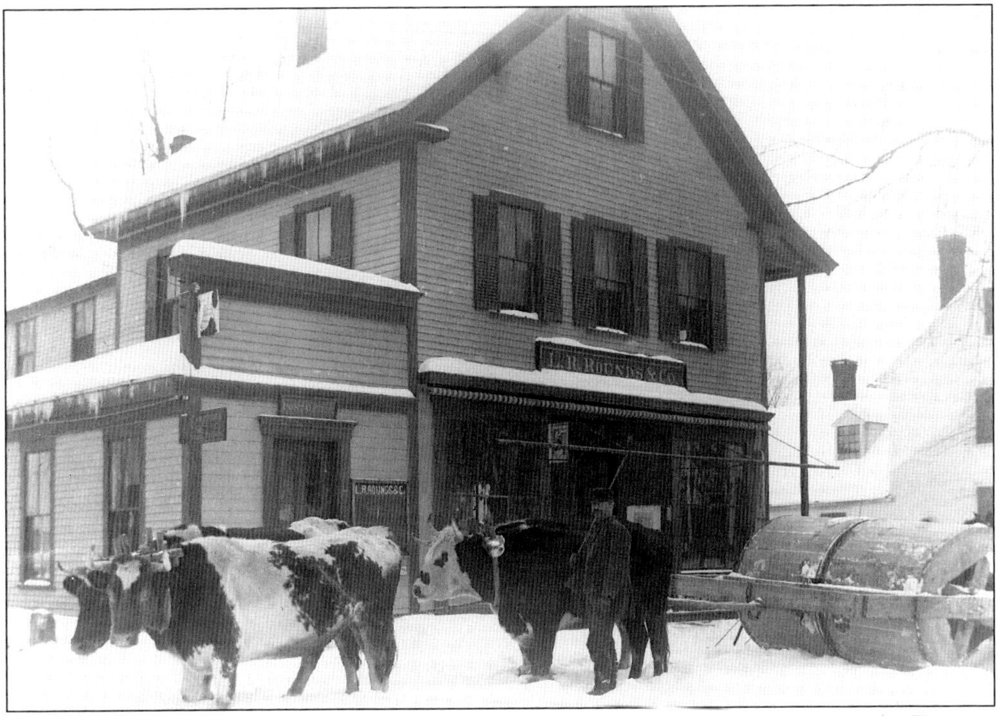

Winter in Waterford Flat, c. 1895. As soon as the first heavy snowfall blanked the Flat and other similar rural hamlets and towns in the 1800s and early 1900s, snow rollers such as this one being drawn by two pair of oxen past Rounds Store in the Flat began packing the roads. Those living on the scattered farms seldom made it to town, however, and often mail and supplies could not reach hamlets like the Flat for days and even weeks after a major storm.

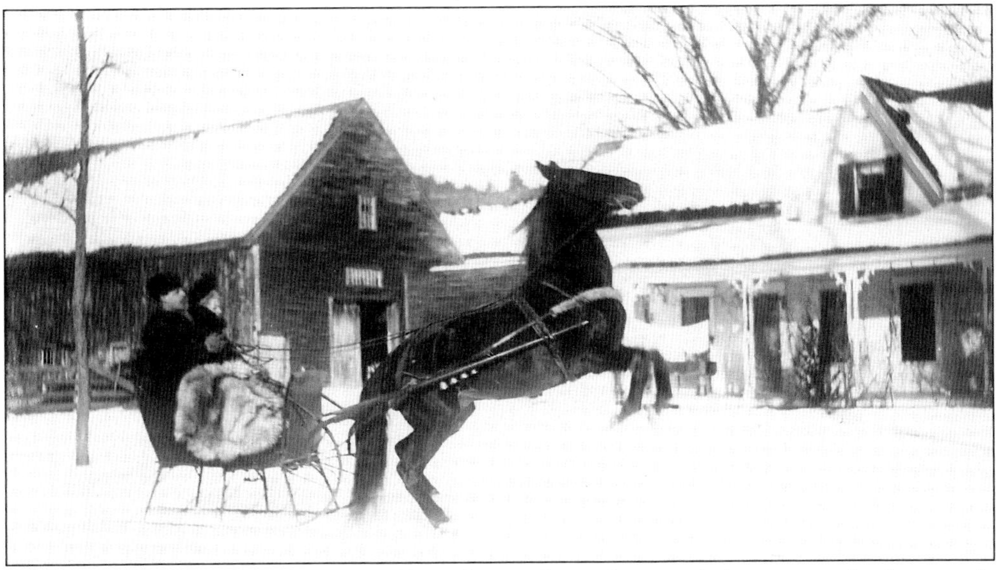

Going for a Sleigh Ride, c. 1910. Even during the early twentieth century, the few people who owned automobiles put them up for the winter and relied upon horses and sleighs. Rex Rounds, the local postmaster, and his wife, Dora, seem unconcerned that their horse is "feeling his oats."

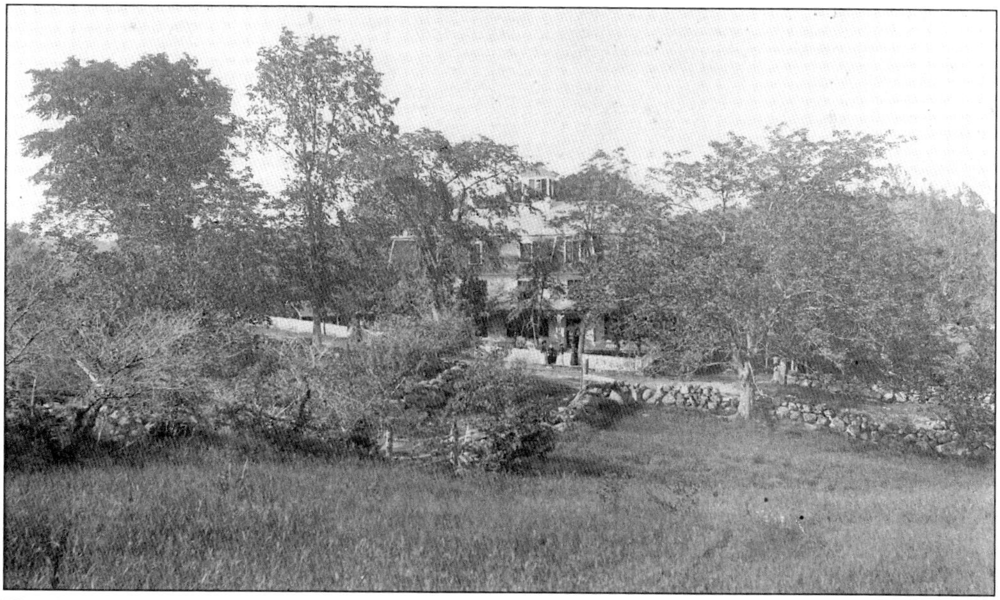

THE DOUGLASS SEMINARY, C. 1890. The Douglass Seminary was founded in 1879 as the Home School for girls. The staff consisted of seven teachers headed by Miss Harriet Douglass, who for a number of years had previously served as the principal for the young women at Gorham Seminary. In 1884 the name of the school was changed to the Douglass Seminary in honor of her father, Rev. John A. Douglass. Students came from Waterford and adjacent towns and occasionally even from Massachusetts. Tuition was $130, fuel included, for 38 weeks. Students taking music paid an additional fee.

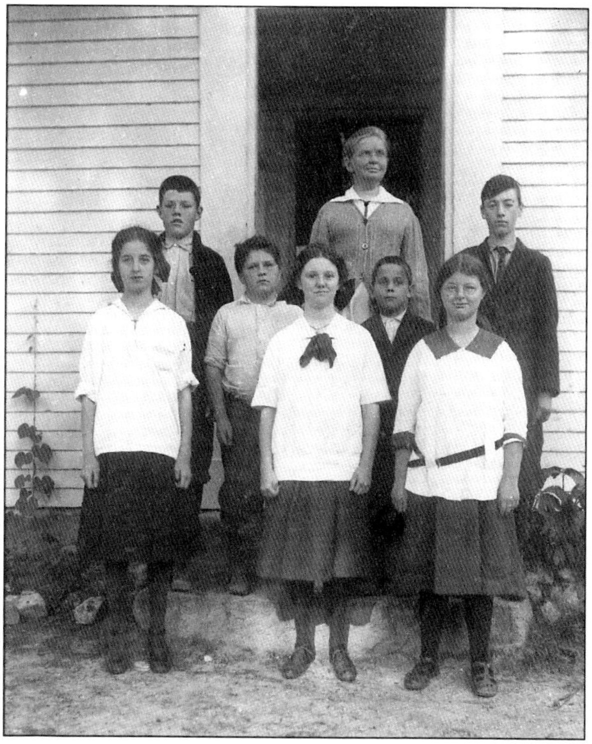

THE WATERFORD FLAT SCHOOL, C. 1915. Many a youngster, who learned the basics in little one-room schools such as this one in the Flat, went on to become prominent in life. These students are, from left to right, as follows: (front row) Julia Morse, Dorothy Stimpson, and Lillian Sanford; (middle row) Bert Heath and Harold Whitcomb; (back row) Horace Green, Agnes Plummer (teacher), and Raymond Cross.

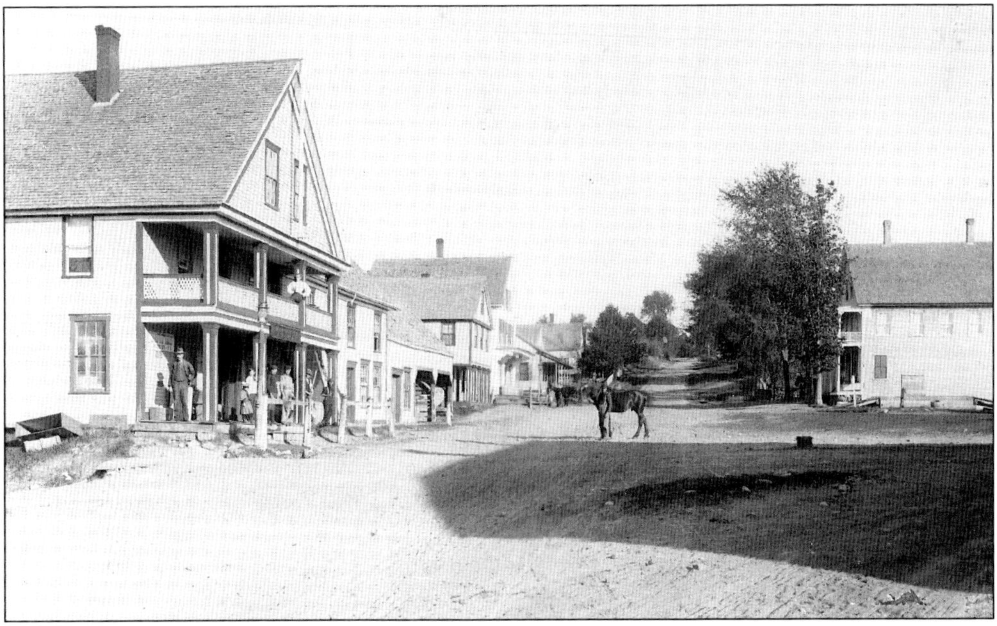

North Waterford before the "Big Fire," c. 1895. It is fortunate indeed that someone captured with a camera this superb view of North Waterford before most of these buildings were destroyed by fire on a cold winter's day, January 8, 1900. The Rand Store (to the left), owned by Harry Brown and Winfield Scott at the time of the fire, was spared because of the quick reaction of some of the local men, who dynamited the shed attached to the main building.

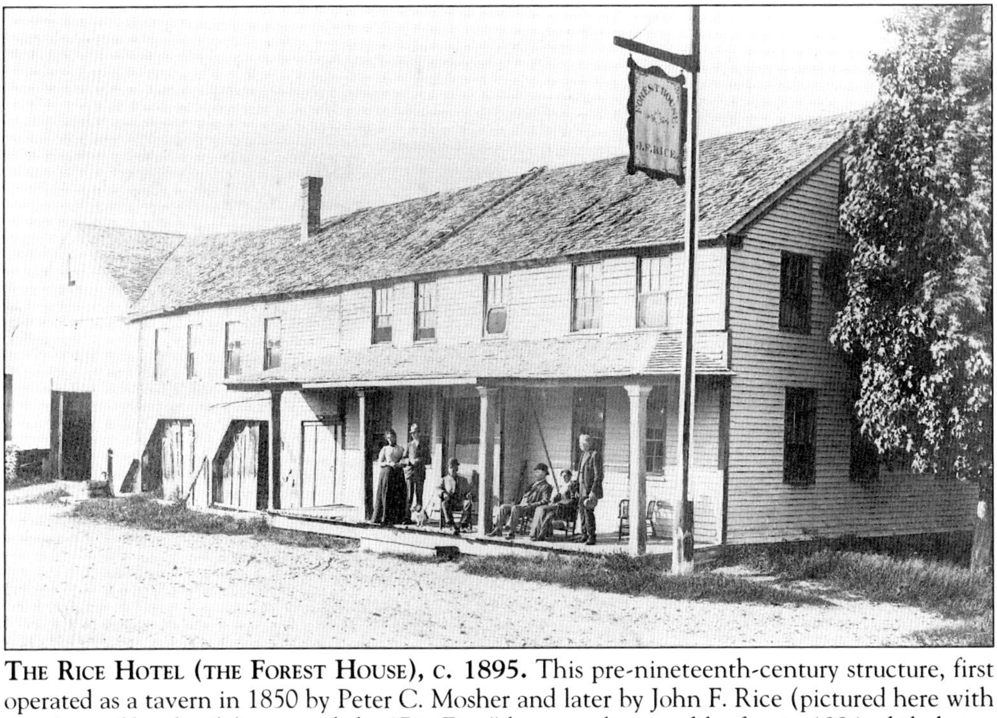

The Rice Hotel (the Forest House), c. 1895. This pre-nineteenth-century structure, first operated as a tavern in 1850 by Peter C. Mosher and later by John F. Rice (pictured here with members of his family), escaped the "Big Fire," but was destroyed by fire in 1994 while being operated as the Old Rowley Inn.

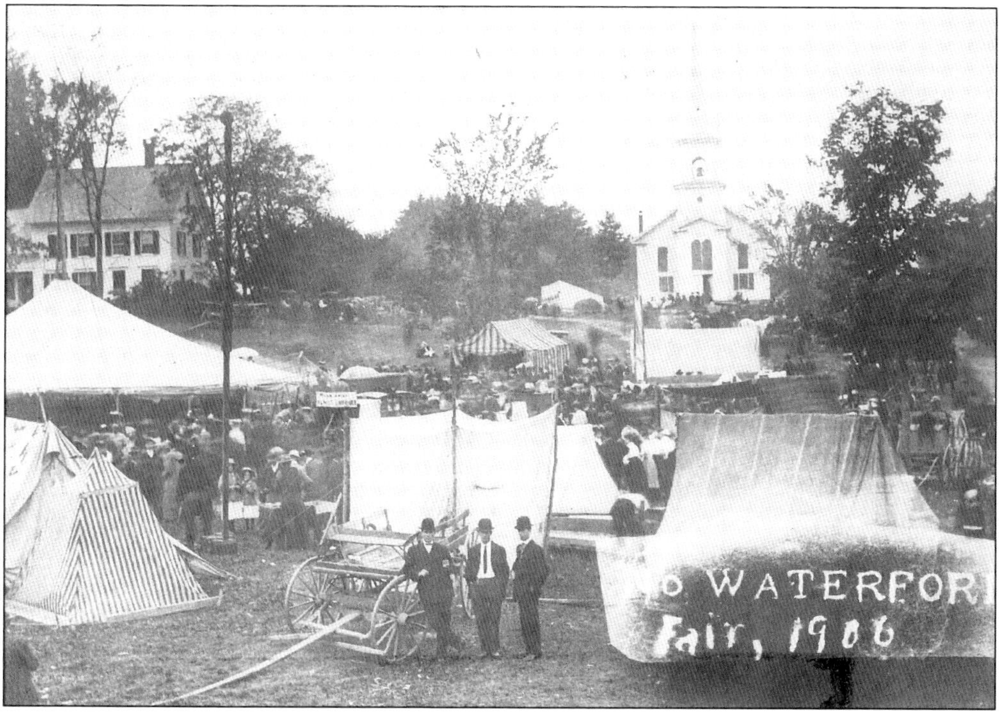

The World's Fair, 1906. Ever since the North Waterford Fair was organized in 1850 (originally called the Tom Greene's Fair), it has been a major annual event in Waterford. Around 1900 the name of the fair was changed to the World's Fair. Because of its growing popularity, due largely to the ever-increasing number of automobiles and the improvement of roads, the site of the fair was changed from the North Waterford Common to the present site.

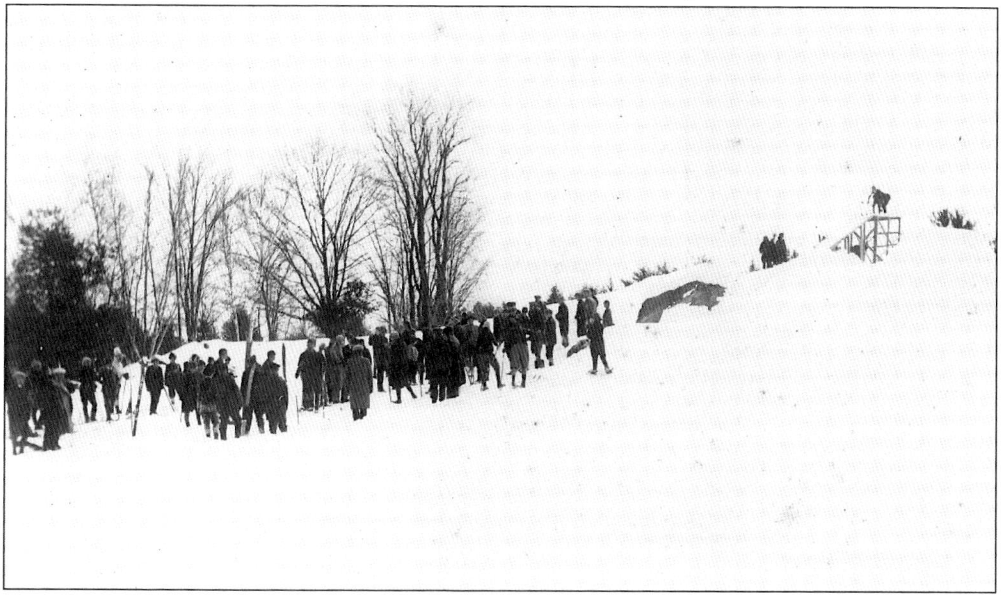

North Waterford's Winter Carnival, c. 1930. Another major event that attracted a crowd to North Waterford for many years beginning in 1926 was the annual Winter Carnival. Here a large gathering of participants and spectators are watching the jumping event.

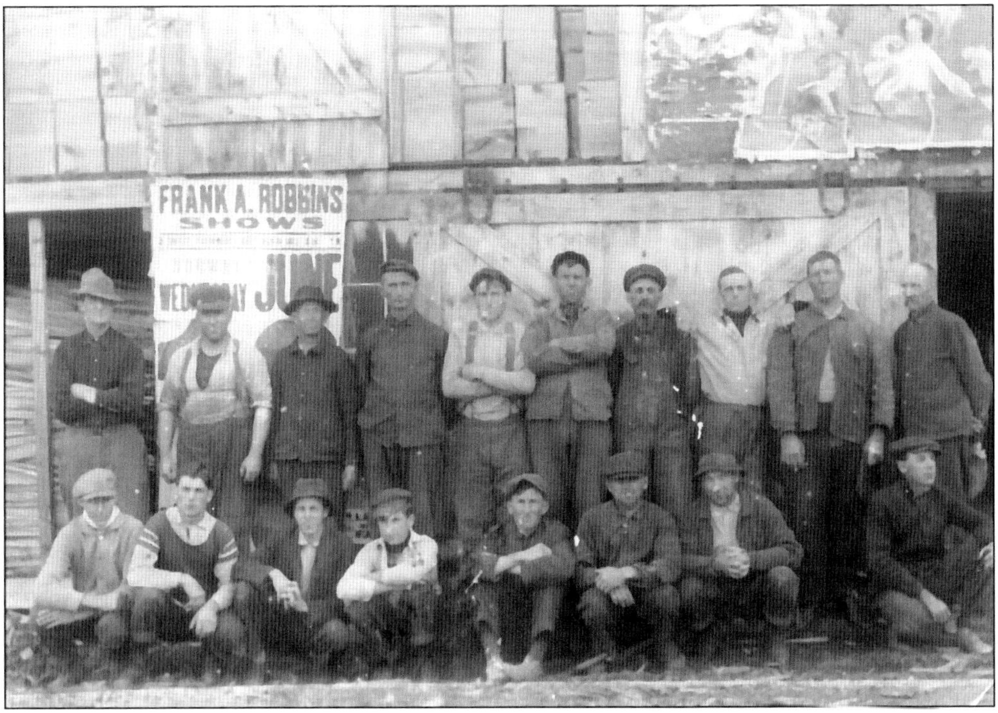

THE CREW AT HARRY BROWN'S BOX FACTORY, C. 1920. Beginning early in the nineteenth century, a number of mills (mostly wood related) operated in North Waterford. Harry Brown, who owned several different mills in the area, purchased this box mill in 1910. In 1923 he abandoned the operation, unable to compete with growing popularity of cardboard cartons.

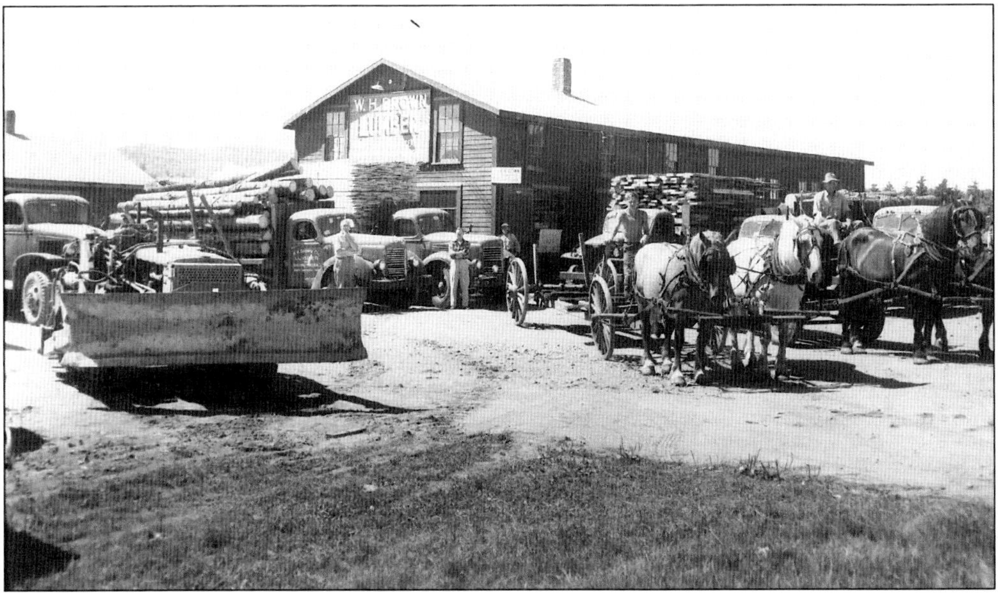

THE W.H. BROWN LUMBER MILL, C. 1945. Harry Brown also owned a sawmill which he sold to his son Winfield in 1932. Winfield moved the mill down to this site on Route 35. By this time he had sold it to the Grover brothers. Note that horses still had not been totally phased out of the operation.

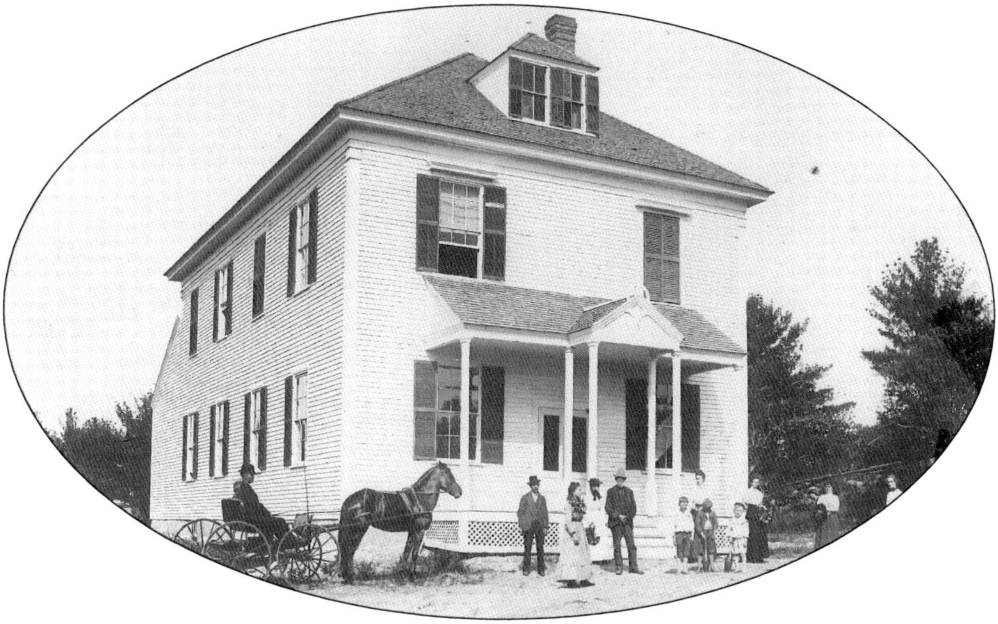

THE IOOF HALL, c. 1910. This structure was built in 1904 in North Waterford for the IOOF (which originated locally in 1875). In 1960 it was taken over by the Daughters of Rebecca who, in 1973, gave the building to the recently organized Westford Historical Society.

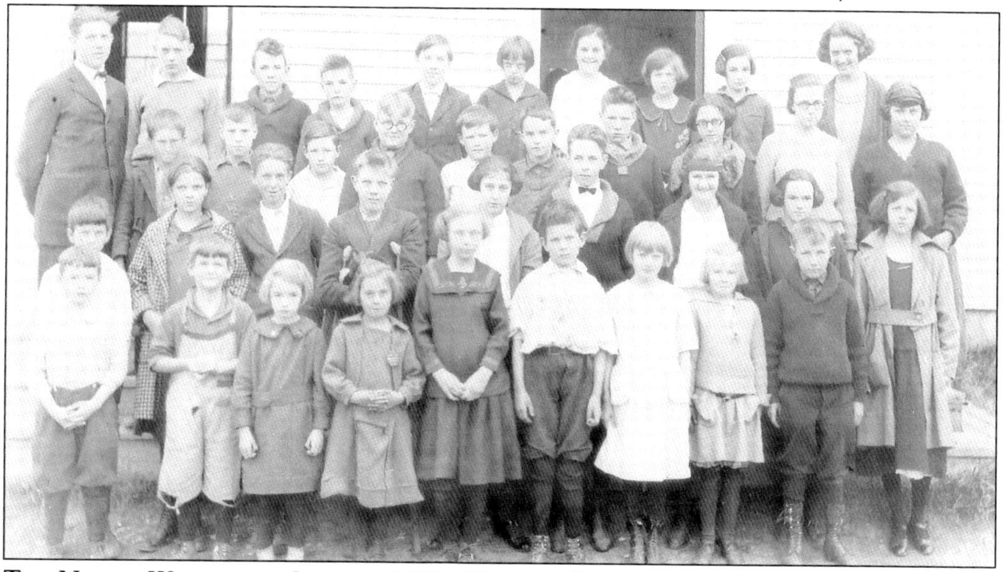

THE NORTH WATERFORD SCHOOL, 1923. These students are, from left to right, as follows: (front row) Alvin Hersey, Jerry Henley, Mabel Hersey, Eunice Morse, Della Libby, Arthur (?) Henley, Betty Holt, Helen Crouse, and Raynor Brown; (second row) Albert (?) Henley, Arline Henley, Guy Morse, Hervey Kimball, Helen Lovejoy, Millard Littlefield, Edith Crouse, Ruth Nason, and Kathleen Lord; (third row) Irving Morse, Stanton Ray, Stanley Lord, Earl Brown, Daniel Nason, Donald Green, Francis McAllister, Thelma Morse, Merline Littlefield, and Sarah Hersey; (back row) Ober Kimball, Lewis Decker, Harlan Willis, Alfred Hersey, Leslie Jones, Leona Kimball, Winola Kilgore, Edith Littlefield, Mary Hersey, and Hazel Kimball. The teachers are Ober and Hazel Kimball.

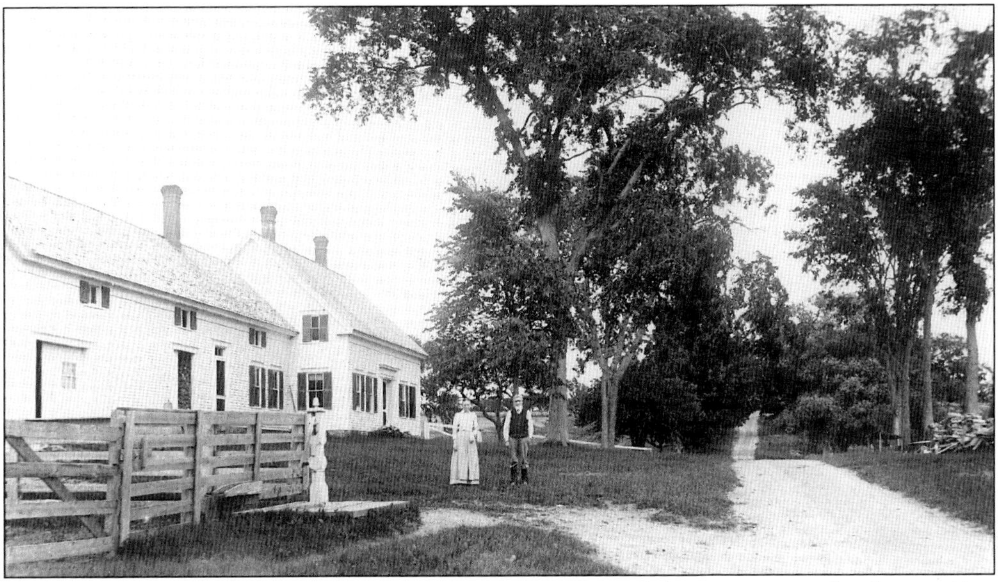

THE JOHNSON FARM, C. 1895. The Johnsons were one of the prominent families in East Waterford. This well-maintained elm-shaded farm is located on the Johnson Road between East Waterford and Waterford Flat.

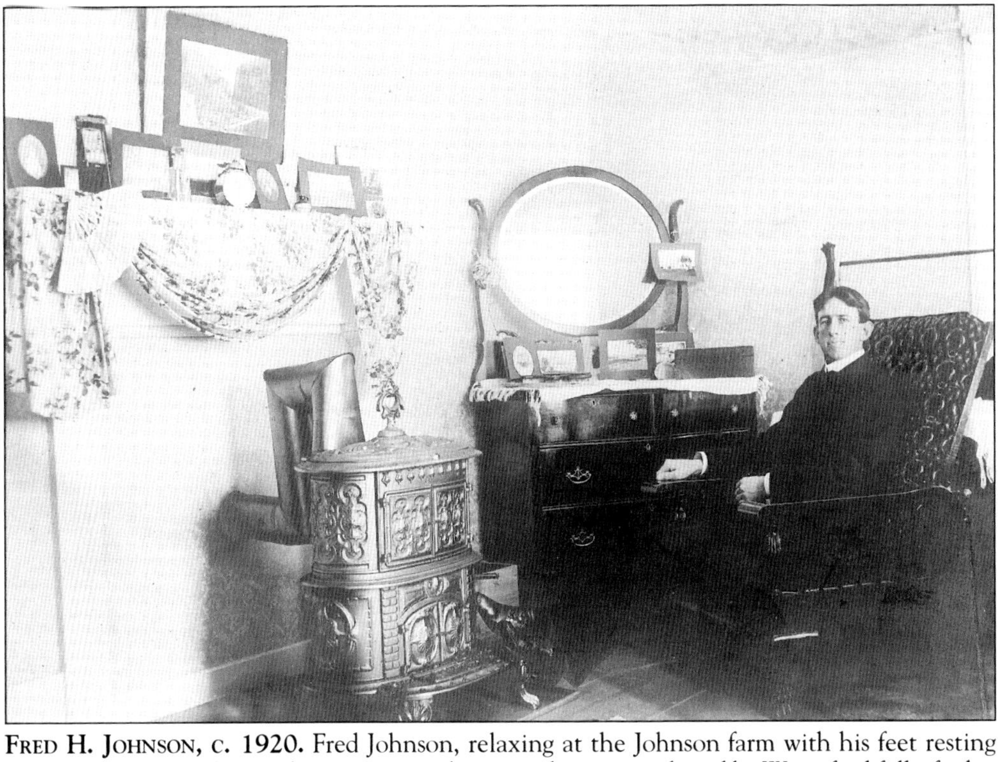

FRED H. JOHNSON, C. 1920. Fred Johnson, relaxing at the Johnson farm with his feet resting upon an intricately designed cast-iron wood stove, is best remembered by Waterford folks for his superb photography. For example, in 1917, when Edgar "Ned" Stone demonstrated his gasoline-run ice-cutting machine on Keoka Lake, Johnson recorded the revolutionary event with his camera, and his photographs and article were published in *Popular Mechanics*.

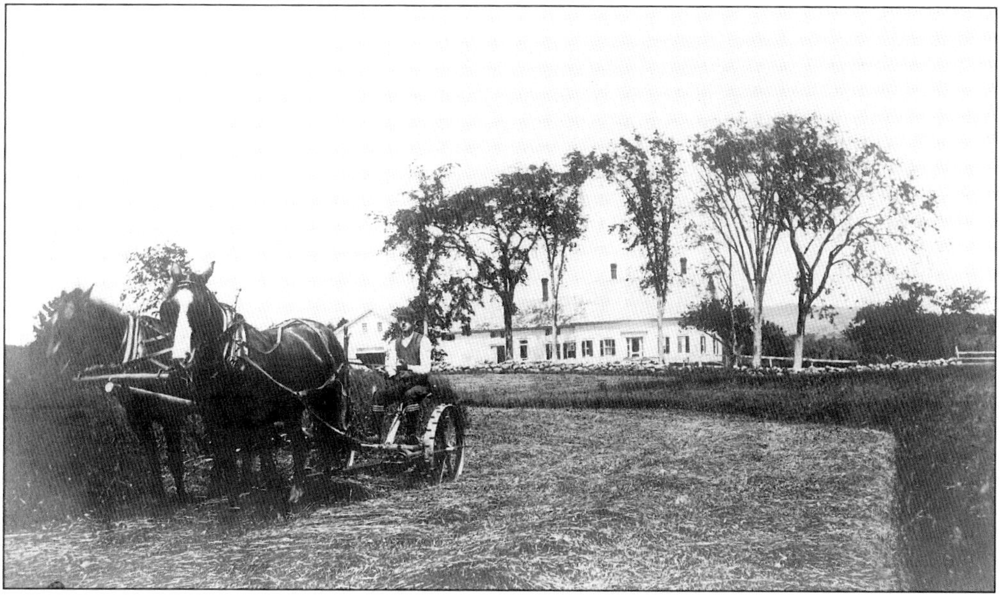

MOWING AT THE JOHNSON FARM, C. 1915. Hay has always been one of Maine's most significant crops, and one of the best ways to judge the prosperity of Maine farms was the quality of their hay fields. Although at the time of this photograph logging camps and urban areas provided a ready market for surplus hay, few farms had a surplus to sell. Farmers relied almost solely upon animal manure for fields and gardens until the early 1930s, when commercial fertilizers began to be more widely used.

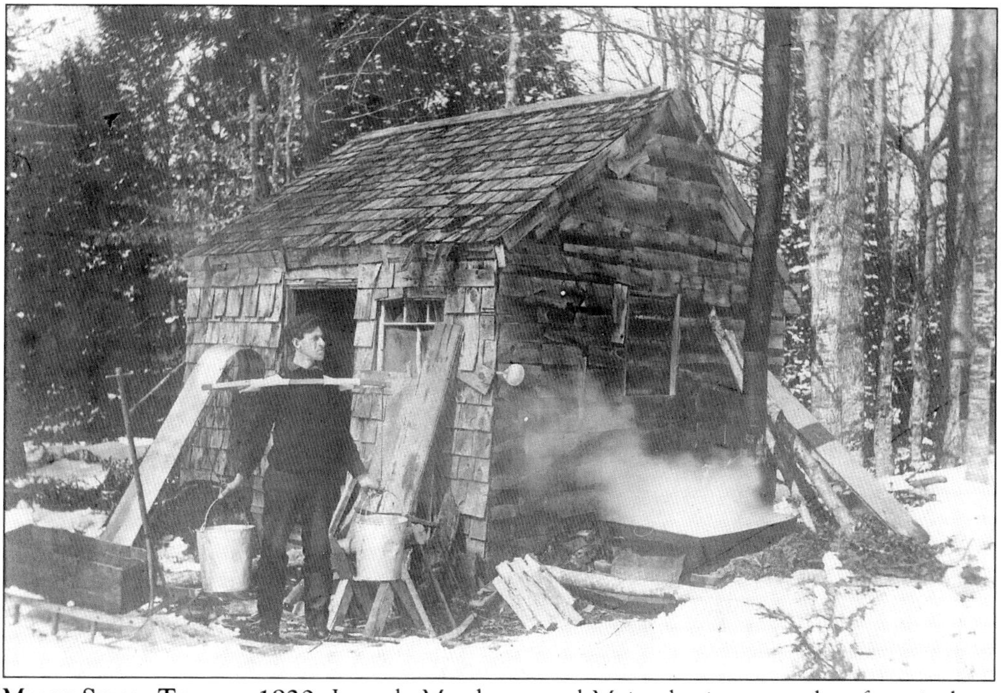

MAPLE SYRUP TIME, C. 1920. In early March, as rural Maine begins to awaken from its long winter hiatus, farmers such as Fred Johnson begin tapping sugar maples and gathering the sap to be boiled down to syrup (and in some instances, sugar) at sugar houses such as this one.

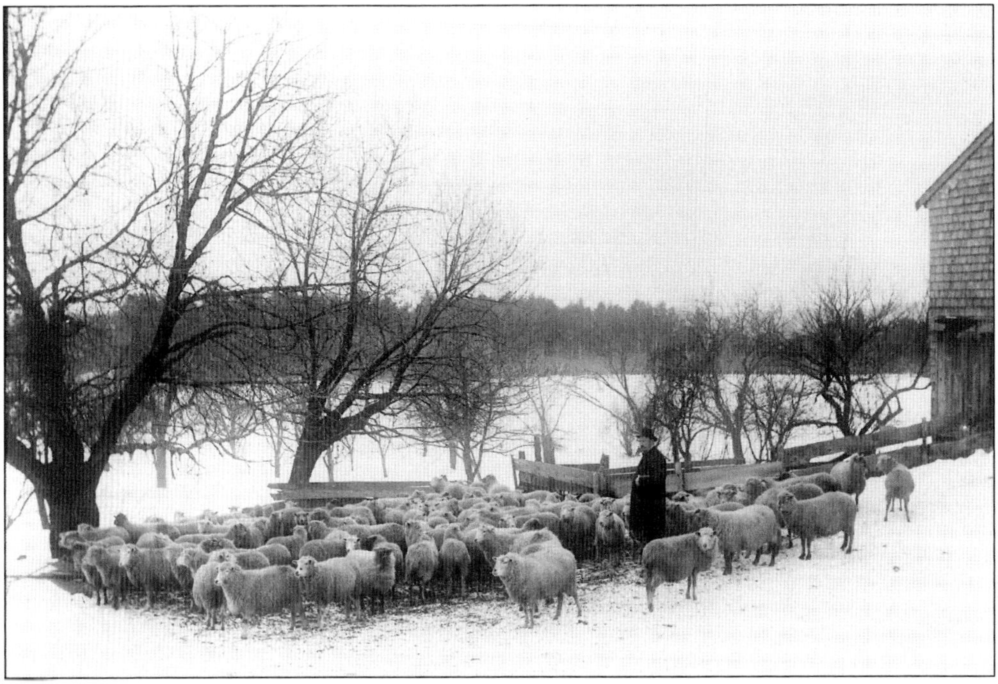

Bertrand G. McIntire Surveys His Flock, c. 1910. B.G. McIntire was a successful farmer and lumberman in East Waterford. His farm included a sizeable flock of sheep. During the Civil War the price of wool was high and, for the most part, fine-wooled Merinos were raised. By 1865 there were about a million sheep in Maine. After the war, the price of wool dropped decisively, but the price of mutton and lamb rose. By 1900 the transition from fine-wool producers to the large English mutton-producing breeds (like those shown here) had taken place.

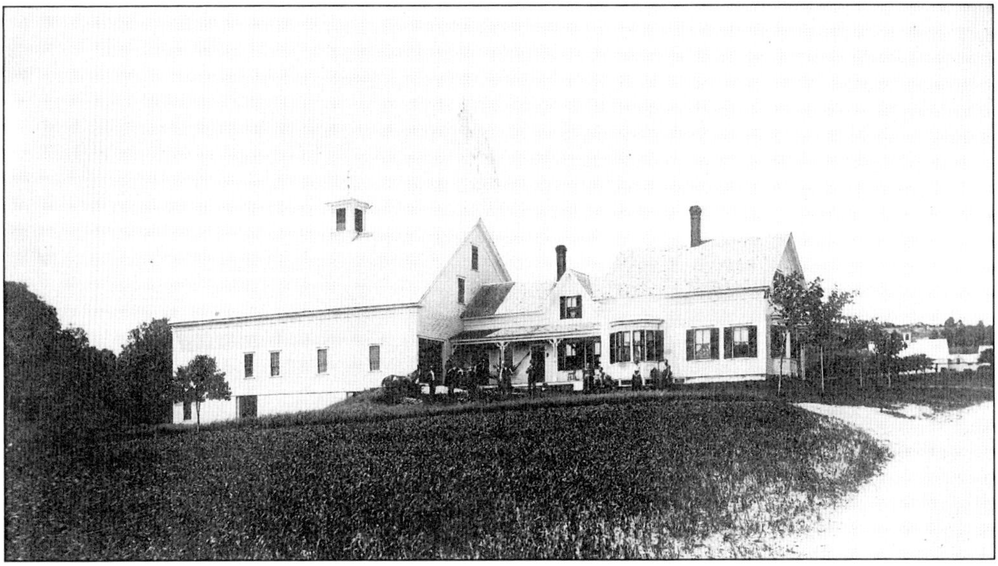

The L.E. McIntire Farm, c. 1890. Leslie, the eldest son of Justin McIntire, a lumberman and farmer, ran his father's meat market in Harrison, with the help of his younger brother Bertrand, before converting this farm into a modern operation in 1918.

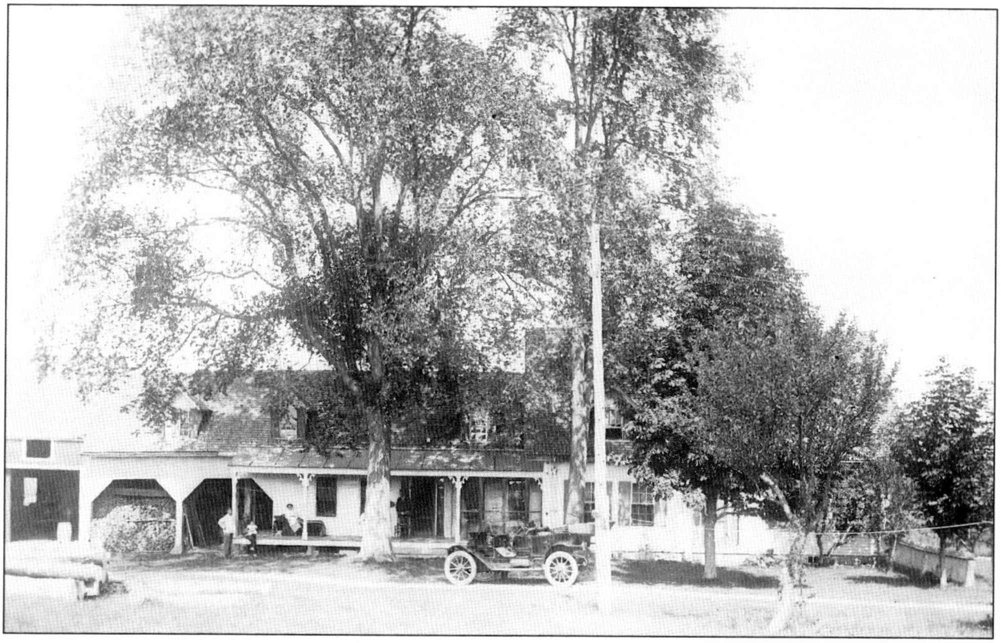

THE SANDERSON FARM, C. 1920. Burton and Minnie Sanderson, both of whom were teachers, lived on this farm in East Waterford. Minnie taught at the Waterford Flat School and was singled out for developing a program on Longfellow's *Evangeline*. Like almost everyone else at this time, they also farmed.

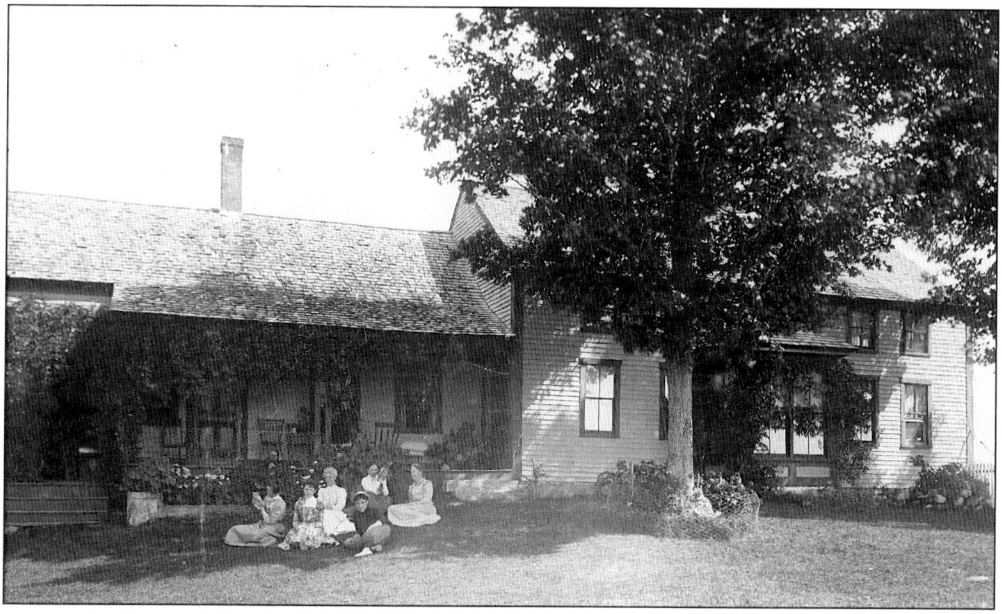

THE WALDO BROWN HOMESTEAD, 1896. The home of Waldo Brown was located in East Waterford. He was related to Charles Farrar Brown (Artemus Ward), the much-beloved Florence Brown Rounds (an educator who excelled in math, English, and Latin and who owned the L.R. Rounds & Co. store in Waterford), and her granddaughter, Ruth Rounds. Pictured here are, from left to right, Louise Brown, Miss Fessenden from Portland, Mrs. L.B. Gerts of Boston, Fred J. Greenhaloh of New York, Miss Alice Brady, and Mrs. Waldo Brown.

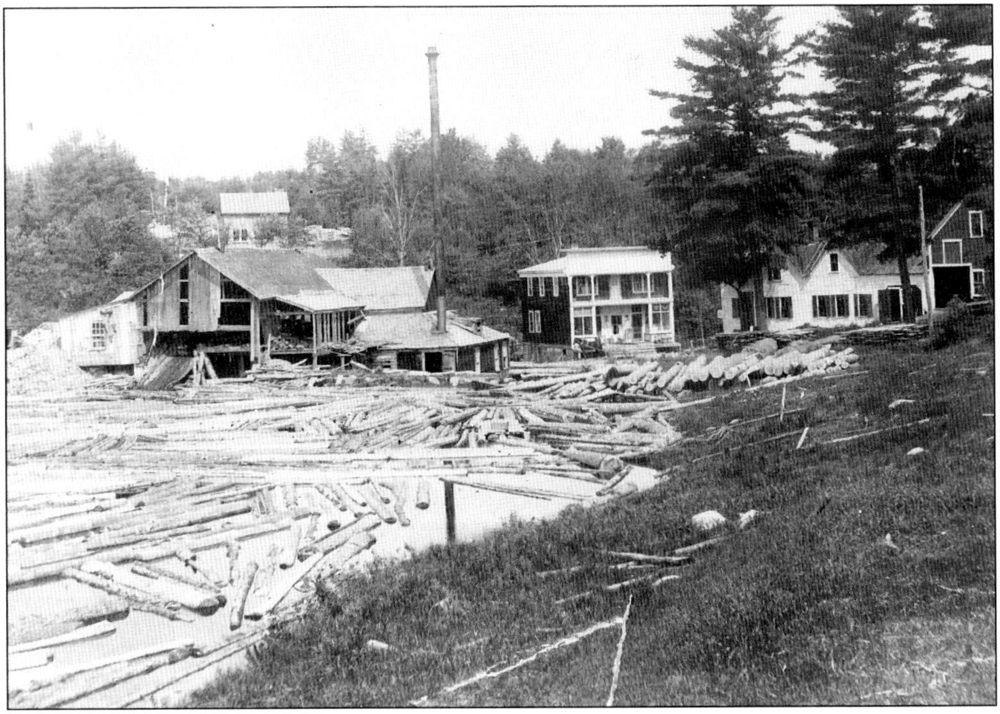

The Haskell (Rolfe) Lumber Mill, c. 1910. At one time East Waterford hummed with industry. Central to this hamlet was the Peter Haskell sawmill, the water for the pond coming from a branch of Crooked River. Haskell also operated a gristmill here. The area at one time also supported a blacksmith shop, a cooper shop, a chair factory, and a corn shop. Next to Springer's Store is the Henry Rolfe place, built by Haskell. Briefly around 1919 a portion of the lower level served as a post office and later as a barbershop.

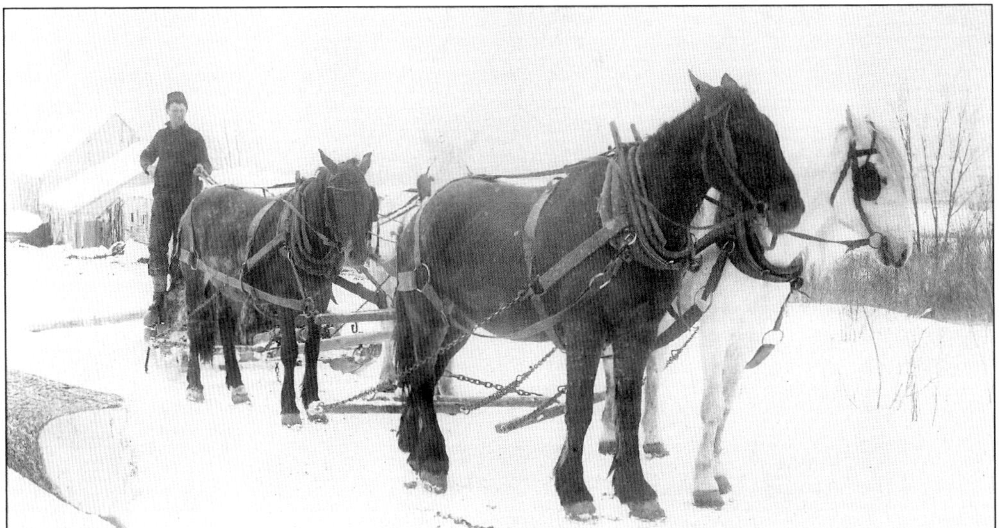

Hauling Logs to the Mill, c. 1910. Dana Berry is hauling logs on a winter's day on a bobsled pulled by four horses to the Haskell (Rolfe) mill to be rolled onto the ice-covered mill pond.

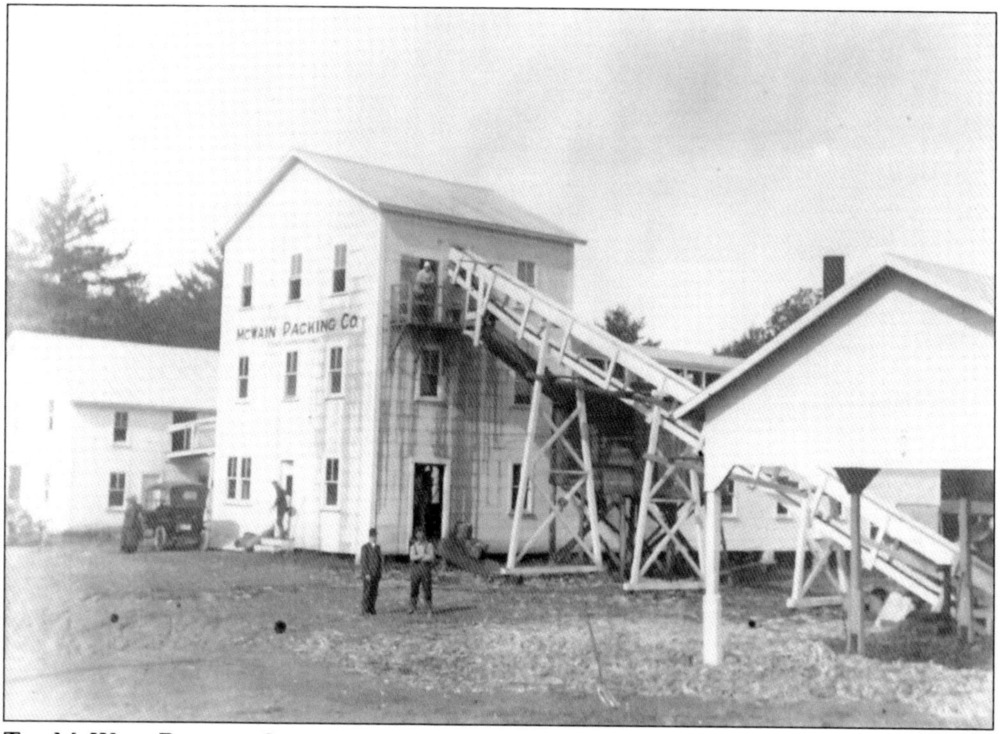

The McWain Packing Company, 1915. In the early part of the twentieth century corn shops were operating in South, East, and North Waterford. The McWain Canning and Packing Company, which processed corn, beans, and apples, was organized December 9, 1911, and constructed at Rice's Junction, now where Routes 37 and 118 converge. The Depression and increased competition brought about its demise in 1931.

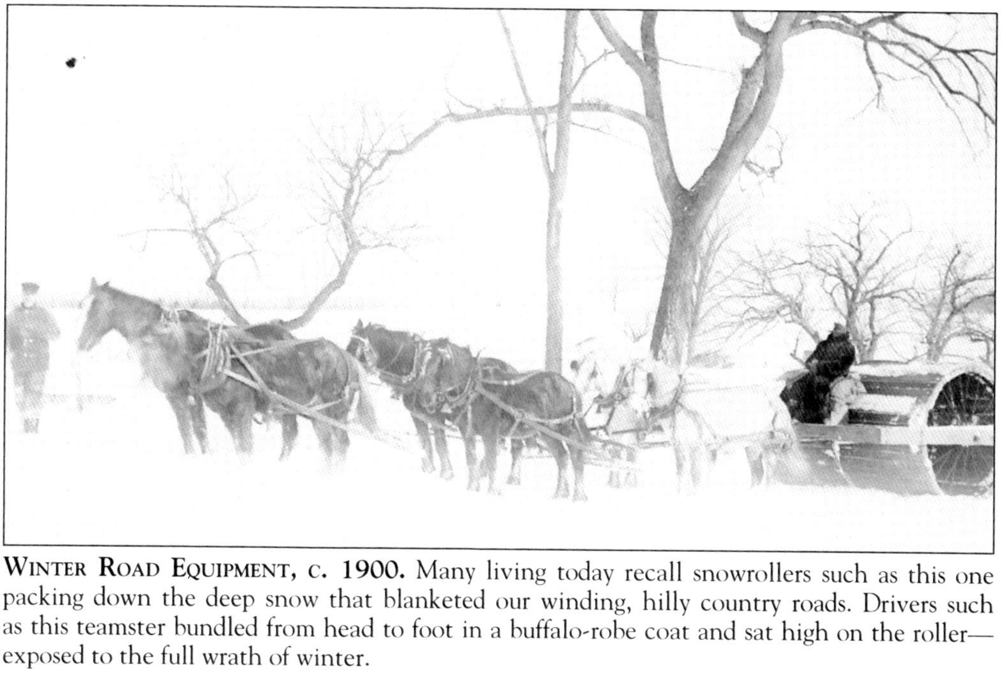

Winter Road Equipment, c. 1900. Many living today recall snowrollers such as this one packing down the deep snow that blanketed our winding, hilly country roads. Drivers such as this teamster bundled from head to foot in a buffalo-robe coat and sat high on the roller—exposed to the full wrath of winter.

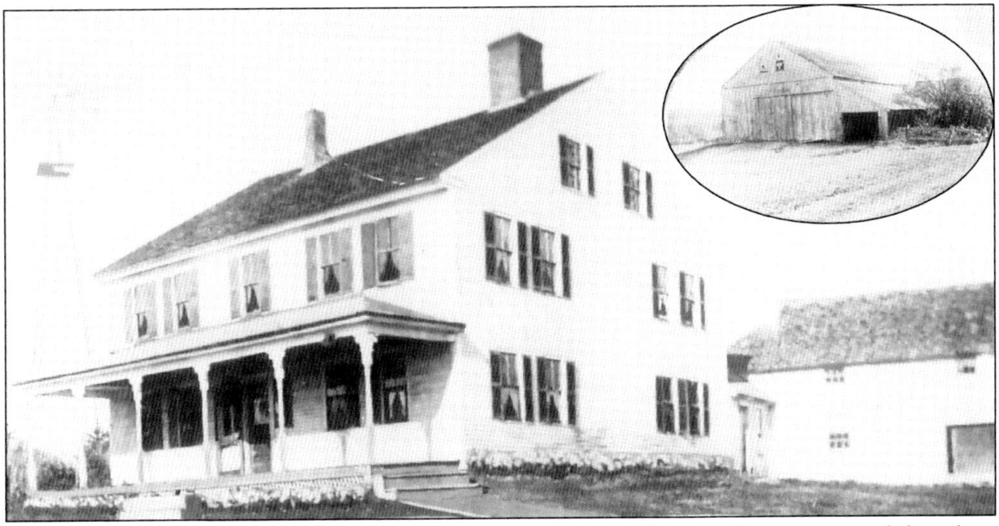

From a Tavern to a Camp for Boys, c. 1920. In the 1820s Sumner Stone operated this place overlooking McWain Pond as a tavern, since at that time the main road to Norway passed by it. In the early twentieth century a number of farms in the area used windmills such as the one to the far left to pump water into houses and barns. In 1932 Arthur and Mary Carlson purchased the farm and operated it as Camp Passaconaway for boys with above average scholastic and social records. Camp Joseph purchased the camp in 1960.

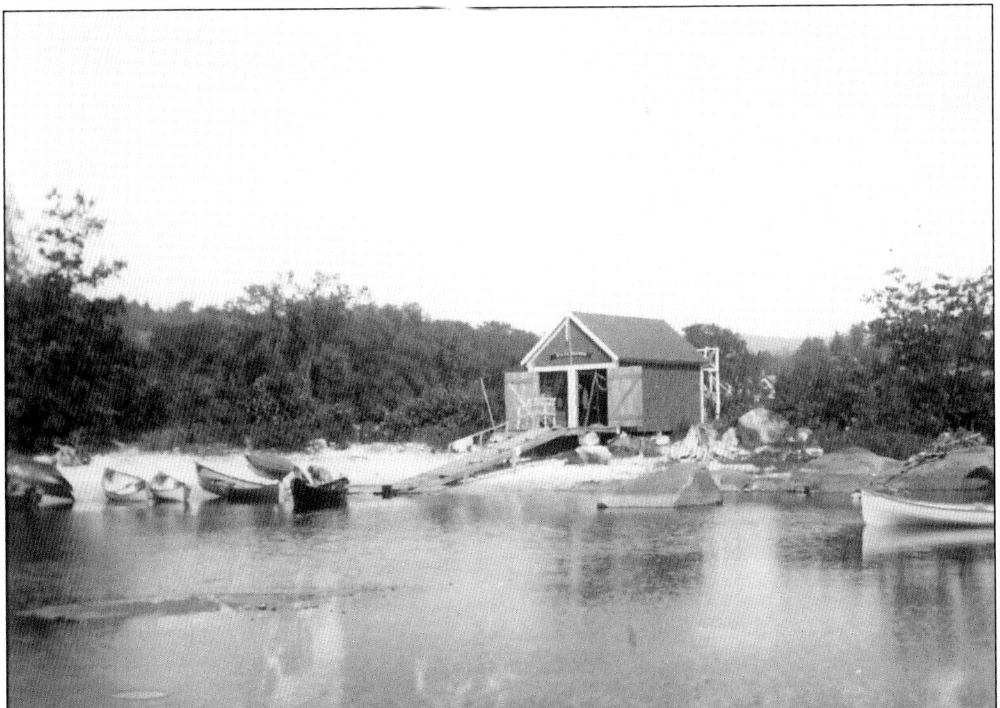

Tom Pond (Lake Keoka), c. 1925. Our lakes and ponds were much quieter in the days when only rowboats and canoes were used. Tom or Thomas Pond is reputed to have been named after Thomas Chamberlain, who killed Chief Paugus in Lovewell's Fight (1724) and later hid from the Native American warriors here at the pond.

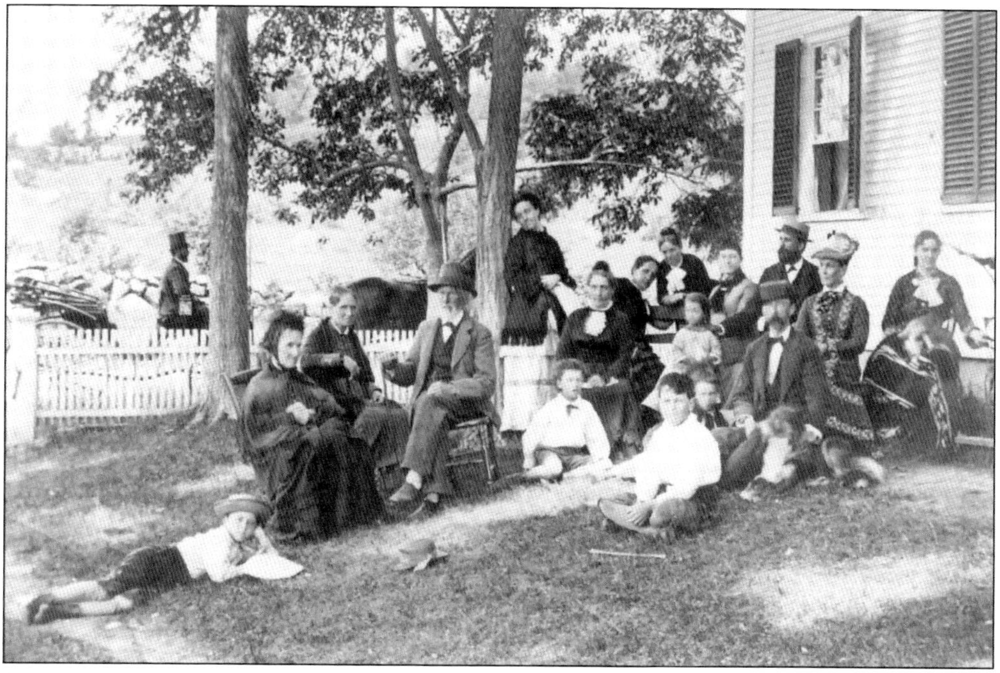

Summer Visitors, c. 1895. Emily Flagg McKeen and her brother, Dr. Carl Flagg, from West Roxbury, Massachusetts, are entertaining a distinguished looking group of friends and relatives up on the Rice Road. They apparently became very attached to Waterford, for both are buried in the Elm Vale Cemetery in South Waterford.

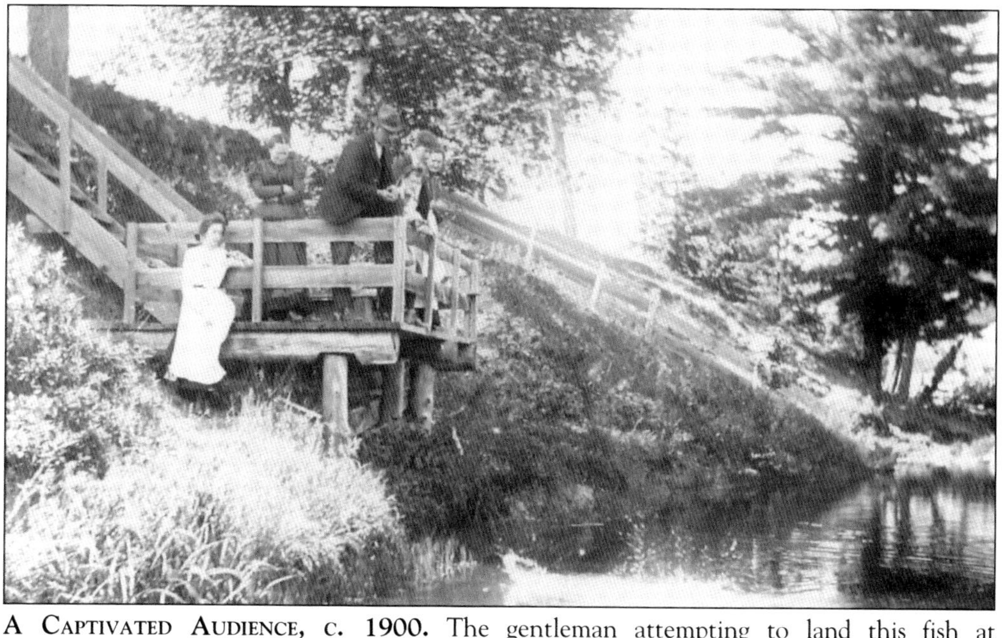

A Captivated Audience, c. 1900. The gentleman attempting to land this fish at McWain Pond near the McIntire Road in East Waterford has a captivated audience. Unfortunately the identity of these people enjoying a summer's outing at the pond remains a mystery. But the photographer was Waldo Brown, who is most remembered in Waterford today for his photography.

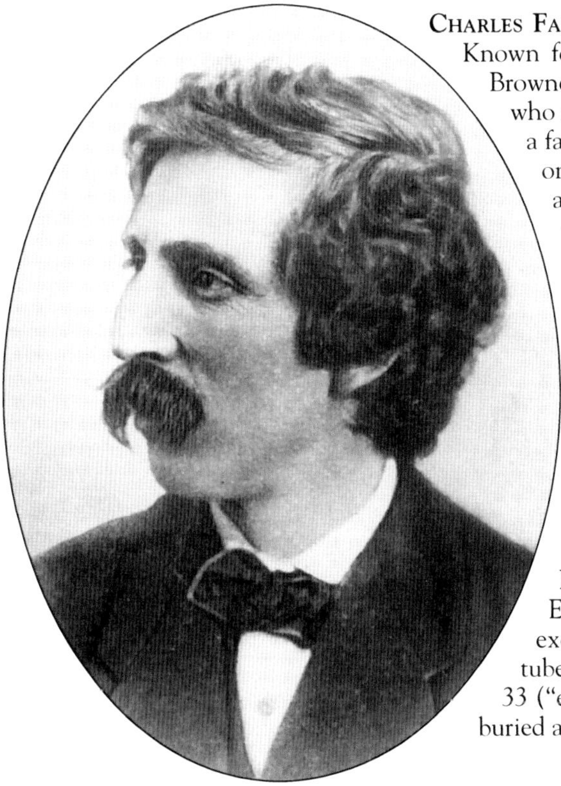

CHARLES FARRAR BROWN(E) OR "ARTEMUS WARD." Known for his captivating satirical wit, Charles Browne—Mark Twain's mentor—was the man who made Lincoln laugh. Charles was born on a farm on the outskirts of Waterford Village on April 23, 1834, the son of Levi Brown and Caroline Eliza Farrar. When Charles was 13, his father died, leaving the family with little money. He left school to become an apprentice typesetter for such local newspapers as the *Oxford County Advertiser* in Norway. At 17, he moved to Boston and worked for the *Carpet Bag*, for whom he wrote his first known piece. In 1857 he was the commercial editor of the Cleveland *Plain Dealer*, and in 1861 he became the editor of *Vanity Fair*. In 1863 he began a series of lecture tours throughout the Far West, and in 1866 he sailed to England, where his popularity far exceeded that in America. He died there of tuberculosis on March 6, 1867, at the age of 33 ("ekalled by few & exceld by none"). He is buried at Elm Vale.

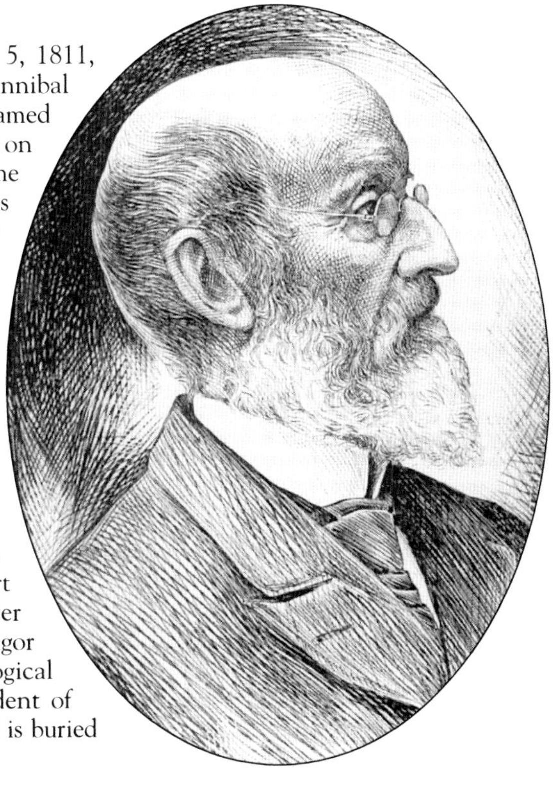

CYRUS HAMLIN. Cyrus was born January 5, 1811, at the family farm in Waterford to Hannibal and Susan Faulkner Hamlin. He was named after his father's twin brother, who resided on Paris Hill and whose son Hannibal became Lincoln's first vice president. When Cyrus was only seven months old, his father died of tuberculosis. Young Cyrus loved farming and would have remained on the farm with his brother Hannibal had the family physician not advised against it. He entered Bridgton Academy at the age of 18; after graduating he went on to graduate from Bowdoin (1834) and Bangor Seminary (1837). Beginning in 1839 he spent most of the next 38 years in Turkey as a missionary, teacher, lecturer, and writer. He is best known for founding and administering Robert College (now Bosphorus U.). After returning to America he taught at Bangor Theological Seminary, Hartford Theological Seminary, and served five years as president of Middlebury College. He died in 1900 and is buried in Waterford.

Five

The Bridgton and Saco River Railroad

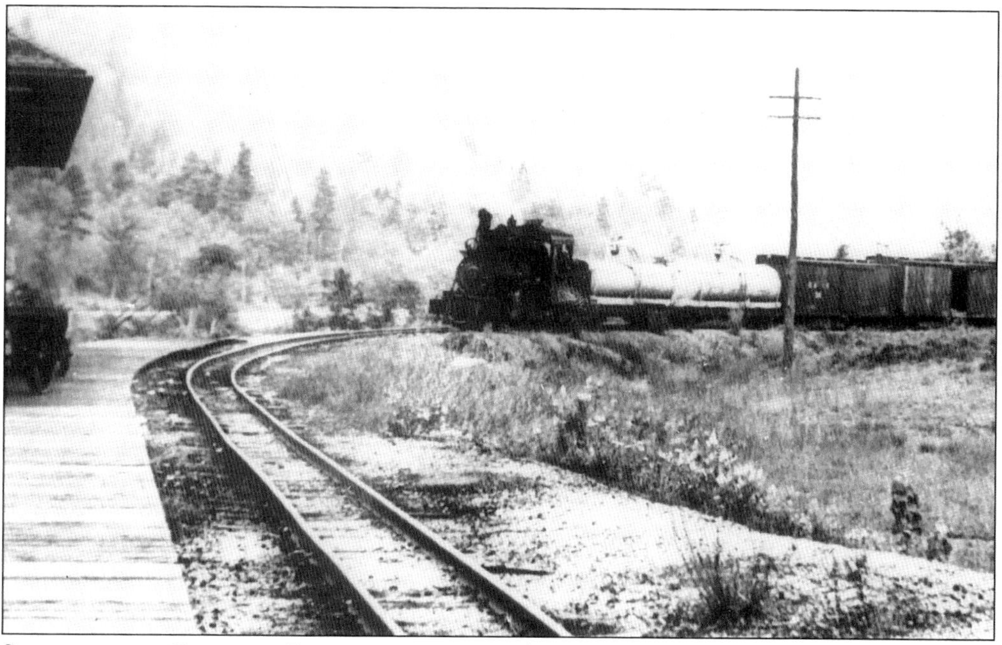

STEAMING INTO BRIDGTON JUNCTION, C. 1922. This mixed train (two tank cars, two box cars, and a passenger coach), which very likely originated in Harrison and added at least the two tank cars at the Bridgton yard, is approaching the station at the junction with the Maine Central Railroad located in Hiram on the edge of the Saco River in the shadows of Mount Cutler. The elfin locomotive very likely is No. 7, built by the Baldwin Locomotive Works in 1913. What is really significant in this photograph, however, is that the two tank cars—mounted on flat cars built in Portland—were the only ones ever to operate on a narrow gauge line in North America.

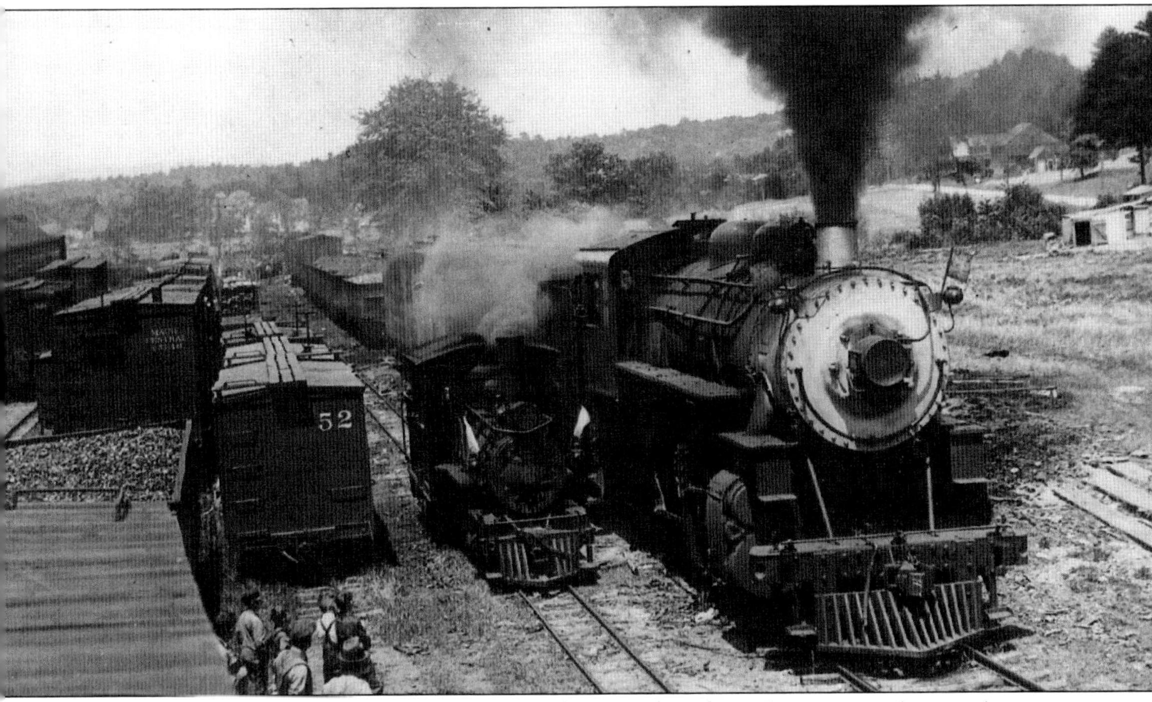

A Study in Contrasts, c. 1915. This photograph, taken during a rendezvous between a Lilliputian Bridgton & Saco freight train and a Central Maine freight on the Mountain Division at the Junction in Hiram, exemplifies the distinction between both rails and equipment of the standard-gauge (4 feet, 8.6 inch) rail and the 2-foot narrow gauge. No. 5 locomotive of the B&SRR is dwarfed by MEC's mighty No. 51—belching a funnel of black smoke skyward. For a period of 40 years or so—beginning in 1830 when the Cumberland and Oxford Canal was opened—Bridgton, Harrison, and South Waterford, via the Bear River (the planned extension of the canal to Thomas Pond in Waterford Flat never materialized), benefitted immensely by having an all-water route to Portland Harbor and beyond. It was a tremendous boon to both agriculture and industry. But it was slow. Canal boats averaged about three days to get from Harrison to Portland. The major drawback, however, was that the waterways could only be used from May to November in an average year.

Then came the railroads. In 1851 the 5-foot, 6-inch gauge Atlantic & St. Lawrence Railroad (Grand Trunk), the first major line to link the U.S. with Canada, reached Bethel from Portland. In 1870 the Portland & Ogdensburg Railroad (Maine Central by 1888) reached Sebago Lake, and by August 1871 freight and passenger trains were running to and from Conway. The canal could not compete with the railroad and shut down completely in 1873.

The four towns in the Lake Region found themselves bypassed by both railroads. Bridgton, which by then had become the hub for both industry and the growing summer resort trade, suffered the most from a lack of rail service. In the case of Bridgton, almost all freight was hauled by teamsters to and from the P&O Brownfield Station, 15 miles away. Freight could also go by water to Sebago Lake Station, and passenger service by steamboat continued until 1932. Little wonder George Mansfield, the man who introduced the narrow gauge to America, found most of Bridgton's leading citizens receptive to the idea of a 2-footer linking their town with the Portland & Ogdensburg at a cost of one-half that of a standard gauge. And although several routes were proposed, the 16-mile route to Hiram was decided upon by the newly formed Bridgton & Saco River Railroad Co. (B&SRR). Construction began at the Junction on July 17, 1882, and the miniature train steamed into Bridgton at 4:45 p.m. on Saturday, January 21, 1883.

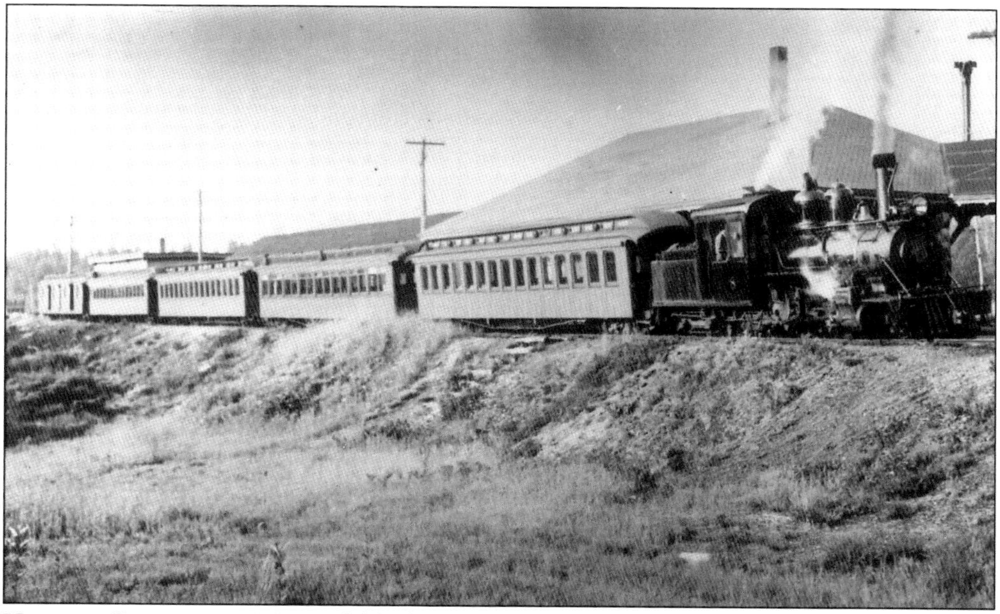

Heading Out, c. 1925. Powerful little No. 8 locomotive, with a string of passenger cars and a baggage car—probably hauling youngsters and their luggage to Camp Wabunaki on Hancock Pond in Sebago—is departing from the Junction. No. 8 was not only the last locomotive purchased (1924) by the B&SRR, which had been acquired by the MEC in 1912, but it was also the last engine manufactured by the Baldwin company for any narrow gauge in North America.

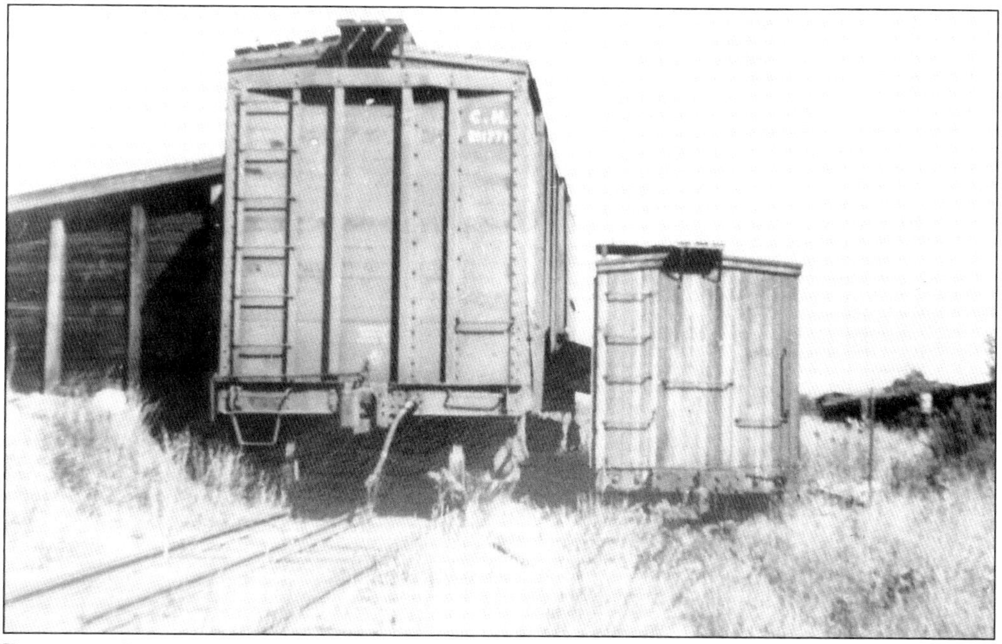

Bridgton Junction, c. 1940. A shipment of oats is being transferred from the huge Maine Central boxcar to the diminutive B&SRR box car, very likely destined for one of the railroad's last good customers, Ingalls & Morrison in Bridgton. Since all bulk items such as grain and coal had to be hand shoveled, labor costs for train shipments were high.

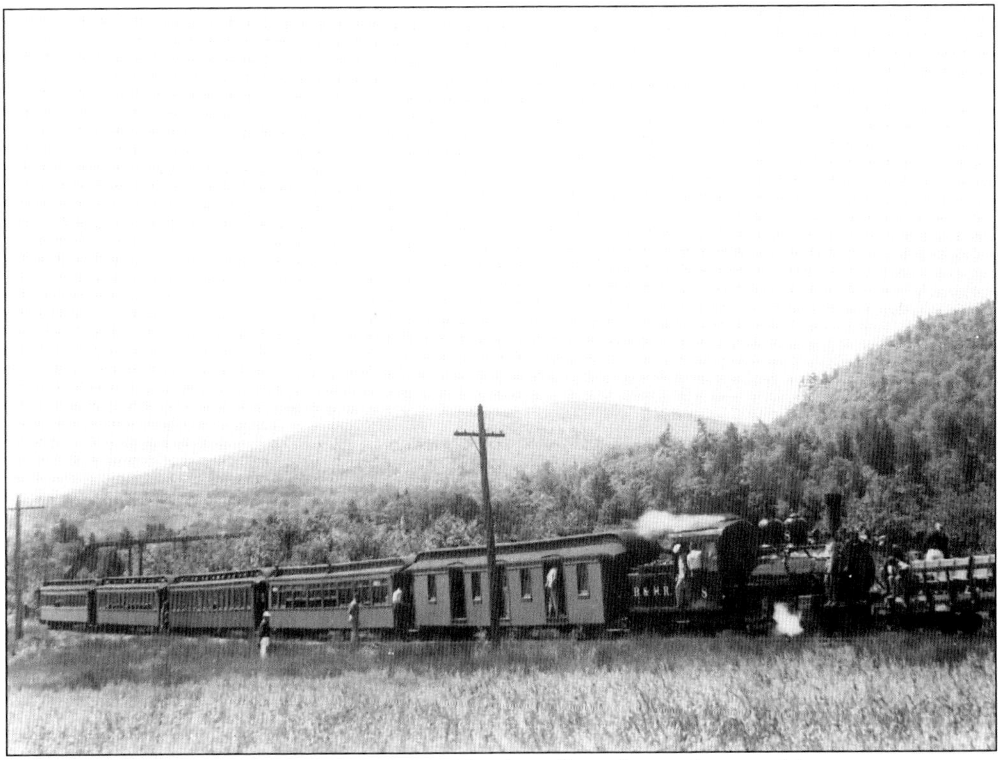

No. 8 Heading out of Hiram, c. 1925. No. 8, pulling the mail car and four passenger cars, has just crossed Route 113 and will soon be passing the Hiram Lumber Co. (formerly the Almon and P.B. Young sawmill). The old covered bridge crossing the Saco at the foot of Mt. Cutler (replaced in 1929) is visible to the right. Although still referred to as "Bustle and Scoot," both the passenger and freight business on the line had begun to decline.

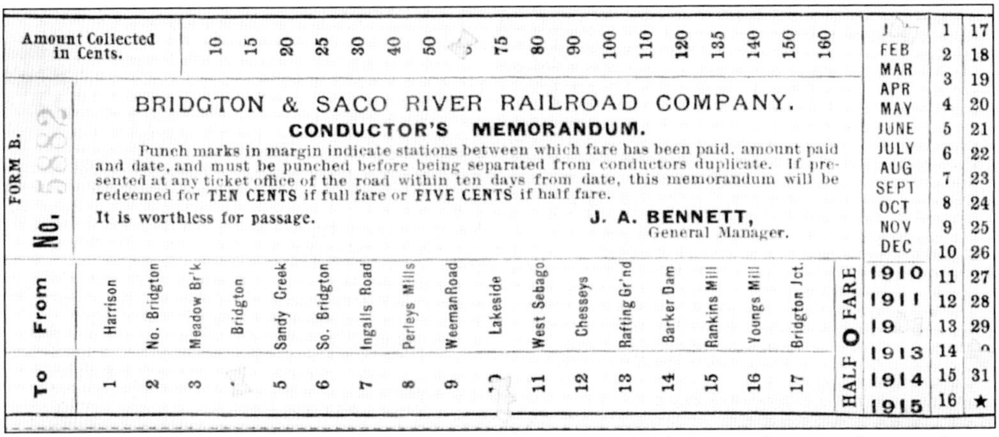

Amount Collected in Cents. 10 15 20 25 30 40 50 75 80 90 100 110 120 135 140 150 160

FORM B. No. 5882

BRIDGTON & SACO RIVER RAILROAD COMPANY.

CONDUCTOR'S MEMORANDUM.

Punch marks in margin indicate stations between which fare has been paid, amount paid and date, and must be punched before being separated from conductors duplicate. If presented at any ticket office of the road within ten days from date, this memorandum will be redeemed for TEN CENTS if full fare or FIVE CENTS if half fare.

It is worthless for passage.

J. A. BENNETT,
General Manager.

From	Harrison	No. Bridgton	Meadow Br'k	Bridgton	Sandy Creek	So. Bridgton	Ingalls Road	Perleys Mills	WeemanRoad	Lakeside	West Sebago	Chesseys	Rafting Gr'nd	Barker Dam	Rankins Mill	Youngs Mill	Bridgton Jct.
To	1	2	3	[illegible]	5	6	7	8	9	[illegible]	11	12	13	14	15	16	17

HALF O FARE

J[illegible] FEB MAR APR MAY JUNE JULY AUG SEPT OCT NOV DEC

1910 1911 19[illegible] 1913 1914 1915

1 2 3 4 5 6 7 8 9 10 11 12 13 14 15 16

17 18 19 20 21 22 23 24 25 26 27 28 29 [illegible] 31 ★

B&SRR Company Passenger Cash Fare Receipt, 1912. This served as a ticket, and was issued a few months before the MEC took over ownership of the line. A ticket from Bridgton to the Junction (16 miles) cost 75¢ and $1 from Harrison.

APPROACHING THE SUMMIT, C. 1920. A locomotive, pulling a string of freight cars, labors to reach the Summit, located near the dam where Barker Pond empties into Hancock Brook. The Summit, 500 feet above sea level and 350 feet from the Junction, had a 2.5% grade and was the highest point on the 21-mile track. Often a portion of a train had to be uncoupled, enabling the remaining cars to be pulled just beyond the Summit and left on a side rail; the locomotive would then back down to pick up the remainder of the cars.

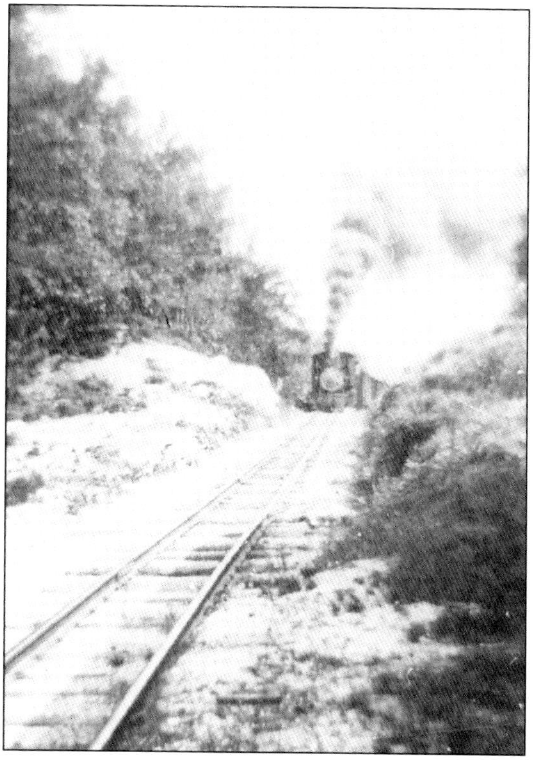

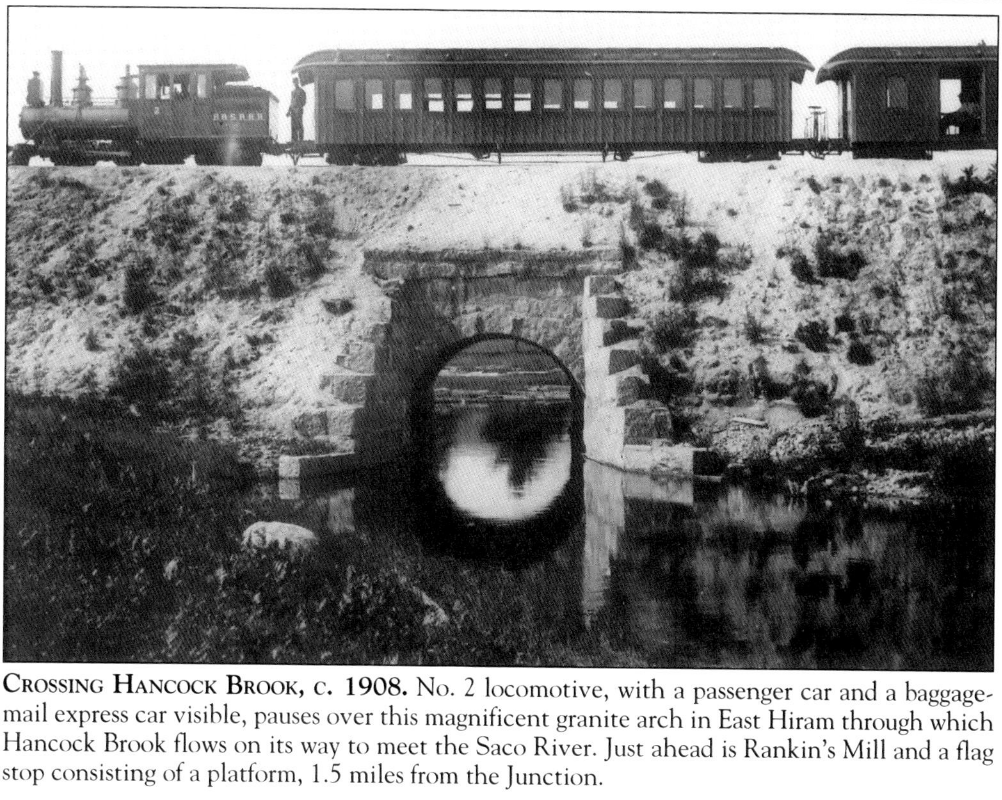

CROSSING HANCOCK BROOK, C. 1908. No. 2 locomotive, with a passenger car and a baggage-mail express car visible, pauses over this magnificent granite arch in East Hiram through which Hancock Brook flows on its way to meet the Saco River. Just ahead is Rankin's Mill and a flag stop consisting of a platform, 1.5 miles from the Junction.

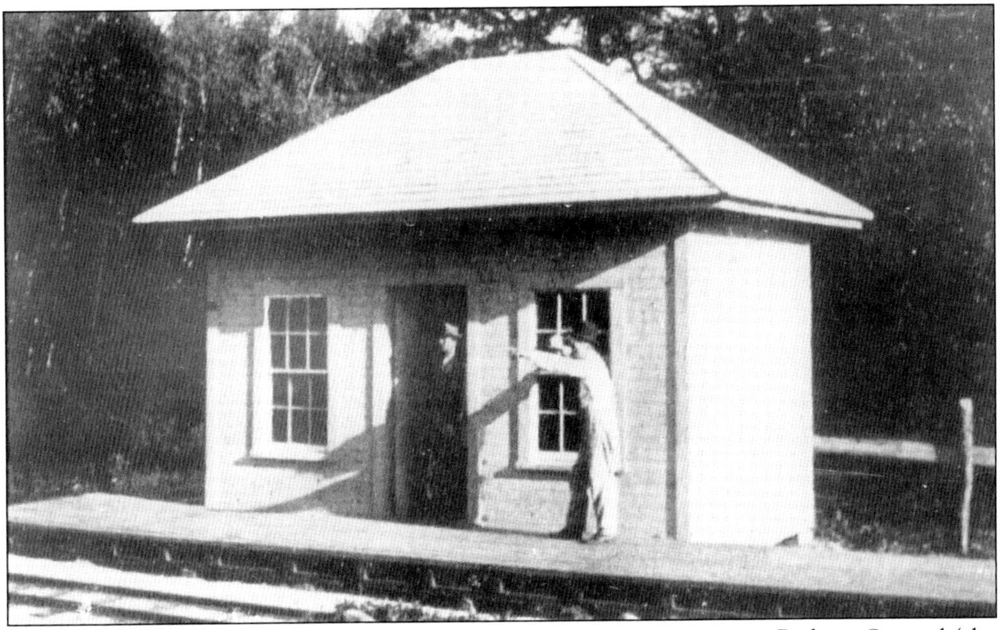

TWIN LAKES STATION, C. 1905. This attractive little flag stop station at Rafting Ground (the head of Barker Pond) was constructed to accommodate summer boarders at the Twin Lake House on Hog Fat Hill in Sebago overlooking Barker and Southeast Ponds. The 40-room boardinghouse was operated by Charles and Annie Douglas Hunt. Guests were transported to and from the station by a horse-drawn hack. The station now serves as a part of Kenney Douglas's workshop near where the Lake House stood until it burned in 1939.

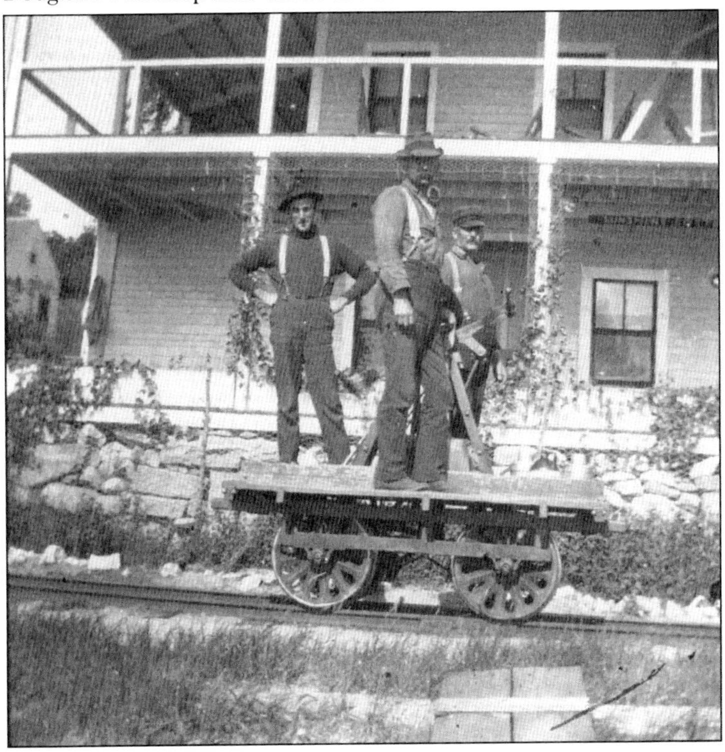

THE SECTION GANG, C. 1910. Three B&SRR section men pause before their boss's cottage (Joe Bennett), called Sunshine Cottage, near the edge of Hancock Pond. Joe Bennett, who built this summer cottage in West Sebago in 1901, worked at one time or another in just about every capacity from the time the railroad was built to his retirement in 1916. By 1894 he was both general manager and superintendent of the line, and in 1908 he became the president of the railroad.

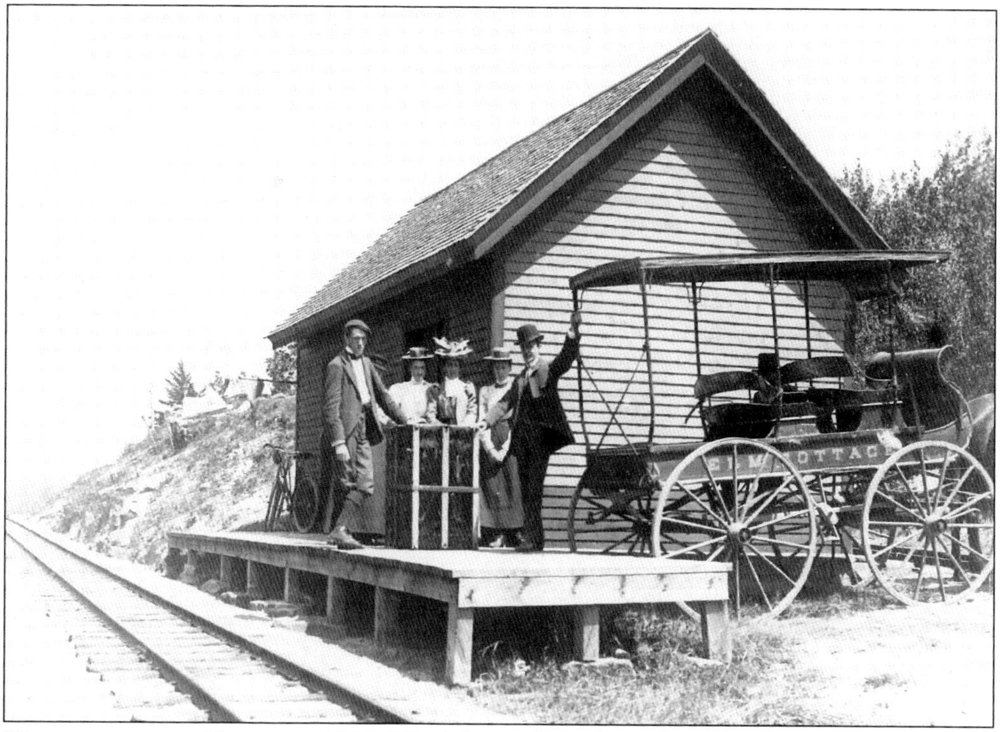

Waiting for the Train, c. 1895. The lakes and ponds in the Lake Region were attracting summer visitors before the turn of the century. Guests of the Elm House at Hancock Pond, owned by the Babbs for many years, appear to be waiting for the arrival of the train. The Lakeside Station, near Joe Bennett's cottage, was constructed in 1894.

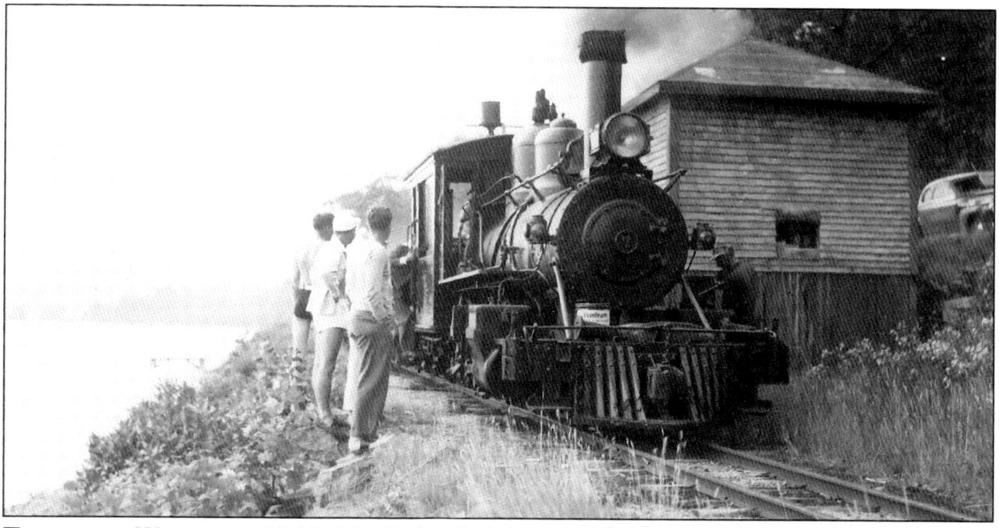

Taking on Water, c. 1941. No. 7, headed down to the Junction, pauses at the Hancock Pond tank in West Sebago long enough for the fireman to fill the engine's tank with water. The model of the automobile up on the Hancock Pond Road indicates that this was the last summer train that would run over the Bridgton & Harrison Railway, as it had been called since the Maine Central relinquished ownership in 1927. The onlookers are very likely rail fans riding on the train.

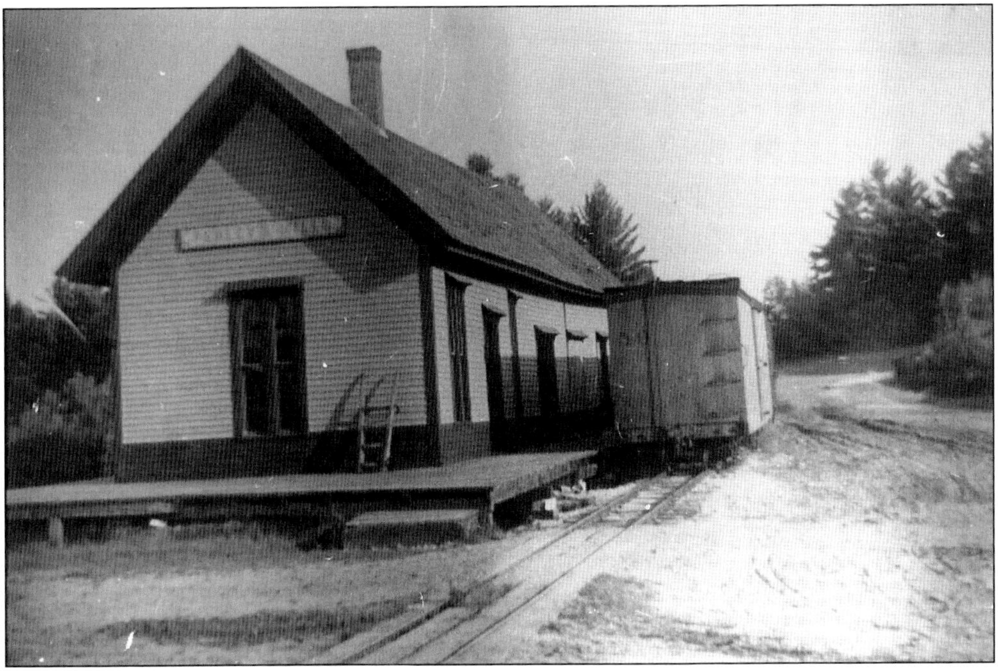

Perley's Mills Station, c. 1910. Until the decline of the railroad in the late 1920s, this well-maintained little station at Perley's Mills (razed in 1930), about 9 miles from the Hiram (Bridgton) Junction and located near the Sebago-Denmark town lines, was a bustling station maintained by a full-time agent. Boxcar 59 was built by the Portland Company in 1900.

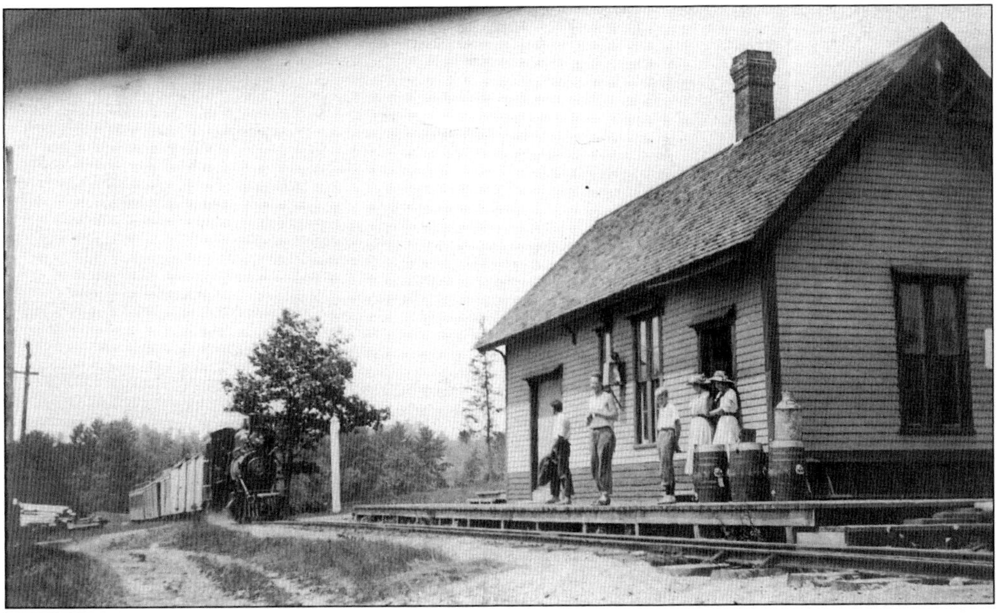

Sandy Creek, c. 1920. Like Perley's Mills, this station at Sandy Creek in Bridgton, the last stop before the Bridgton terminal, maintained a full-time station agent. In the early years of the railroad, Sandy Creek was a significant lumber and wood products community that provided the line with considerable freight business. Passengers are shown here awaiting the arrival of a mixed train from the Junction.

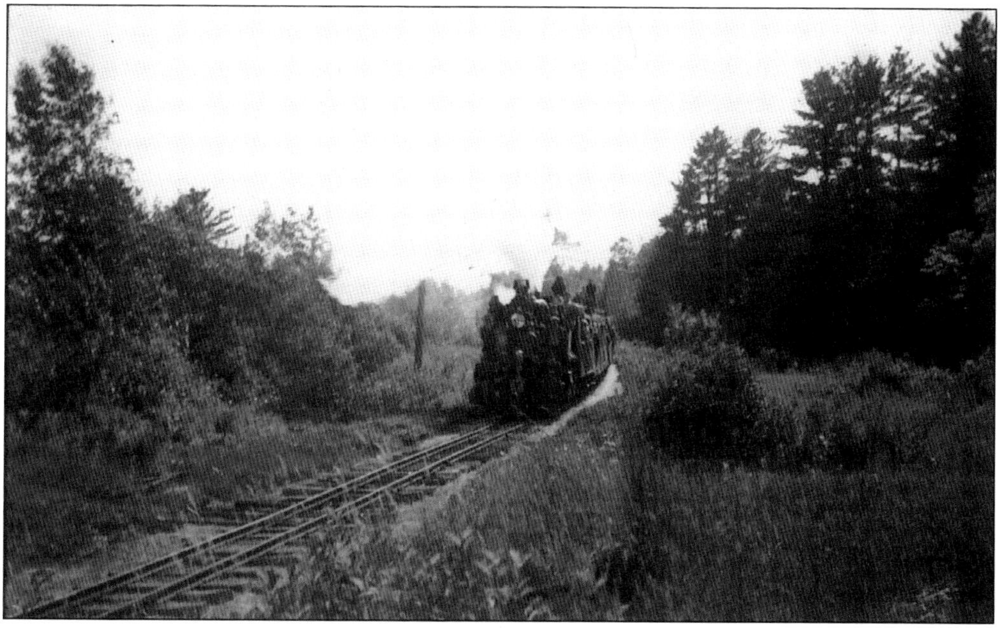

APPROACHING THE BRIDGTON STATION. The train has departed from the Sandy Creek station and is approaching the rail yard in Bridgton. The locomotive is probably either No. 7 or 8 and is conveying a group of rail fans on an excursion. If so, the photograph could have been taken as late as 1941.

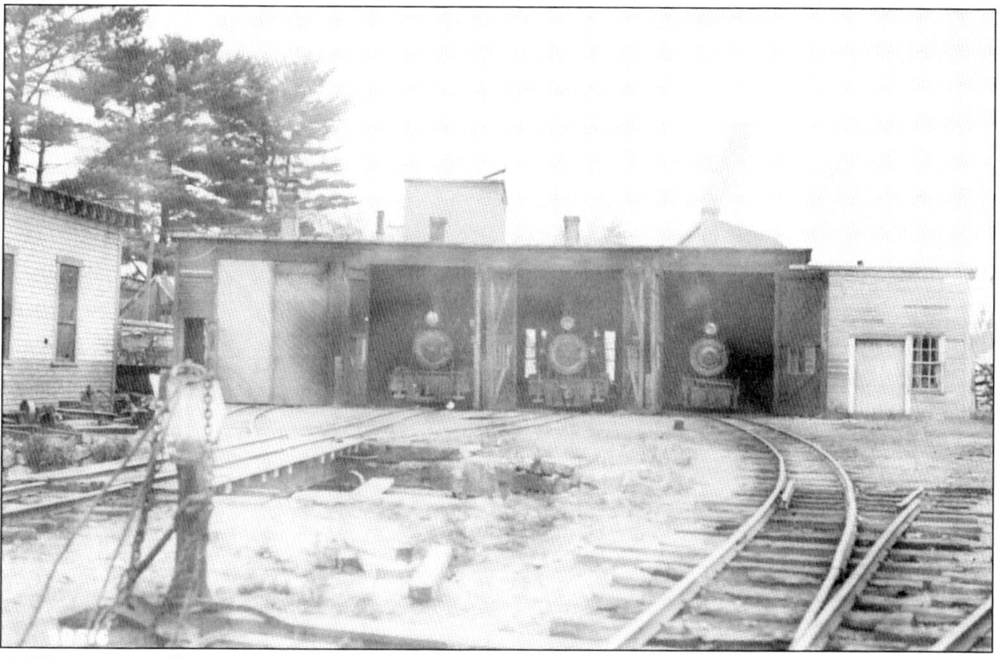

A VIEW OF THE BRIDGTON YARD, C. 1933. Some of the most prosperous years for the B&SRR were between 1901 and 1922, when it was kept the busiest hauling freight and passengers to and from the Junction. But soon afterward it became obvious that the railroad's most profitable years were behind it. Engines 6, 7, 8 are visible inside the engine house. A simple hand-powered turntable enabled the crews to turn the engines around to head south.

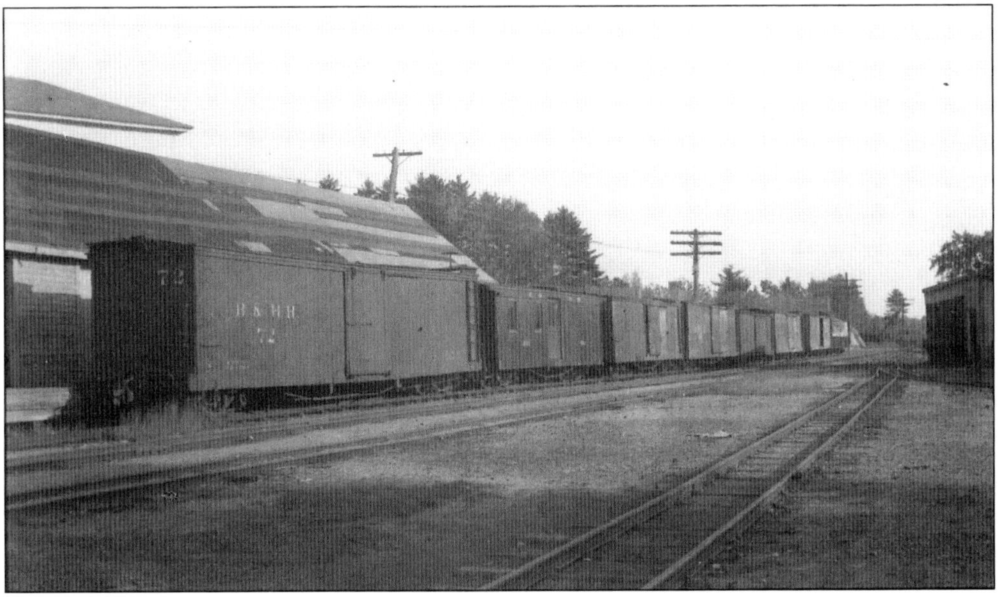

The Bridgton Terminus, c. 1936. A long string of boxcars sits idly on the tracks beside the freight house in the Bridgton yard. The building looming above the freight house appears to be the baseball grandstand, built in 1936.

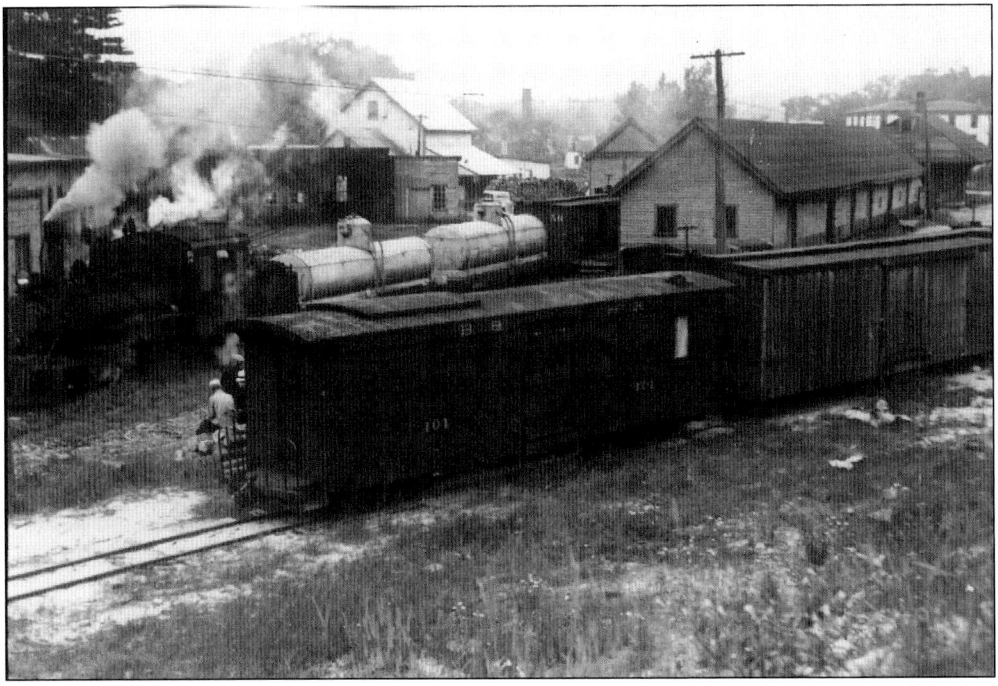

Heading up a Freight Train for the Junction (1935). No. 8 is building up a good head of steam in the Bridgton yard before heading down the line to the Bridgton Junction with a freight train which includes the two Standard Oil cars that kept the storage tanks of a local dealer filled with oil. A caboose and more freight cars are visible on the spur in the foreground. Beyond the engine house is Ingalls & Morrison, owned by Harold Morrison, a coal and grain customer of the line to the very end.

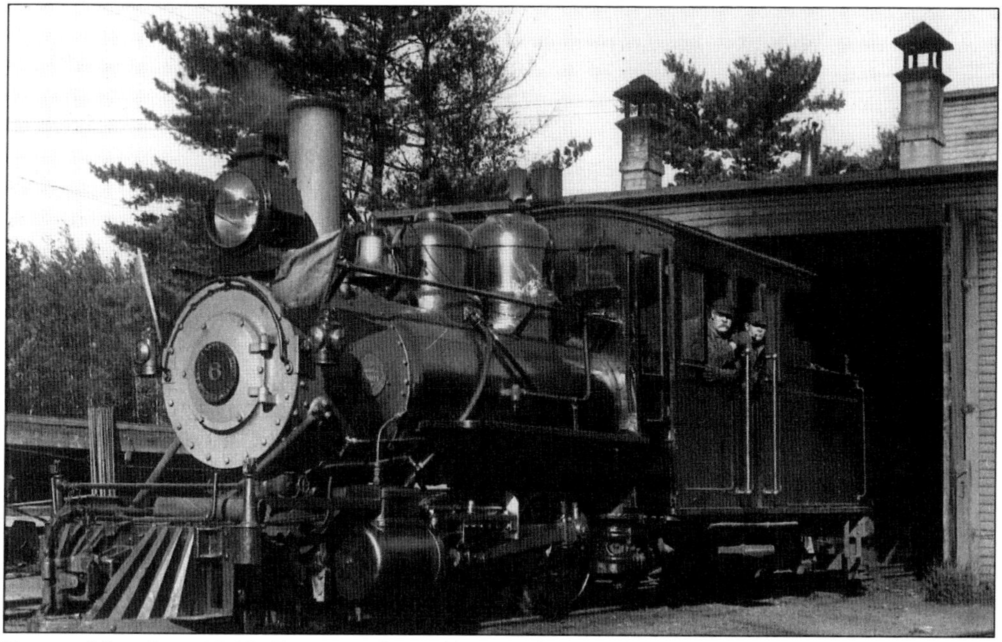

ENGINE NO. 6, C. 1907. Engineer Oscar Ham and an unidentified fireman are visible as they peer from the windows of Engine No. 6 in front of the engine house. This shiny new locomotive built by the Baldwin Locomotive works in 1907 was the heaviest locomotive used on the line until No. 7 was added in 1913.

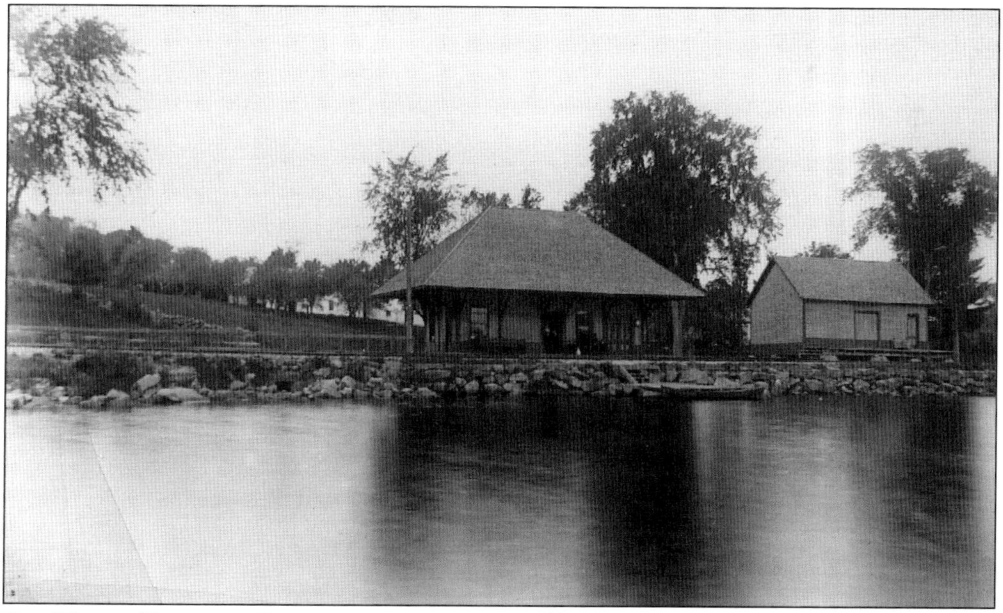

THE NORTH BRIDGTON STATION, C. 1915. Spurred by the Portland Railroad's proposal to lay a trolley line from Westbrook to Windham, Naples, and Harrison, plans were set in motion in 1897 to extend the Bridgton line 5.5 miles to Harrison. On August 3, 1898, the first little train pulled into this station at the edge of Long Lake on its way to Harrison. Meanwhile, plans were under way to extend the Norway & Paris Street Railway to Waterford and beyond, linking that area with the Grand Trunk. Bizarre circumstances aborted this proposal.

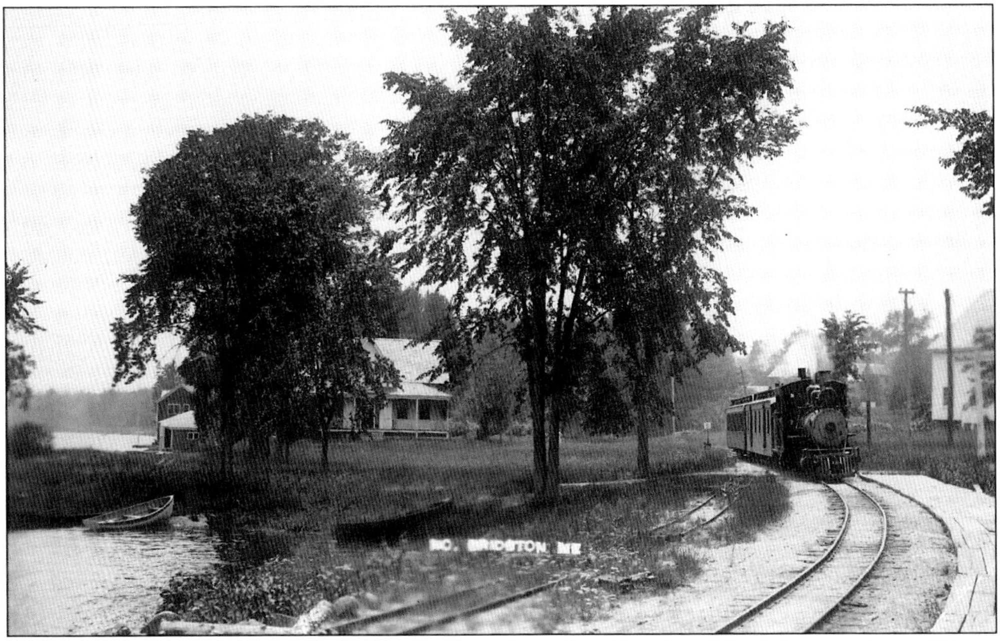

Rounding the Bend, c. 1909. What looks to be either No. 5 or No. 6 locomotive pulling a two-car passenger train is approaching the North Bridgton Station, where the 35-pound rail curved around the head of Long Lake in the direction of Harrison, about a mile up the line.

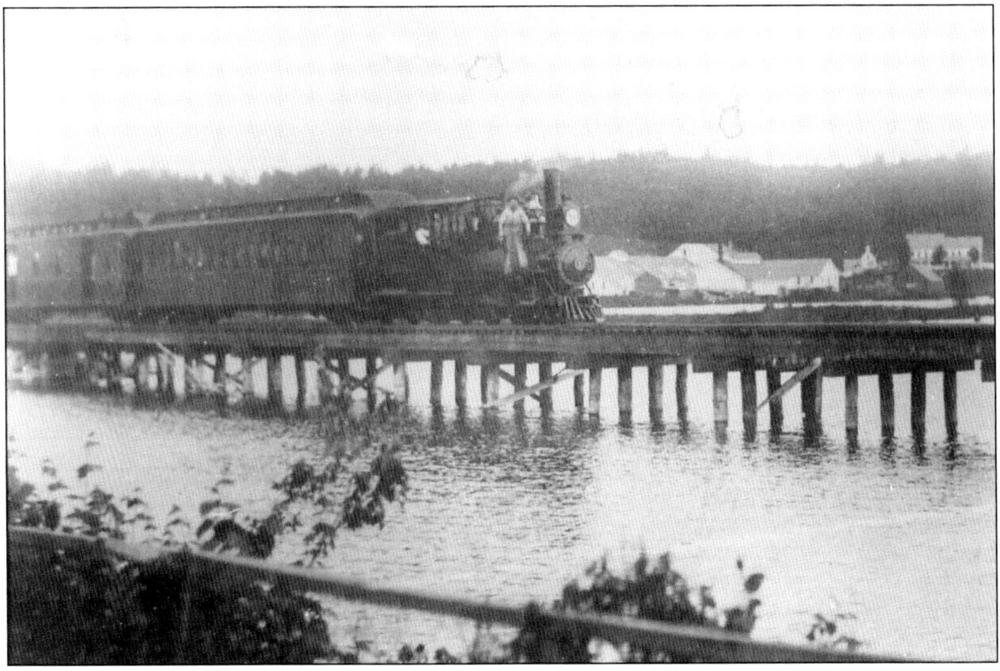

Crossing Long Lake, c. 1900. Diminutive No. 2 and two passenger cars pause on the imposing 800-foot trestle, supported by about 260 wooden piles driven deep into the bed of Long Lake in Harrison, before heading down to Bridgton and on to the Junction—a distance of nearly 22 miles. A shorter trestle was also constructed at North Bridgton. The Harrison Corn Shop is visible in the distance.

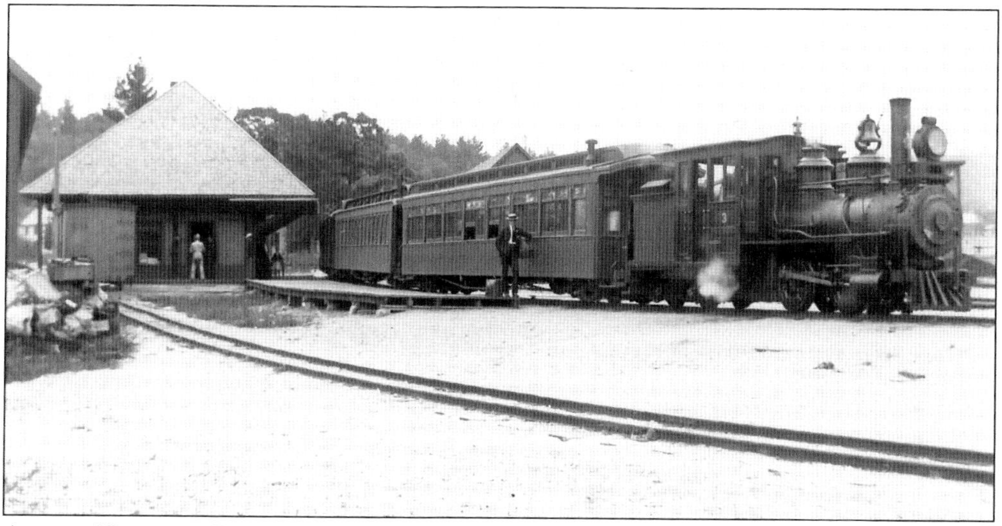

AT THE HARRISON DEPOT, C. 1900. No. 3, added to the line in 1892, has just been turned around on the turntable and is ready to depart for Bridgton, pick up more passengers, and head down to Hiram. The early 1900s were busy times for the B&SRR line. Three passenger trains a day were scheduled to Hiram and back, and a fourth was added summers during the peak of the steamboat excursions. Factories, mills, and farms in the Lake Region kept the freight business booming.

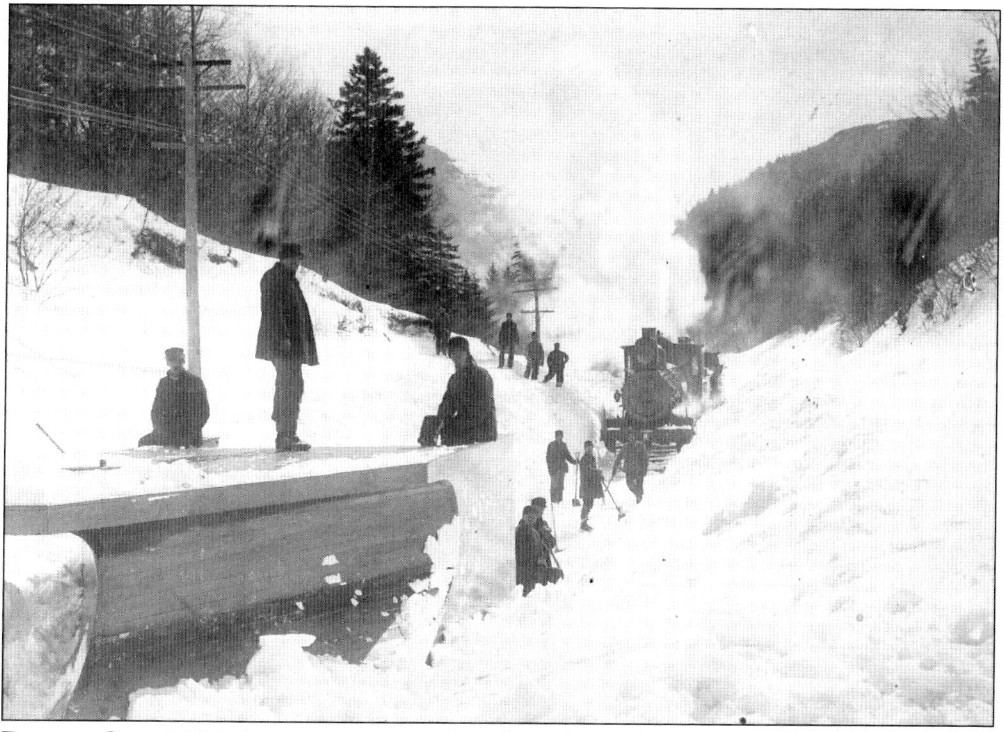

DIGGING OUT, 1927. But snowstorms such as this February blizzard in 1927, which buried the Lake Region under 22 inches of wet snow, were extremely costly to the railroad, which by then was struggling. Here the plow and the flange digger were almost useless. Nearly the entire line had to be picked and shoveled by hand.

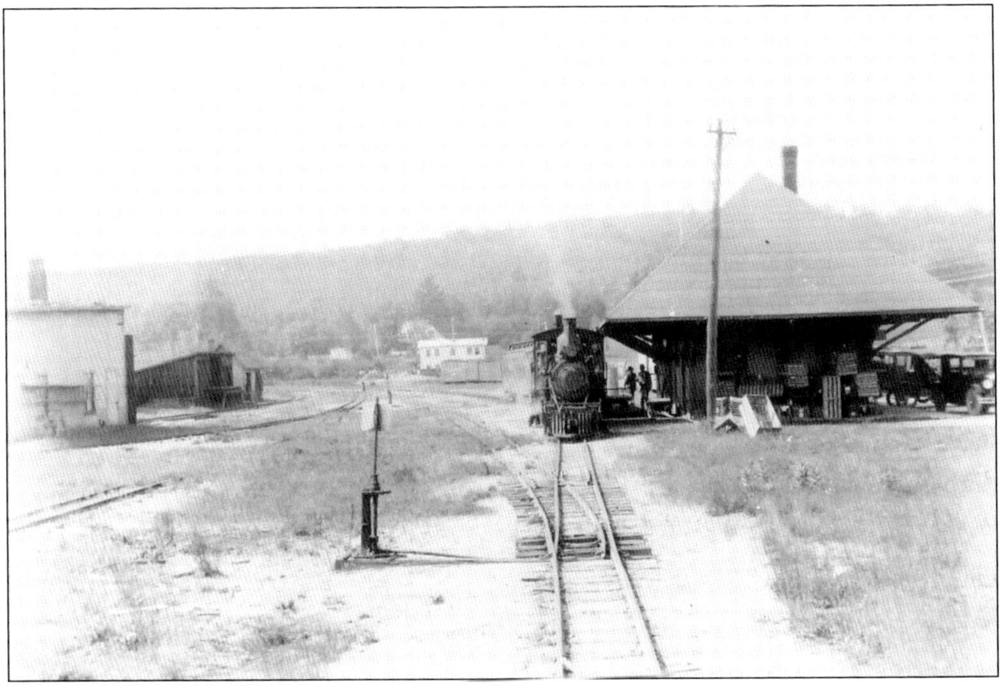

AT THE HARRISON STATION, 1929. No. 6 has just arrived with a short freight. The pile of crates in front of the station indicate that the poultry business still provided the line with revenue, but the automobiles are a bad omen.

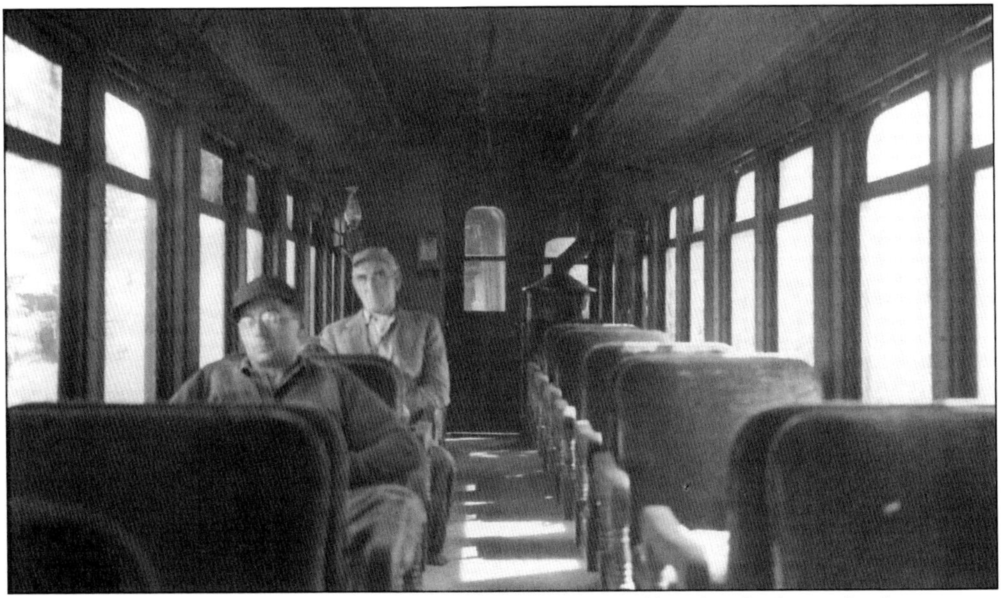

A VETERAN ENGINEER RELAXES, C. 1930. Everett T. Brown (front), who began his long career with the B&SRR as a brakeman but spent most of his career as an engineer, replaced the venerable Mel Caswell when the latter retired as master mechanic in 1926. He is shown here sharing a passenger car with Guy Andrews. The kerosene lamp is a reminder that when Brown started out as a lowly brakeman, one of his more unpleasant duties was very likely cleaning the lamp chimneys.

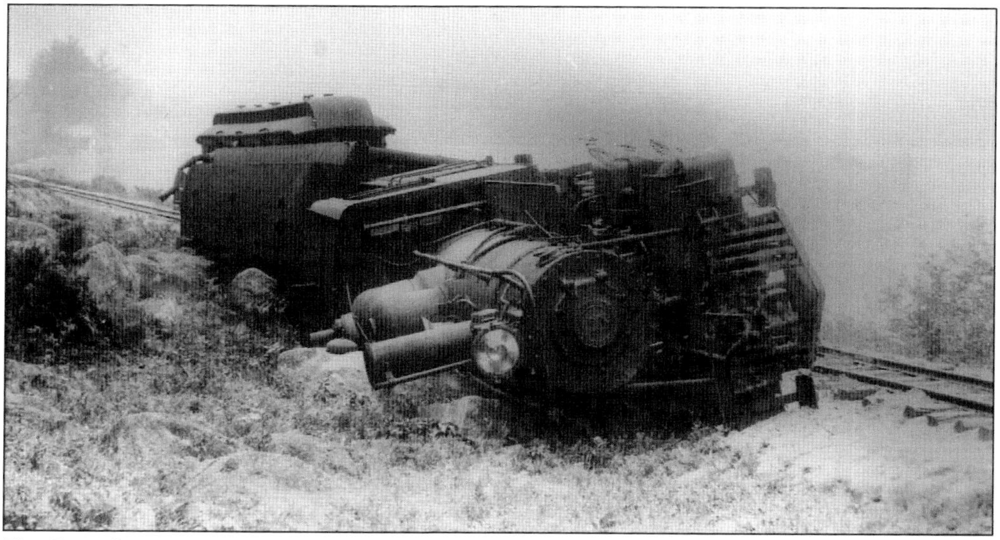

THE LAST STRAW, JUNE 15, 1930. Over the years, train derailments were a common occurrence. But when powerful No. 8 and two passenger cars hit a soft spot between North Bridgton and Harrison and flipped over, the Bridgton & Harrison Railroad Co. (B&HR), which hours before had purchased the line from the B&SRR, terminated the Harrison extension. Originally, 35-pound rails were laid from the Junction to Harrison. Beginning in 1908 the lighter rails were replaced by 50-pound rails, but only as far as Bridgton. No. 7 & 8 were too heavy for the 35-pound Harrison stretch.

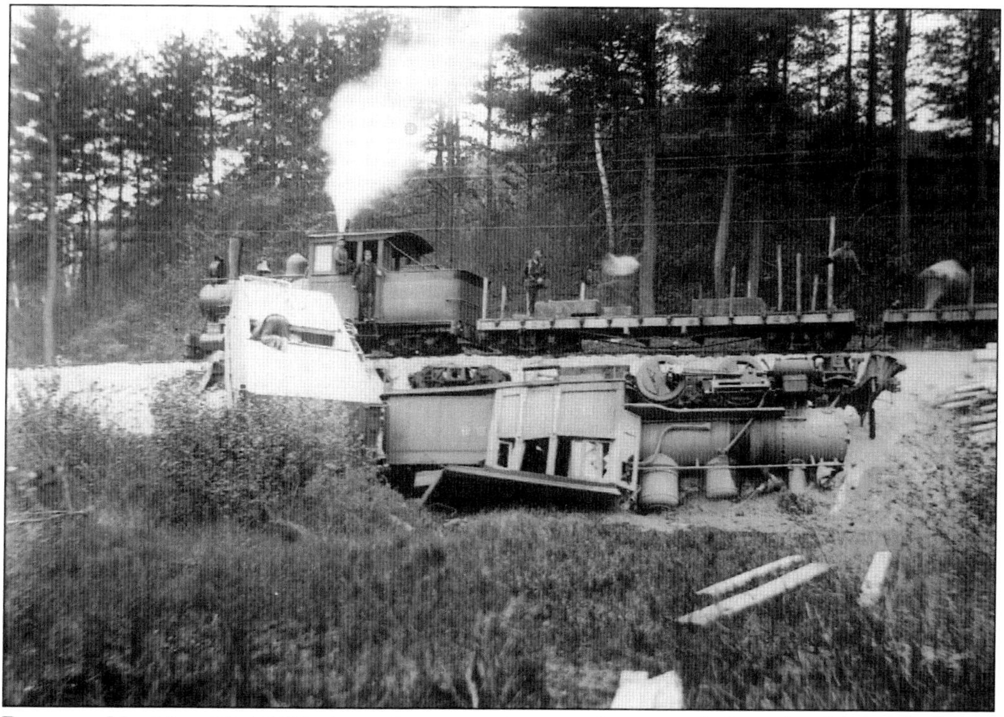

BOTTOMS UP, MAY 11, 1911. A much more serious wreck occurred along this Denmark stretch between Ingall's Road and Perley's Mill when No. 5 hit a sunkink and upended. Engineer Roland Woodbury was seriously scalded. No. 4 and a work train have just arrived.

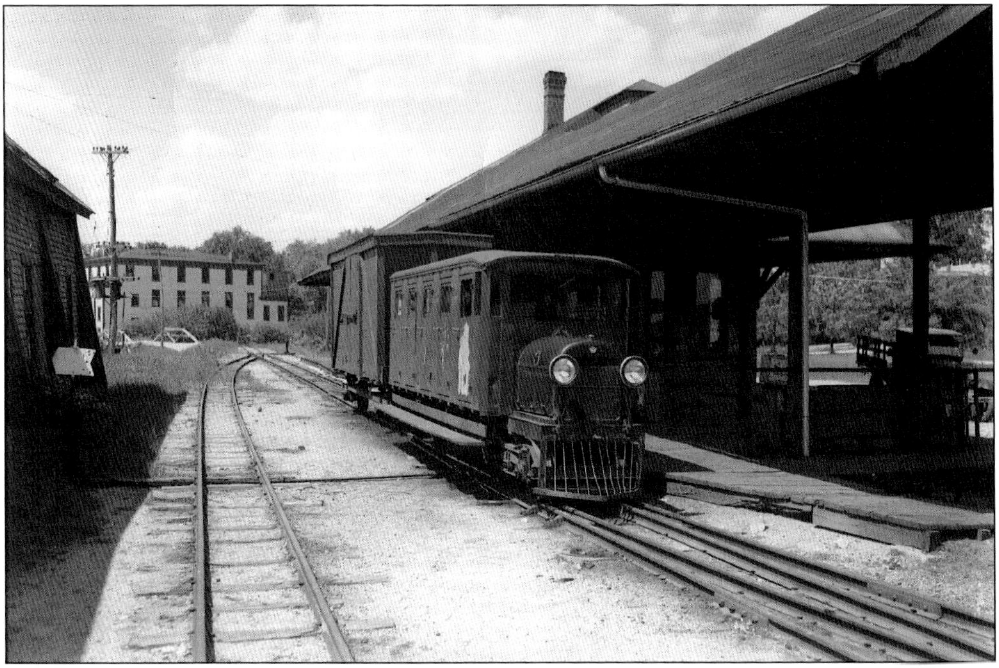

"Busted and Still Running," c. 1936. The B&HR was hit hard by the Great Depression when most of the mills in Bridgton shut down. The acquisition of this railbus (No. 3), with a four-speed drive Chevrolet truck engine (originally a Reo) and a metal cow-catcher, enabled the struggling line to cut operation costs. It carried both freight and passengers.

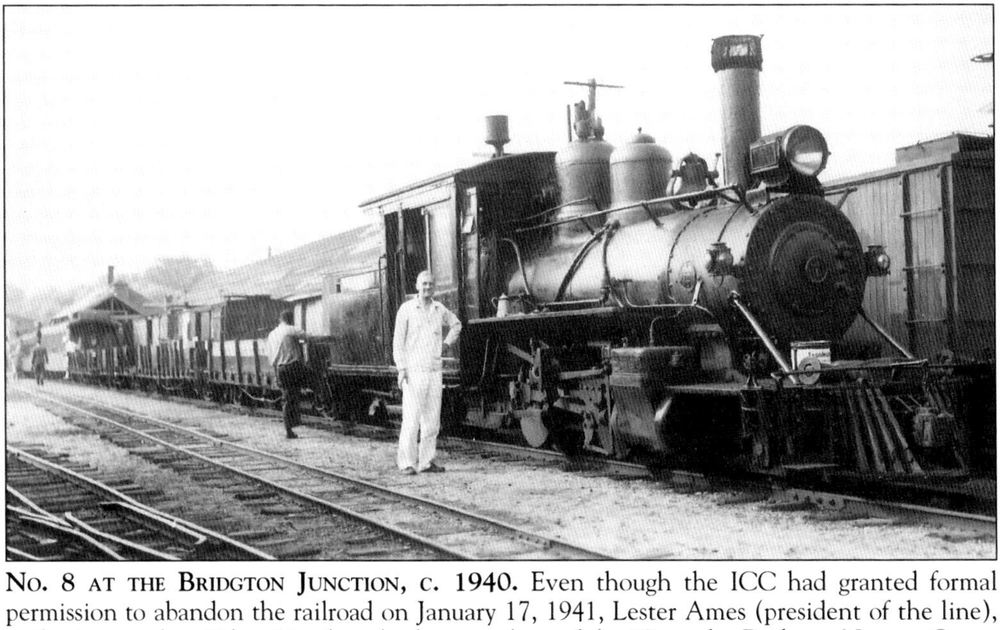

No. 8 at the Bridgton Junction, c. 1940. Even though the ICC had granted formal permission to abandon the railroad on January 17, 1941, Lester Ames (president of the line), enthusiasts such as Edgar Mead, and other members of the "Save the Bridgton Narrow Gauge Railroad Club" continued the fight to keep the line running. They were encouraged by the growing numbers of rail fans patronizing the line.

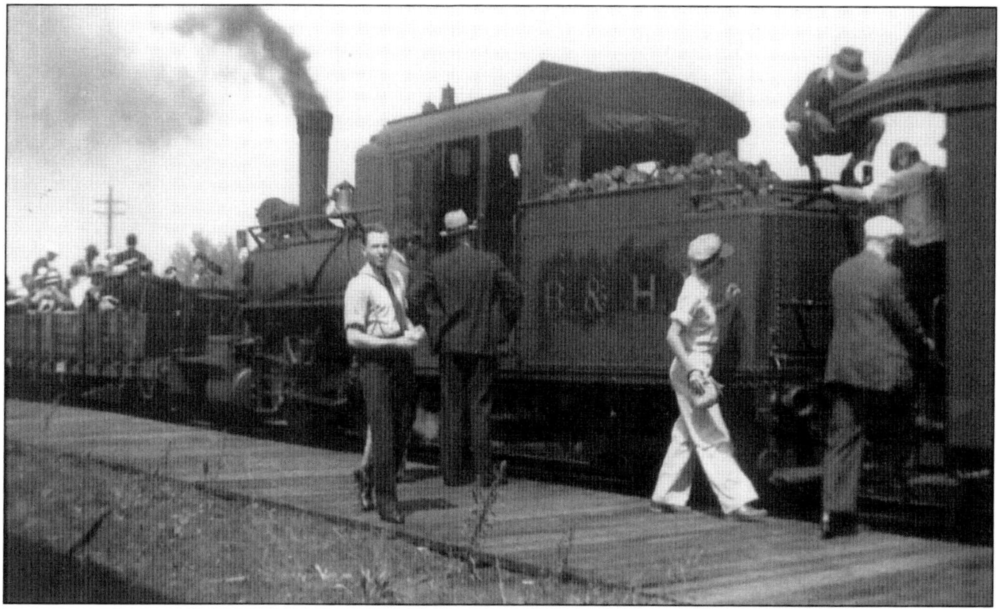

A LAST HARRAH, SUMMER 1941. The beehive of activity at the Bridgton yard on this particular summer's day seems euphoric. Ominous clouds were fast approaching—the end of the railroad and Pearl Harbor. On this day every available passenger car was put into service, gondolas or flatcars were fitted with sideboards and seats, and some enthusiasts gladly road on the top of the coal car.

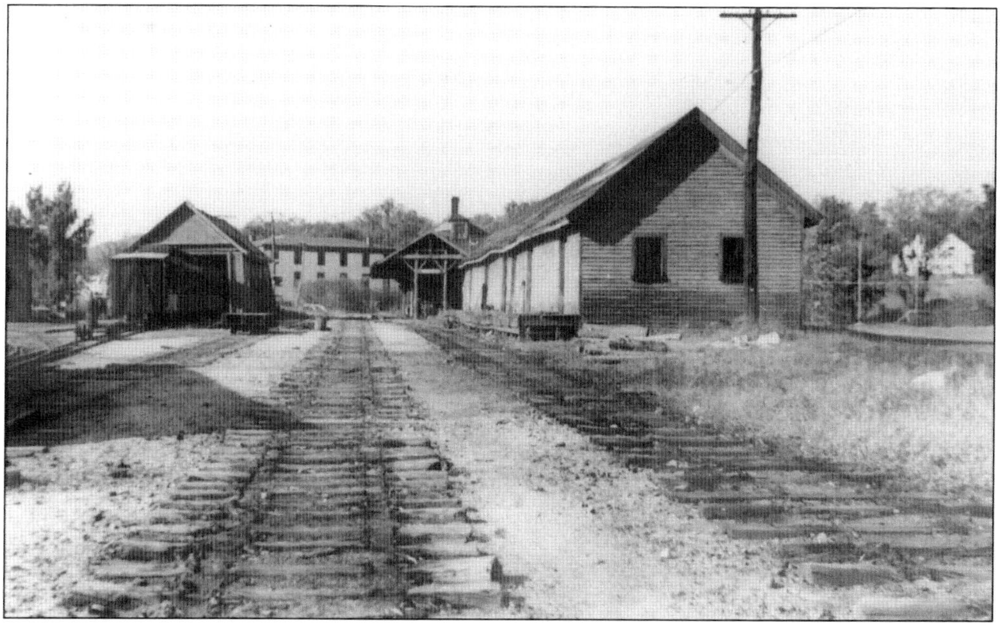

Scrapped, 1942. Despite a last-minute offer by a group of New York investors to purchase the railroad, the local "progressives," who looked upon the line as an anachronism, and Ben Checkowa, a junk dealer from Newburyport, Massachusetts, triumphed. For $20,001, a promising tourist attraction was sold for scrap. On September 7, 1941, No. 7 puffed into Bridgton for the last time. Then began the slow process of ripping up the rails.

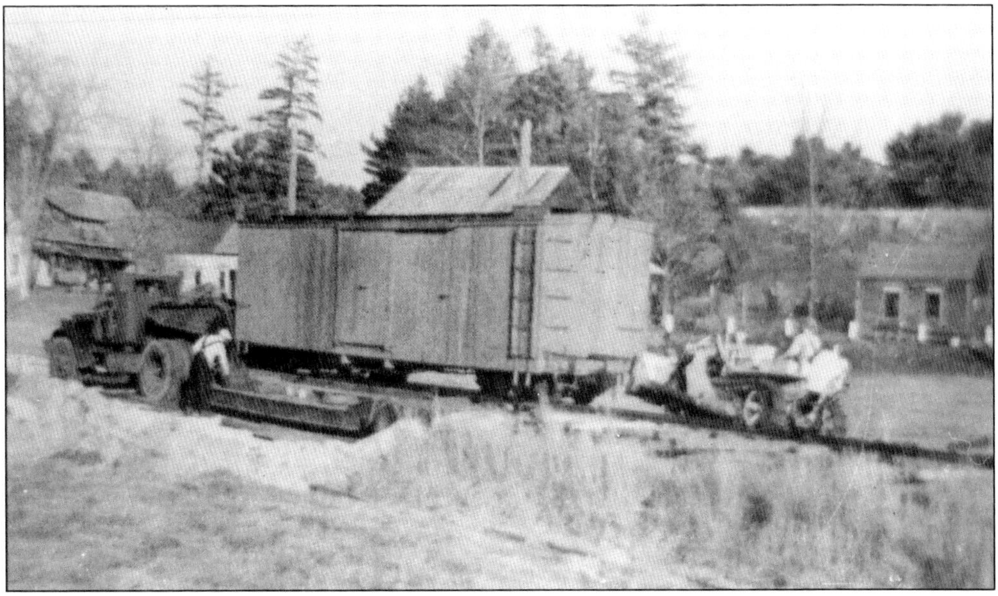

Headed for South Carver, c. 1946. But the good news was that Ellis D. Atwood, a rail buff who owned 1,800 acres of cranberry bogs in South Carver, Massachusetts, succeeded in purchasing all the rolling stock. After World War II, he began moving all but the rails to his newly constructed Edaville Railroad. The two mighty "railbreakers" were put to work transporting tourists and cranberries.

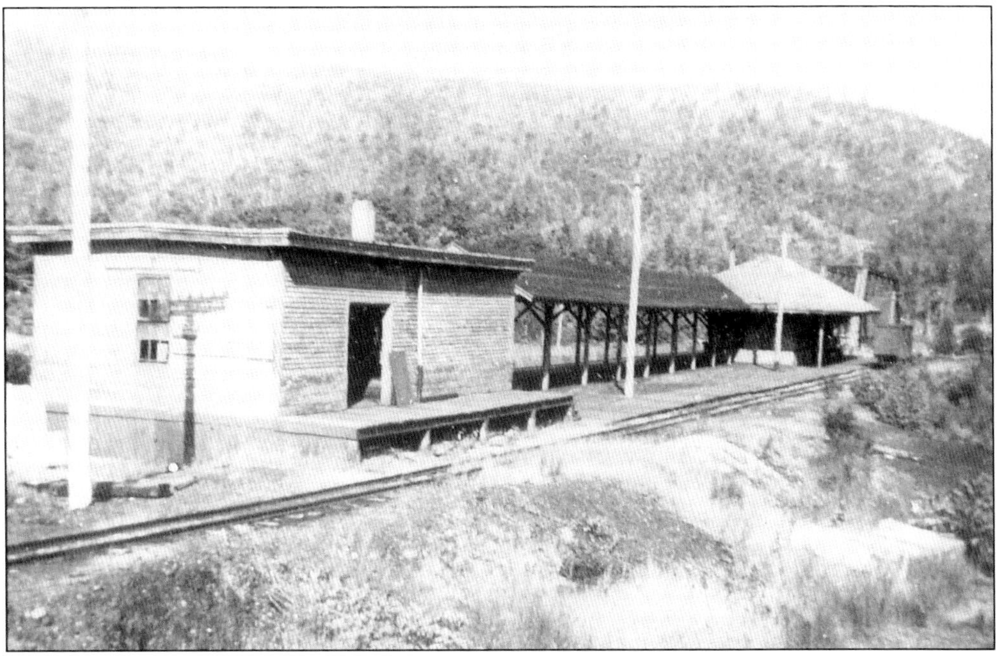

The End of an Era, 1941. The passenger and freight stations at the Junction in Hiram, to which the B&SRR had paid one-third of the maintenance cost, await the inevitable wrecking crew. And since 1985 no train has passed over the Mountain Division from Westbrook to North Conway. Fortunately, the Maine Narrow Gauge Railroad Museum in Portland now owns and operates much of the rolling stock of the old Narrow Gauge.